EXTREME SPACE

THE DOMINATION & SUBMISSION HANDBOOK

F.R.R. MALLORY

EDITED BY: LYNN MARIE BLAKE

15 YEAR ANNIVERSARY EDITION

Copyright ©1996, ©1998, © 2001, ©2013
By F.R.R. Mallory All Rights Reserved

No part of this book may be reproduced or utilized
in any form or by any means, electronic or mechanical,
including photocopying, recording or by any
information storage and retrieval system
without written permission from the author,
except for the inclusion of brief quotations in a review.

This book is protected
Under International and Pan-American Copyright Conventions.

Published in the United States of America by
F.R.R. Mallory

If you purchased this book without a cover
You should be aware that this book is stolen property.
Neither the publisher nor the author has
Received any payment for this 'stripped' book.

Selected portions of this book have been drawn
From the extensive highly acclaimed articles
Featured in the D/s BDSM newsletter
The Steel Door.

Mallory, F.R.R.
   Extreme space : the domination and submission handbook / by F.R.R. Mallory -- Edited / Lynn Marie Blake – Rohnert Park, CA : Unbound Books, 1998.
   i-v, 284 p. ; 23 cm
   Includes glossary
   ISBN 1-893006-48-4
   1. Sexual dominance and submission – United States. 2. Man woman relationships – United States.

HQ79.M34 1998   LCCN
                               98-090971

Cover Image & Design by F.R.R. Mallory
Interior Design by F.R.R. Mallory

10 9 8 7 6 5 4

Dedication

This book is dedicated to every person who is asking questions about kink, BDSM and alternative sexual practices. It is my hope that this content will provide insight and awaken curiosity about the potentials hidden inside each of us as we explore our sexuality, as well as our body, mind and spirit.

WARNING – DISCLAIMER

This book explores controversial issues. Some of the activities described in this book may be illegal in some jurisdictions or countries. All sadomasochistic practices hold a substantial risk of physical or mental injury. Neither this book nor this author advocate nor suggest that any reader should attempt anything found inside this book. Neither the author nor the publishers assume any liability or responsibility for the exercise or misuse of the practices described herein. The author provides only basic and incomplete health and safety warnings to remind readers of the serious hazards involved.

The content, ideology, expressions and opinions within this book are the product of the author's personal life explorations and curiosity regarding questions outside the scope of mainstream informational resources at the time this work was originally created. The analysis and summaries are not offered as scientific fact nor are they designed to imply that other people's analysis may not be equally valid.

It is not the purpose of this book to include all of the information that may be available to the author but to complement, amplify and supplement other texts. You are urged to read all of the available material to learn as much as possible to meet your individual needs. This book is sold with the understanding that the publisher and author are not engaged in rendering legal, or any other form of professional service or advice. If legal or other expert assistance is required by the reader they should seek out the services of a competent professional.

The purpose of this book is to entertain and educate. The author and the publisher shall have neither liability nor responsibility to any person or entity with respect to any loss or damage caused, or alleged to be caused directly or indirectly by the information contained within this book.

Contents

	Acknowledgments	i
	Introduction	1
1	D/s	3
2	Balance	13
3	Discovery of Self	36
4	Emergence	48
5	Dominant vs Master	65
6	Alpha Submissive	81
7	SSC: Safe, Sane, Consensual	97
8	Hard Limits	118
9	Abuse	142
10	Respect	149
11	Space	160
12	High End Submissive	200
13	Alpha Dominant	230
14	Threshold of Flight	240
15	Submissive Frenzies	249
16	Dominant Drop	262
17	Shifting Roles	303

18	Humble	337
19	Collars	361
20	Scene Building	367
21	Sterile Safety	370
22	Kinky Menopause	376
23	Enhancing Traits	381
	Recommended Reading	397

Acknowledgements

*I gratefully acknowledge the invaluable assistance
provided by Chelsea Donnelly
to bring this book back into print
in 2012-2013.*

*I am also very grateful to my wonderful son
David S. Romesburg II
for his encouragement and
support.*

F.R.R. Mallory

This book originated in 1996 and a large portion of the content was drawn from articles that were released as a newsletter. These later became accessible directly from my Steel Door website. This is the fourth edition of this book and over the years the content has been edited, updated and revised during each publication. It has been almost 12 years since the last version was published and in this 15th year Anniversary Edition I have once again updated the content as well as revised and expanded the content. This version is 100 pages longer than the original version.

At the same time, although my personal focus and perspective has altered, I have made every effort to retain the integrity of the original text because so many people have told me that the content was very helpful for them.

I am very pleased to be able to publish this book once more in a form that should make it readily available well into the future. Because I hope to keep it in print indefinitely, I have tried to clarify the content so that it remains useful indefinitely. I thank you so much for choosing to read my works.

A very brief bio:
I have degrees in English and Psychology from the University of California at Berkeley. I have written and published more than 2,000 nonfiction tutorials, novels, short stories, poetry and screenplays. I have a continuing interest in behavior mechanics, non-violence, altered states of consciousness and the seductive mysteries of kink.

Introduction

This is the 15th year Anniversary Edition of this book. During the interim this title went out of print for many years and I received frequent requests from readers to locate copies or identify where they could find one. During those same years I continued my exploration of kink as well as professionally publishing thousands of tutorials, novels, short stories, poetry and plays. Recently I've been writing screenplays and moving my work towards film. Still, kink remains a powerful interest in my life and in the last year I again undertook the effort to write about kink from my current perspective and viewpoint. This work produced two new manuscripts: *Extreme Space II: Kink Secrets*, and *The Kinky Feminist*. Extreme Space II was published in February of 2013 and The Kinky Feminist is due for public release in March of 2013.

Each time I write about kink I am driven by both the cultural environment surrounding me and by my own passions and curiosity. In the intervening years BDSM has blown up all over the world. Great new materials have been produced and yet, new questions and concerns erupt as well. Still, the entry of a newcomer into kink remains quite similar to the conditions that were present when I first published this book in 1996.

Because of this, I have chosen to maintain most of the original text. I have added more than 100 pages of completely new content and revised much of the original content. I have tried to honor the integrity of my earlier viewpoint and allow the content to retain its substance as much as possible. For those of you who have read this book before, there are some changes, some updates and hopefully improvements. Most of this book explores kink and D/s role play from a primarily heterosexual viewpoint but I have expanded some areas to include other perspectives as well.

I encourage you to use this book as a resource during your own journey into kink, particularly if you are new and inexperienced. I also encourage you to continue on to my two new books. Both of my new books are more advanced both in scientific support, details and far-reaching implications. When you are ready, they are waiting for you.

D/S

Deliverance/slavery

I bet you have heard rumors and whispers of people subjecting themselves to torture, whippings, spankings, humiliation, bondage, and even more bizarre acts.

Hello. That isn't D/s (Domination and submission). D/s is far simpler, requires no accouterments, no implements, no fancy gear or elaborate workshop training. Domination and submission can be quite simple. When a heterosexual man looks down into the eyes of a woman and within him surges the desire to possess, to own, to control, or to protect, he is expressing (patriarchal sexism) and maybe domination. When a heterosexual woman looks up into the eyes of this man and within her surges the desire to be held, coveted, desired, possessed, owned, controlled and protected, she is expressing (patriarchal sexism) and maybe submission. "Ah Ha!" you say. But, isn't that sort of everyone?

Indeed. D/s traits are common to any human raised in a patriarchal culture which at present is most humans in most cultures in the world. It is a characteristic that can be seen across many species. So why the whips and chains? Aren't they D/s?

No. D/s is domination and submission. This is the idea that each person in a relationship has dominion over some areas of the relationship and is not dominant in other areas of the relationship. Within kink there is a tendency for newcomers to want to isolate all dominant activities towards one person and all submissive activities towards the other person but this isn't exactly how it works.

Whips and chains are the territory of BDSM or (Bondage, Discipline, Sadism, Masochism). BDSM and D/s are actually very separate things. In heterosexual relationships a man can and often does dominate a woman physically. He may not know that he is doing so, but he responds based on his conditioning and personality. A woman can and often does submit to the man's will, she may resent it, challenge it or even deny it but she has typically been conditioned by the same culture so submission is familiar. Essentially, though both people are autonomous and separate they must come together as a team in order to successfully propagate their species. If you have two captains on a ship you will most likely have conflict. In a conflictive relationship little is achieved except polarity, division and stress. You can have two captains who share control of the ship on different schedules if their journey and direction are the same, then they will act as a team in the best interest of both.

So let us address what D/s people term the vanilla life. Vanilla is a colloquial term used to identify any person who isn't attracted to or participating in kink. Using the word 'vanilla' is supposed to suggest that people in kink are more sexually expressive and active whereas non-kink participants are more staid and less sexually active. Like most generalizations, this isn't true.

Essentially, all Americans are conditioned inside a patriarchal sexist power structure with prominent features of male dominance and female subjugation. However, the relationship dynamic within kink known as D/s is seeking to modify or reinvent this traditional relationship model using old ideas in different, often more extreme, ways. Most dominants and submissives will collectively tell you that they have already tried to establish and maintain a romantic or sexual relationship following the conventional parameters currently common in the mainstream culture, usually with limited success. A large number of people exploring kink are divorced or single after the failure of one or many relationships. They may not be looking for a committed relationship when they begin exploring kink. Instead, it is fairly common for newcomers to be looking for new sexual experiences that might lead to a relationship.

> *Is heterosexual D/s just the latest 'new' way to impose a sexist power structure on women?*

Most people acknowledge a deep yearning for more from their interactions. They may want more attention, more time, a stronger response from their partner, a deeper sense of connection and better sex. They are hopeful that the sexy, naughty rumors they've heard about BDSM might hold some answers or at the very least some interesting sexual experiences. In a nutshell, people are looking for deliverance from the inadequate relationship and sexual experiences of their past.

All of this sounds great, easy and safe except for the pain thing. What is that all about?

D/s isn't about pain or suffering but most people conflate D/s with **BDSM** and **BDSM** *is* about stimulating or applying intense sensory stimulation to the body or mind (usually on the submissive). Is it abuse? It might be as there are always people who seek to use any relationship framework as an opportunity to oppress or negatively control others. But, for the most part D/s participants are not domestic abusers. They have no need to abuse their partner. "Ahhh." Say what?

From the Submissive: I intertwine my arms around my man's neck, look up into his eyes and ask him or even beg him to spank me. His arms tighten around my waist, and with a loving grin in his eyes, he replies, "perhaps."

Every single aspect of a relationship is important. The respect, the disrespect, the elevation and the reduction.

I know that when he focuses his attention lovingly upon me, uses his hands or a paddle, flogger or whip against my skin, that it will hurt, will burn, will alter, will arouse me. This allows me the freedom to connect directly with my pain and respond with sharp cries, wanton desires and pure raw passion. His behavior towards me helps to free me from the inhibitions I may have about my body, attractiveness or conditioned constraints against my own sexual nature. I feel free.

So, to be very simple here, pain enhances arousal. Pain and pleasure share the same nerve endings in the human body, they send messages to the brain on the same conduit. How the body interprets sensory signals depends on many surprising factors. People exploring their body this way are drawn to kink

From the Dominant: I feel the laughter bubbling inside her, the way her eyes dance when she looks up at me. Her attention is like the sun surrounding me, enveloping me. She freely offers to me the promise of herself. Between us, when I express control of her, it is by mutual consent. And the pain? When I touch her, intentionally bringing her to an edge, I see and smell the musk of her arousal, she excites me and I can tell I excite her. This offers a freedom, a connection I don't have to guess at or wonder about. When her body and mind begin to fly, she takes me with her. She carries me with her, together we ascend.

This is part of the lure, this desire to co-experience what every body is capable of experiencing.

So, what about bondage and discipline?

This is a potentially prickly subject. Bondage and discipline are often practiced by long-term real life Dominants and submissives. Bondage can range from silk scarves to iron shackles and everything in between. Discipline can represent correction or be a feature of play, a fetish. There are no right or wrong rules about what works for any couple.

Most people enjoy physical bondage, skin-on-skin. It's primal and fun to struggle one body against the other. It's immediate and free. It's natural to most intimate relationships and it isn't specifically associated with kink.

Other couples love to experiment with the toys, the straps, the devices. Part of the attraction to domination is the opportunity to *play* with a person you find attractive and interesting. What's not to like? The very idea of tying up a woman or man and flogging them is mentally erotic and very stimulating for most dominants male or female. Frequently both people will collaborate on creating or trying new things. Many people make their own stuff.

This isn't experimentation by one person on another person. This is two people deciding on what sounds interesting and fun, together. Many people like bondage, collars, and commands. This is very much like a theatrical production where the two people control the script, the props and the set design. It's a departure from the imposed script of everyday life. It's sexual theater.

You can consider D/s (with BDSM features) as a role that includes a series of discrete fetishes and challenges. Neither person knows, in advance, how it will play out. The mystery is part of the excitement. Discipline (as part of fetish) is a reward, a treat, a totally desirable pleasure. A submissive may want to be reduced (with love), played with, used, everything that was or is forbidden in mainstream society.

Most females are told, "good girls *don't like anything sexual.*" Women are told they have a low sex drive and that sexual experimentation with numerous partners will reduce their *value* as a female in society. Value is equated to potential marital status acquired by the perceived status of the man.

How many sexual partners is too many for a female? Conventionally a woman is told she should only have one sexual partner in her life. If she loses that relationship, she is allowed to have one more, but only if it is oriented towards long-term monogamy. And, she should only pretend to like sex because virtuous women don't really like sex, they tolerate sex in order to maintain the relationship and to provide children.

To be erotic is to be nothing more than a slut. For a woman to get past all that conditioning it really helps if she is tied up and can't help herself. Really! So, the man ties her up and voila she becomes a wanton slut. This is a simplistic view of an experience which is always about sex and about inhibitions, self advocacy, empowerment and discovery of self.

As you explore D/s you will discover that not everyone actually has intercourse or the acts commonly described as sex. Does this mean what they are doing isn't sexual? No. It can and often does involve eroticism and deep orgasmic pleasures. But sometimes the sex is just a vehicle, the method, or a pathway.

Sexual interactions play many roles in life. Sex mediates conflicts, reassures, reduces tension, aids in pair bonding, reduces loneliness, combats depression and these are just a few of its attributes. Sex is anything that the body, mind or spirit identify as sex. It's important to understand that the systems that are activated in kink are connected with sexuality. This is why all of kink relates to sex. It doesn't matter if you engage in sex directly, it is always activated indirectly in any kink encounter.

> *Are male submissives the same as female submissives?*

But sex is only a part of D/s. It is within the giving of direction and compliance with direction, the sharing of mutual devotion, and through the blending focus on a specific goal that transformation occurs. This is the moment when a dominant and submissive truly come into their own. The roles exist because both people agree that they exist. If either cease to participate or believe then the construct ceases to exist.

Are things the same when the dominant is female and the submissive is male? Not exactly. In general most men tend to be physically larger and stronger than most women. So women don't usually rely on physical size or might in the same ways that a male dominant might use them. In addition, female dominants have the opportunity to work professionally. This means they can earn money by scening male submissives professionally. This also alters the dynamic.

In a 'lifestyle' situation D/s can be managed in similar ways so far as giving and receiving direction. However, there are often substantial differences in the fetishes and interests of male submissives from female submissives. Some of these are technical based on different physical attributes but the stronger differences are emotional and psychological. Male dominants are more likely to engage in kink in anticipation of sexual intercourse while female dominants are often interested in kink in anticipation of power exchange. These differences reflect some of the different issues men and women face or are conditioned towards in childhood. Women are more likely to have a strong reaction to male authority and overt sexism and this informs their orientation towards kink.

It is also important to recognize that modern kink in America has primarily been led by the male homosexual community. It is an error to think that D/s is oriented sexually or by gender. It is fairly common for issues of gender and sexual orientation to be more fluid. A man can express dominances as a female dominant over other men and women. A female dominant can equally choose to dominate from a masculine perspective. The same is true for submissives. Because a submissive has male genitals does not make them a male submissive. Care should be taken to refrain from assumptions of role, gender and orientation in anything related to kink.

To understand the dynamics involved in D/s it is helpful to move past the surface messages of why people react intimately with each other as dominants and submissives. Avoid accepting the easy answers that are typically based in the patriarchal mindset rather than the realities of kink. The picture I have offered above is all about the mysterious nature of kink and how it expands during exploration. You can't easily solve it. I encourage you to set aside conclusions you may have drawn about how and why the dominant and submissive model enjoys such enormous popularity within kink. I invite you to join me in this wondrous adventure of the mind, body and spirit.

This is called a triskelion or three-sided symbol.

A version of this symbol is commonly used to represent persons interested in kink.

Balance

There are those who believe that balance is composed of two parts such as Yin-Yang, black and white, top and bottom. I have always felt that this was incomplete. There is black, white and the absence or union of both together forming a unity of the greater whole.

It makes more sense for me to imagine balance being composed of three parts: body, mind and spirit or the symbol of kink, the triskelion. For a person to reach their inner potentials they must not neglect any of these aspects. Too often people focus totally on one of the three sides taking them further and further out of balance in the areas they don't tend to. This causes their viewpoint to twist, become myopic or opaque and rigid.

It has also never made sense to me why people subject themselves to forcible denial of one or more of their aspects in order to advance the aspects they favor. How can your whole self grow if parts are stunted? How can you even approach a valid understanding of self if you only allow yourself to access *some* of yourself?

Denial creates pressure, and pressure creates stress, and stress creates failure. We are all familiar with stress, we understand how it negatively affects our health, wellbeing, perceptions of self, and personal successes. We tell ourselves that by enduring stress, say from a difficult job, that we are creating wellbeing in our future at that vague time when we will be successful enough to escape our current stressors. But this isn't truthful, it is merely our way of justifying why we must endure the stress and the suffering it produces.

An unpleasant example of sexual denial can be found by looking at the imposition of celibacy upon individuals in some religious communities. Every few months the media reveals allegations or charges being brought against a person of religious authority for inappropriate sexual activity. Some involve children. Would these assaults have occurred if the religious person had normal access to sex? I can't answer that. But, there is evidence that normal access to sex reduces sexual assaults. It seems reasonable to me. Just because a person intellectually chooses a religious calling doesn't mean their body ceases to produce the hormones that elevate sexual urges.

I also question how denial acts upon the person mentally and psychologically. It is certainly an imbalance of the person's natural state. Does sexual denial promote spiritual growth?

There is truth in the old saying *'Do things in moderation'*. Abstinence is not moderation. A well-rounded person actively seeks out a wide variety of stimuli in their life. The trick is not to obsess totally on any single aspect of your life to the exclusion of or detriment of the other aspects you also possess. This includes your passion and interest in kink.

In many ways kink offers incredibly unique opportunities for stimulation and potential growth, but, only if you disperse kink across your entire self. Is it all about sex or sexual access or relationships? No.

Many people experience dissatisfaction with their

romantic or sexual relationships. Often the level of commitment is more surface than substance. There is also a growing level of role confusion. What is a man supposed to do? What is a woman supposed to do? This confusion translates into communication drama and epic relationship failures. It's best to say that current relationship models are unstable. It's not possible to roll back time to some era where roles were more fixed, nor is this desirable. Forcible imposition of patriarchal roles added to kink activities create domestic violence, not kink.

But, instability is stressful. Many people feel alone, insecure, doubtful of themselves and others, disconnected and a little bit angry. No one prepared them for how to engage in a relationship with non-patriarchal roles. It's like wearing a shoe that suddenly doesn't fit.

Instability can lead to feelings of depression and inadequacy, an increase in nonconsensual verbal, emotional and physical violence directed towards relationship partners and others and a deep fear that there is something profoundly wrong with you as an individual.

All of this is how any person shows up looking through the blurry glass of kink. On the inside it sure looks like kinky people have defined roles. Won't that simplify everything? But, everywhere a person looks the media and society are now telling them that defined unequal roles are exactly what society is trying to move away from. Is kink just a reversion to a traditional patriarchal role? Its participants, quite a lot of them, don't exactly appear traditional, at least not in the photos you like to look at. The mental challenges within kink are almost immediately obvious. What are you supposed to do with your beliefs in equal rights? Is kink just another bedroom sex game?

At the very least it is pretty clear that some if not all of a person's prior relationship knowledge will probably not work very well inside kink. It isn't that the man or woman wants to go back to patriarchal-style domination. Most don't. The reason they don't want to go back is because history provides pretty clear evidence that patriarchal-style domination made a lot of women very unhappy. So many women were unhappy that there were enormous demonstrations for equal rights. When women are unhappy men know that their sex life is going to suck. That means forced domination sucked. But, perhaps in your experience modern relationships suck too. Can you have kink and equal rights? Why not?

Kink is about overcoming, adapting and transforming sex, relationship models and behaviors. The trick is, can *you* do it? It may look like all of the work is done on the submissive side of things, like the female (in the conventional heterosexual model) must be able to submerge their ego during interactions within the relationship. This sounds suspiciously like the same old crap. Is it?

Does the male dominant simply need to show up and give orders to the female? Well, they can, if they want a relationship that lasts about five minutes. Neither person can escape being a modern human being raised in an evolving culture. Both know better. The dominant has their own problems. They have to sustain the attributes their submissive desires for the submissive to maintain the submersion of ego sufficiently for the relationship to be satisfying for both people. The submersion of ego requires continuous acts of investing belief. Belief requires continuous acts of sustained role immersion. If the dominant guy only shows up when the submissive female is annoyed because the dominant guy is mooching off her paycheck while he kicks back on the recliner playing a video game all day when he is supposed to be job hunting, then there is a problem. Domination is no escape from bad behaviors.

Each person will actually be testing their belief in the integrity of the investment in role on a daily or even minute-by-minute basis. Will the belief stand up to close scrutiny during difficult moments? For belief to be sustained the individual has to weigh a preponderance of the evidence. Is the dominant inhabiting the role 60% of the time? Is it enough? When it ceases to be enough the submissive ceases to submit and the relationship ends.

> *Why does a submissive need to submerge their ego?*
>
> *Is it necessary?*
>
> *Are there negative consequences?*

The submissive doesn't escape this process either. If she can't submerge her ego sufficiently to meet the dominant's invested belief in her role then he can cease dominating her as well. Belief goes both ways. Investment and immersion go both ways. No one will rise to the level of 100% and they shouldn't try. You can't force who you are and you shouldn't stuff everything that doesn't fit. Stuffing leads to suffering and suffering leads to relationship failure.

Belief changes. When you were seven years old you believed many things that you don't believe today. New evidence and experiences inform belief constantly. You will never have complete belief in anything, if you do it means that whatever you believe in moves into the past, it ends, it dies because it no longer grows.

This means that your role of choice is something you must continue to grow into, grow out of or transform around you. Any one role is unlikely to be completely fulfilling across the whole of your life. It is equally likely that as you explore roles you discover a desire to try more than one or to relinquish all roles in favor of the fluid flexibility of the versatile self. Such possibilities do not threaten the actions or potentials of submission or domination within daily life but reflect a healthy perspective that remains open to growth and change, no matter how you might feel in the moment.

Many people try to view submission as the role of the weaker person. This is an error. While it may look easy to be led it is actually very difficult to submerge the ego for even a short time. Submission can feel more comfortable early on in the exploration of kink. Most women within the American culture are conditioned to align with many of the behaviors and attitudes common to submission from birth. Because of this conditioning it is less difficult to conform with familiar cues. During the early stages of a D/s relationship when the body is also flooded with oxytocin, *the love hormone,* both people will tend to attempt to 'be' exactly what they believe their partner wants them to be. But, this hormone fades and over time the natural cynicism of the individual will need to confront all of the conflicts that engaging in kink from a submissive standpoint produces.

Each submissive must conquer fear, shame, guilt, embarrassment and the criticisms of family, friends and society as a whole. As they struggle to maintain the new relationship these pressures do not lessen but become more intense, particularly if engagement in kink is sporadic, unsatisfying or complicated by other factors. Often the submissive may feel a desire to immerse themselves into the dominant, like a total release. Functionally they are always a separate individual and this relinquishment of responsibility over self may mask other issues that the individual isn't dealing with and wishes to foist onto the dominant. You can't actually share the space of another human being as if you only respond to or comply with direction.

What actually happens is a constant inquiry of self, a constant compliance in the moment. Some of this becomes habit and routine, fading into inconsequential. Some will remain difficult.

In order to offer freely of the self, the self needs to be whole unto itself. If you are trying to fill a need, a void inside of yourself, you will fail. You may find it romantic to believe that you are incomplete without sharing your life with another person and that you like the idea that another person *completes* you. But, this is only and ever a romantic notion. You can't really give of yourself if you are already incomplete. If you take from another person does this sound as romantic? If there were something *to* take wouldn't your *taking* remove something of value from the other person? So, you fill yourself up and leave them incomplete? It's illogical. It's an error.

The more needy you are, the more desperate you are for attention, the more you will attempt to steal from other people their time, energy and attention. This isn't the path you take in a relationship that survives or thrives.

As an adult you know that you have failed relationships and unpleasant personal experiences in your past. These are called emotional wounds. You arrive at kink with all of these informing your thoughts and wishes. This is where everyone starts.

Our issues don't magically vanish because we find someone to give or receive directions. Back before you arrived at kink, at experimenting with intentional domination and submission, you were in some kind of relationship where someone gave you directions and orders. If you go back far enough it will be your parents or the people who cared for you in childhood. Later, it may have been a spouse or a relationship partner.

You can't cure or eradicate the past by choosing D/s. But, in any new relationship and particularly a relationship where you can define boundaries, it is possible to attempt to adopt practices more conducive to healing, self-nurturing and cherishment. As you grapple with identifying and confronting hurtful language and actions, this intentional process can aid you in reducing the levels of damage that continue to inform your life.

> *Is a bratty person actually submissive, or are they pretending just to get attention?*

But, it is equally easy to perpetuate damage as well.

How we receive experiences and the meaning we apply to those experiences differentiates whether the experience is hurtful or non-hurtful. When a person delivers words with the intention of causing injury, usually both persons in the exchange know that the attempt to injure is occurring. The desire to cause real injury is assault. It doesn't matter if a person apologizes later. Imagine words as if they are baseball bats. If you swing words at another person and hit them (words that can be heard always make contact with their intended victim) you are committing assault. You can't call them back or nullify their impact.

I've already said that every person is working on issues and wounding from their past. Everyone! How old are you? If you are 30, it means it took you 30 years to accumulate your collection of personal issues. This means it is fair to guess it will take you equally long to heal and process this junk if you start right now and if you don't keep creating more junk.

Here's the positive news, during the process of self-healing you will gradually improve the way you feel and deal with your world. The important issue here is to understand that you have to actively and intentionally go after this process.

The act of constantly submerging your ego places pressure on your psyche. You are likely to feel bratty or the desire to question and you will feel every other feeling you probably had as a teenager. Moving into a dependency effectively positions you, an adult, at the stage immediately before full adulthood. The struggle will have many of the identical features of this natural development stage.

Part of the attraction towards submission is in the desire to relinquish adult responsibility to another person. However, as attractive as this may appear to be, you will remain adult and you will continue to possess responsibility.

Cleaning up wounding or areas in the past where you might be stuck takes many forms. D/s, because it is often focused and experienced as intense, can propel issues to the surface intentionally or accidentally. The greatest battle that any submissive faces is internally as they struggle with issues of trust, insecurity, low self-esteem, and the continuously changing landscape of their self. Often a submissive will discover new territory in their psyche as they work to inhabit the role of submissive.

The physical challenges within D/s are also clearly and easily visible. People within the lifestyle view the body as a tapestry to be worked. It is a living work of art, an instrument that can be tuned to deliver the submissive from the normal range of sensory response through a mental and physical door into the range of the extra normal. This blending of the mental and physical ranges operates as a gateway to open the mind and body to entirely new experiences, many of them transcendent and quite spiritual.

The physical imagery of kink often horrifies outside observers with its graphic depiction of living physical torment. The less informed will almost invariably equate what they see using the only language they have to describe what is happening. They will call it abuse or assault.

Today any physical contact between two people can

be described legally as some kind of assault. Touch is rapidly becoming a legal battleground. Kink is all about touch, often harsh pain-inflicting, tissue-bruising touch. This is exactly the type of touch described as domestic violence and criminal assault in every legal court in the country. There are laws to protect one human from the infliction of assault by another human. These are good laws, important laws, necessary laws. There is one key difference. Consent. However, you should know that consent is not defensible in court. Before you engage in any BDSM aspects of kink you should understand the legal ramifications in your location. What do your local laws say about it?

Understanding what abuse (assault) is and what abuse (assault) isn't becomes very important to this discussion and indeed to your understanding of the fundamentals of domination and submission. As an example: if two men are fighting, pounding each other brutally with their fists, are they committing assault against each other?

You cannot make a legal distinction until you know if their fight is consensual. I don't mean did both agree to go into the alley and fight, that would still potentially be assault. However, if both men have signed contracts exempting the other from liability to harm in the context of a legal boxing match then consent separates the event from meeting the legal definition of assault, even if one man dies.

In this example you begin to see that the activities engaged in by consenting adults cannot be evaluated based on a surface description. But, it is also important to realize that our court system sees your kink activities not as a legal boxing match but more like an alley fight. You can consent all you like but your legal rights to protection from assault continue to exist.

This doesn't mean that someone will send you to jail for spanking your partner's butt in the bedroom of your home, unless some other condition elevates your action to the threshold necessary for legal action. My point is that risk is constant if you engage in kink.

In general, abuse is the non-voluntary, coerced, assault of one human upon another. It is the removal of choice, disregard for health and welfare and the imposition of nonconsensual violence from one human being upon another.

You may have noted that I am using two words here somewhat interchangeably: abuse and assault. Abuse is a deceitful, corrupt or misuse by one person towards another. Assault is a violent verbal or physical attack. In my opinion both rise to equal potential damage in frequently identical ways.

Sexual assaults used to frequently be called abuse in the past. This conveyed a less damaging perspective favoring the perpetrator in courts and in the public eye. Today the Bureau of Justice of the United States of America recognizes these crimes as assaults. Although a sexual assault may appear to be about sex, it is often also about power differentials between the perpetrator and the victim.

Early in this section I talked about the destabilization of relationships. One of the consequences of change in a society is the difficulty individuals experience adapting to change. Often a person will be raised and conditioned to believe one set of rules or ideas only to discover that these rules have dramatically changed by the time the individual reaches adulthood. The information and behaviors they were conditioned to understand no longer work. This causes deep anxiety, fear, distrust and other emotional experiences that the same individual was not taught to manage well. These are just some of the reasons that sexual assault escalates during periods of societal changes around status and rights.

Sexual violence often includes death threats, mental, verbal, emotional and physical abuse and injury. This violence is typically forced upon the victim by a person who often has little or no control over their emotional state who seeks out some person to control for a period of time in an effort to stabilize or exorcise their dissonant feelings. Causing fear also triggers sadism, not the sadism of kink but the diagnostical mental illness of sadism associated with gaining pleasure from hurting others non-consensually.

Is the perpetrator a dominant? It is certainly true that they are forcibly exerting control which can be used to say that they are dominating the situation. But, it is the dominance of a bully. A bully derives and maintains power only through a continuous use of force or the threat of force. The bully will only receive compliance while the threat is present or believed to be true. This means that the bully doesn't have a sustainable position of dominance. The victim will cease to comply with the bully as soon as possible. This means the perpetrator doesn't meet the description of a dominant.

If a dominant uses fear, intimidation, manipulation, guilt, shame or pain to attempt to control a submissive, the relationship will fail. While a dominant may appear to control a submissive this is actually an illusion. A submissive is an autonomous human being, they control themselves. They choose to comply with direction from moment to moment.

I haven't skirted the issue of pain or punishment. What's really going on here?

First, a D/s relationship doesn't need to have any aspects of BDSM. Many people enjoy the dynamic on its own. Some people have physical limitations and they cannot engage in BDSM. But, many people like both the role dynamic and BDSM.

There are two basic variations on the D/s dynamic. In the first variation the couple uses BDSM as both a device for punishment and as a stimulant for sexual pleasure. In the second variation the couple uses BDSM as a reward or only for sexual pleasure.

The first variation is more difficult to accomplish in a long term successful relationship primarily because it requires both people to differentiate between punishment and reward. I will look at this more in a later section. The second variation is easier to use because it reserves kink solely as a reward.

You are possibly wondering how pain can be a reward. How can it cause ecstasy or even bliss? Isn't pain, pain?

The simple answer to that question is that there are different kinds of pain messages. The brain is an exquisite instrument whose capacities we barely understand. What kinky people have discovered is that how a person responds to stimulation changes or transforms based on consent, intention and support. This is the same secret mystics and devoutly religious sects have used for thousands of years to attain transcendent mental states.

Within the D/s BDSM relationship dynamic the submissive actively wants, desires and needs the application of sensory stimulation from their dominant just as the dominant actively wants, desires and needs to apply techniques of mental and sensory stimulation upon their submissive partner. This *need* has many of the features of any habitual physical, mental or spiritual practice. If you go to the gym on a regular schedule and suddenly cannot go for several weeks, it is likely that you will begin to experience a deep desire to go. The need may show up as both physical and mental and even sometimes spiritual. While you are going to the gym you potentially don't notice the positive experience of endorphins triggered by physical exertion and you may not notice the rhythmic relaxation of walking or running on a treadmill or how this combination of factors shifts your mental state. You don't really notice until the experience is gone. Then you notice. This is what it is like with kink.

A kinky scene can activate the body and mind in very similar ways to exercise. The most profound difference is not the application of sensory stimulation but how that stimulation elevates the energy of the submissive. As a submissive experiences stimulation their body produces a series of complex chemicals designed to help them 'survive' the stimulation. The brain doesn't exactly know that the experience is voluntary, it simply recognizes that certain sensations are occurring that could potentially cause damage if they are not halted. So, the brain sets off warnings (pain) deploys chemicals (to help manage the pain) and elevates the energy in preparation for potential flight (escape).

As the situation and experience continues, the brain elevates its signals, sends more chemicals and jacks up the energy even more. The result is tricky.

In many cases the submissive will achieve a floaty state where the stimulation no longer feels painful. Most people call this sub-space.

Sometimes the submissive will experience a deep emotional surge. The reaction will be far beyond the range of the stimulation and may often require the scene to immediately end.

A submissive may also continue to feel pain until they yell out their safeword and force the dominant to stop. All of these experiences are normal and only a few of the possible experiences the submissive will have. Each time the submissive and dominant do something, anything, it will be different from the last time they did the same thing. Each day the body, mind and spirit is in a different space. This variation is part of the attraction and part of why kink is also challenging.

Any attempt to grasp D/s tightly will inevitably wreck havoc. It's easy to conceptualize the roles of dominant and submissive. It's even pretty easy to theorize how the dynamic will work. After all, each of us has a partial model inside our cultural conditioning. But, the more you think you *get it*, the more you will be pushed

> *Does the madness of kink affect your competence?*
>
> *If it does, if you become incompetent, how can you offer reasoned consent to kink?*

out of your comfort zone when you actually try to apply what you think will work. Your partner isn't a parent or child no matter how you set up your dynamic. Both of you are modern, most likely born beyond the pre-birth control era. The trick is being authentic in who you are while at the same time prioritizing making the dynamic work. You have to allow room for change, for challenge, for mistakes. You have to be able to communicate effectively and it is highly likely you don't have a lot of experience being a good communicator.

The really difficult part of trying to form a sustainable D/s relationship is your lack of experience coupled to all of the deceiving excitement augmented by hormones cocktail that is the composition of any new relationship. You have to be able to overcome the madness inside your body and brain to still hammer out the foundations of a good relationship. The madness is the additional boost of connection that occurs during a scene when two people share the intensity of the experience. This is like going on a first date where you do a dual bungie jump off a bridge that makes you scream the whole way down while you cling together tethered upside down above life and death.

It is common for a submissive to feel as if they are a physical part of the dominant during and immediately after an intense scene with a dominant. Their emotions and mental state will be so intense that they feel too big for one person to contain. It is less common for the dominant to have the same intensity during the experience so the connection is likely to be unequal. It may be very pleasurable for the dominant and often it may end in a sexual interaction that is likely to be experienced as hot. But, it's important to know that the experiences are distinctly different and how the body and brain of each person process the scene will always be at odds.

It's also important to talk about spirituality here. When you activate the parts of the body and brain that are designed to respond to survival questions, you also activate elements that we comprehend or describe as akin to mystical or spiritual. It isn't intentional for many people and often when it happens it surprises and sometimes disturbs people. Often kink is intentionally positioned to have an element of crude sexuality. This, juxtaposed against elevated spirituality don't usually appear to go together. In fact our culture is rife with messages that they can't go together. But, here you are feeling both and it's like mixing sweet and sour in a savory dish, when both are present it's way beyond what either element is by itself.

Still, it is disturbing when a submissive experiences the dominant as a god. The dominant may not know what to do with this type of unexpected result. Often the dominant will play it off as a momentary strangeness and they will carry on telling themselves its really not about spirituality, not really. This is part of the reality of kink, it will upset everything you've been told or taught about your body, your sexuality and even how you think about your relationship with spirit.

Most organized religions have invested in controlling the sexual behaviors of their participants, usually by controlling female sexuality more than male sexuality. There is a perspective that humans should elevate themselves above the crass or profane physical body. This is a type of denial of man's physical nature, of man's sexual nature. There continues to be an idea that it is necessary to deny physical pleasure or enjoyment of the flesh in order to attain spiritual states. In some religions this concept goes so far as to remove the clitoris of young women so that they cannot experience sexual pleasure. This is designed, not to promote spiritual excellence, but to prevent females from desiring and pursuing multiple sexual partners.

There is at least one tiny culture that practices radical penis modification but the modification is not shown to diminish pleasure or to prevent sexual activities, it is designed to make the penis look larger. Many cultures seek to control or limit a females access to sexual experiences while actively promoting a males access to sexual experiences and multiple sexual partners, all in the name of spirituality.

Sexual promiscuity is primarily focused as the sin of women. Men are merely succumbing to the sinfully displayed or offered sexual temptations of unscrupulous and heinously fallen women. What exactly are the men who typically govern these religions so very much afraid of? What is it about female sexual experience that requires such extreme measures?

I used to hear that the modern applications of female sin were derived from Medieval times both to ensure the parentage of male children and to maintain a steady stream of money into church coffers. After all, until DNA came around it wasn't possible to identify the actual male contributor to the genetic makeup of any child. When parentage is tracked through the female lineage this issue becomes less of an issue. Is it really all about money and power?

I used to think so, until I had my first kink experiences. Denial is a tricky business. When a female is raised in a patriarchal culture everything about her sexuality is secret or a lie. Her vagina might as well be a distant planet for as much as she knows about it. Sure, she can look up technical drawings that show every organ, blood vessel and fold but it doesn't look the least like what she feels. Touch – don't touch. Leak. Blood. Clean – unclean. Sin. Whore. Orgasm – smelly. What is it?

Unfortunately for the prevailing religious organizations in America, the 1960s saw the development and availability of the birth control pill. With the threat of pregnancy now preventable or off the table women suddenly became aware that their crotch was no longer in the rigid grip of some stranger yelling about vaginal sin from the pulpit. But, so what?

Do you know that women in the 1920s knew so little about their body and sexual potentials that doctors used to routinely visit a woman in her home when she was suffering from 'hysteria' described as genital distress, what we call being horny. The doctor would then administer treatment by manually rubbing the female's clitoris until her hysteria was relieved. This is the state of women's knowledge of their vagina, right up to some women today. What do you think happens when a woman discovers the sin of common orgasm? How about when she discovers the greater sin of the perverted sexual experience? What about when she feels like she is communing with god? Or when she feels like she might *be* a god?

As science informs the public about basic human sexuality the role of organized religion is in decline. The concepts of sexual denial are directed towards the congregation but all too often they are not followed by the men giving the directions from the pulpits. As the hypocrisy becomes more prevalent, more women are raising simple questions about the widespread focus on controlling the sexuality of women by religions and by men. Does having good or even great sex mean you are spiritually bankrupt? Is sex a moral issue? When is sex not a moral issue?

Kink may look like a very strange place to look for religious and spiritual answers, but appearances are often deceiving. Because kink places extraordinary pressures on the body and mind of its practitioners, it exceeds the common range of sexual experiences and enters territories of the mind and body that are truly extraordinary. The submissive in a BDSM encounter literally places their life and welfare into the hands of another human being. This is beyond the trust offered between two people in a marriage. Everyone is going to fight, to have bad days, to be pissy with each other. Still, the moment they decide to do kink that trust has to be there. Is it always there. No. For as much as I would like to tell you that kink is good, it isn't. Kink is kink. The individual will bring their stuff to kink for better or worse. Some people shouldn't be trusted, they cannot manage themselves well enough to maintain trust against the temptations of their own desires.

When you explore D/s you will encounter and probably have at least one interaction with a person who violates trust or violates consent. It doesn't mean they are a bad person, it means they have poor behavior management. You need to know how common it is. Think about every person in your immediate circle of friends and family. Now, ask yourself how many of those people have broken their word about something important, a violation you know about. There, I bet you realized it was all or nearly everyone has done something. This means that everyone you meet is working on these issues, including you.

It is very rare to meet someone who will violate your trust in a critical way so that you experience serious harm. The trick is to try to work with or form a relationship with a person who is trustworthy enough and honest enough to maintain your physical health and to communicate well enough to work through emotional and mental violations when they occur. Because they will happen.

BDSM provides unique opportunities for violations, particularly of sexual violations. Unfortunately it is pretty hard to identify who will cross the line when you are tied with your genitals exposed and your brain floating on chemicals. It is just as likely to be the really wonderful person you think who would never do such a thing as it would be the guy you are sure would always do such a thing. Remember that BDSM will act like a dis-inhibitor on both the submissive and the dominant. It is like giving the dominant several stiff drinks and then offering them a banquet of genitals. Some can resist. Some can't.

Kink isn't safe. I can't make it safe for you. I can't tell you that you will be safe and protected or that everything will work out the way you want it to in your fantasies. It won't. This doesn't mean it will be bad. It doesn't mean bad or good are the measures you should be using to evaluate your experiences.

D/s offers both people the opportunity to intentionally create the type of interaction they want to explore. But, to do this you have to be able to communicate clearly and directly and you have to know what to communicate. In the beginning you won't really know what this might be. So, you try to select the type of person who demonstrates the qualities you believe are the minimums of what you need and want. Try to prepare for the onset of your own madness, when your capability of discerning reasonable from unreasonable will fly out the window. If you select well, you will learn the right words to use to communicate well to move in the direction you want. If not, you can select again.

DISCOVERY OF SELF

The discovery of self is an active process of personal growth. Becoming a dominant or a submissive often starts out as a choice. It is likely you have already decided which aspect of domination and submission fits you. After all, you know yourself. You know what you like and dislike, feel or don't feel and it seems important to clarify as soon as possible which role you will present to the people you are meeting or desire to meet within kink.

That seems logical and fairly simple, only, the self is seldom logical or simple. The roles we like to identify as dominant or submissive from the outside seem very clear cut with distinct differences. Perhaps you have thought that by selecting the side you *'must'* be then you can keep from wasting time by exploring the ideas presented by the other side. Or perhaps the idea of the other role makes you uncomfortable, uneasy or embarrassed, sensations you are certain are clear signals that you cannot possibly be or share much in common with that *'other'* role.

What is less obvious is that the stirring of emotion, feelings or sensations is often an indicator of something within you that is sensitized. Exploring what you are not comfortable with feels dangerous, risky, maybe even a bit scary. If you instantly adopt the role of least resistance you can often retreat into safety, feel yourself hidden, unexposed.

The simple truth is that what you know about yourself is often limited to what feels comfortable. The aspects that you hide or deny are usually those that feel awkward and uncomfortable.

The dominant and the submissive are two sides of the same coin, sometimes so closely similar in nature that the distinctions of role become blurry or vague. Both the dominant and the submissive share the same traits, characteristics, mannerisms, behaviors, actions and inactions. To some degree a submissive is a dominant and a dominant is a submissive, that is the fundamental secret to how they blend into each other or act upon each other. A submissive will dominate any person who demonstrates they are submissive to that submissive, effectively triggering the submissive to respond in their dominant aspect. The same goes for the dominant. A dominant will submit to any person who actively demonstrates that they are dominant to that dominant, effectively triggering the dominant to respond in their submissive aspect.

How we identify who is on top depends upon the circumstances we are presented with.

To understand this more clearly we need to look at how challenge acts within each of us on a daily basis. Challenge is when a held opinion, belief, idea or thought is overtly tested. If, as an individual, we react to the presence of challenge then we are to some degree identifying that challenge of that opinion, belief, idea or thought is possible. This means that within that specific framework we do not fully possess that opinion, belief, idea or thought. Lack of possession makes us subject to outside or external challenge. It means we are in a position of possible modification of that idea, opinion, belief or idea. When we are fully possessed of our opinions, beliefs, ideas or thoughts we are no longer reactive to challenge around that challenge. It ceases to retain an energetic charge. What we possess fully cannot be challenged except from within since we also constantly test our own belief and opinions for validity in an ever changing world.

However, possession of the self is not a decision, in many ways it is a process of change and transformation that exists in a state of unresolved permanent continuation. You may find this idea somewhat contradictory and it is a conflictive idea if you believe that who you are can be finitely identified, labeled and solved. If you are a submissive then you are to some degree stating that your growth or state of becoming, transforming or evolving as an individual has ended. You are declaring that you have reached an attained state or the end of the process. Are you really done growing? If you are alive then you are never done growing.

This means that you are not 100% submissive. If the individual identifies that they are a complex and diverse being with infinite aspects of the self coming together in ever changing patterns as the events and circumstances of their lives change then that individual is stating that they are within the constant process of change, development, growth and transformation and that the aspect of their self which is prevailing at this moment in time presents itself loosely within the framework of the aspect most recognizable as submissive. Quite a mouthful, huh?

If you declare that you will always be submissive or be 'a' submissive then you are not being truthful or honest to yourself. You know that if you are thrust into a circumstance where your survival or the survival of your children or loved ones demands that the dominant aspect of yourself rise to the surface and direct action, in that moment you will willfully, willingly and completely become the dominant that you need to be to protect those you love and cherish.

You may be sitting there arguing with me right now saying, it isn't the same thing. But it is. Acknowledging the existence of all sides of the self is fundamental to discovery of the self and to accepting the fullness of whom you are in your entirety. If you deny or reject any aspect of yourself then you can not possibly reach the center of yourself and achieve that state of balance within yourself that is necessary both for mental health and to explore the real potentials of your gift of humanity.

> *Roles are artificial labels that describe a partial identity.*
>
> *Roles limit your potentials and while this may be fine in the short term, eventually you will need or want access to all of your potentials.*

If you are beginning the journey of the discovery of self then you must begin by forming the understanding that you are millions of aspects and you can present yourself as either dominant, submissive, switch or all or none of the above.

By refusing to reduce yourself to a single label you do not force yourself to acknowledge only the traits or aspects which fit into your idea of what you are supposed to be. If you are allowed to experience all sides of yourself without internal censure then you will truly have all the means to discover who you are and how to integrate what you discover into the changing landscape of your life.

Over the course of time you will find that the reality of what exists within you will surface to make itself known. Many people struggle with this emergence and the difficulty that this knowing awareness immediately brings to their lives. It is in part putting a name to previously inexplicable feelings, sensations and beliefs.

Once an awareness of your individual potentials becomes part of your consciousness you will never feel the same. For many people finding multiple potential identities of their intimate nature and realizing that they are not alone is an overwhelming experience. It's okay to be the wildly varied human being that you are.

In this way the discovery of kink can feel comfortable. We want to believe that this is a place where we no long have to hide our thoughts or fantasies, particularly around sex. This seems like the entirety of what we need. But, it isn't.

While finding your 'tribe' can allow you to feel accepted and more valued, kink is not really a community and it certainly isn't a utopia. It is merely a space where censure is less immediate and less obvious. The people who engage in kink are all flawed and if you stick around for a few minutes you will quickly discover that all of the same issues that exist in mainstream culture continue to exist because the people practicing kink have these issues.

So, your feeling of comfort and support is not reliable. Instead of investing in the idea of a co-culture, invest in individuals.

The following descriptions and definitions are to aide you in understanding the most common characteristics which are attributed to each personality aspect. I urge you to recognize that these are only partial descriptions to be used to guide you in understanding the broader scope of how D/s is typically viewed by many in kink

- The metrics commonly used to measure dominance in the American culture include:
  - Money, power, physical size, culture-centric attractiveness and celebrity.
  - Mastery of a craft or skill.
  - Gender, race, ethnicity, sexual orientation and agency.

It is important to recognize that most of these *attributes* can be inherited as an accident of birth and reflect no characteristics on the part of the individual.

Dominant

Dominant: commanding, controlling or prevailing over all the others. Overlooking and commanding from a superior elevation. Of relating to or exerting ecological dominance. Being the more effective or predominant one in action. Of relating to, or exerting genetic dominance.

Dominant, Predominant, Paramount Preponderant, Sovereign...superior to all others in power, influence or importance.

To peer backward through the shrouds of time itself we look into the heart of humankind. It is important to consider genetics when searching for understanding in the actions of the human psyche. There are clues to consider in how and why humanity currently favors a patriarchal sexist power structure over other options.

A dominant in historical terms was likely to be the *'beast'*. That being capable of standing atop the crushed, mangled bodies of others in the pursuance of their objective. Historically the dominant was the individual who had the size, health, strength, capacity, timing and will to overcome, outmaneuver or conquer others.

Some dominants lead through fear, using hatred, pain and threat to control and drive those within their realm into compliance with their wishes. I call such people tyrants. Some dominants lead through physical dominance, using their physical attributes to physically overpower less endowed individuals. This is another type of bully.

A third type of dominant will lead through cunning, deceit and manipulation. Often all three of these types of dominants inherit the means to forcibly impose their will on others in a tyrannical framework.

Every person is the living manifestation of thousands of years of evolution, quite literally we are each genetic history. Some families developed early 'bully' traits that allowed the family to acquire the means to maintain dominance across centuries. These beginnings were crude but effective. Over time, in the interest of continuing power, many families connected through marriages. This created traits weighted in the behaviors and characteristics that proved successful in earlier times. Physical might and unscrupulous behaviors began to be trumped by cunning and intellect. These characteristics were also married into the bloodlines. As you might imagine these genetic characteristics, while successful, do not produce human beings that are strongly interested in the health and wellbeing of others. These characteristics can produce the brutalities that humankind is suffering with today and attempting to overcome. But, the forces against the concerns of common humans is substantial and unscrupulous.

Humans have design features that encourage the individual to align with authority. This means that confronting or challenging unscrupulous wealth and power is incredibly difficult and dangerous to accomplish. Frequently the individual or group that does manage to remove the power base of a major authority figure will simply adopt the same heinous position, revealing their nature is as corrupt as the regime they challenged.

In modern terms America is currently suffering from increasing political corruption by shadowy corporations and individuals of great wealth who seek to govern from hiding. This is the state of our affairs. It is no different in kink. In most cases the individual that seeks dominant status over others has no inherent skills of mastery.

Humans align with power in order to survive. It's a very simple formula. Among the spoils of this struggle are the rest of us, the full array of human designs and potentials. Under these conditions humans who were not in direct power or authority, developed strategies and behaviors likely to increase their survival into the future. These people often desired to retain their personal power and increase it if possible. How? By adapting to the ways of authority and seeking paths to add to personal value, all in the effort to successfully reproduce into the future.

It's helpful to remember that just because a person is born into wealth and privilege, it doesn't make them adept at anything. In fact, wealth and privilege often lead to sloth and a lack of motivation. So, the capabilities that may exist genetically don't respond the same when evolutionary pressure ceases.

This means that inherited positions are also in constant decay and the individual who possesses such a position may often be oblivious to the pressures of those seeking to acquire the role of authority. The dogs at the door are frequently more vicious than the dog inside.

> *Does the desire to submit and serve identify you as a submissive?*
>
> *What are the limits of role?*

This is the evolution and continuing production of bully-style dominants that are so common in every phase of human life today.

A less-successful dominant will role-play submission to a more-successful dominant until they devise the means to overcome the more-successful dominant. So, from this perspective you can see that the submissive isn't particularly submissive, nor are they automatically in service or maintaining the care and welfare of the dominant as their primary concern.

Of course, not all human beings display such extremes in behavior. Other forms of relating exist as well. To identify individuals who are engaged in the acquisition of personal power and wealth through this type of process, merely look at your behaviors, the behaviors of your friends, family, associates and others. What are you attracted to watching on television? Do your television show choices center on celebrity, wealth acquisition, sports, warfare or other status related subjects? For most people the answer is yes. The argument might be that this is what is available to view but in this age of media proliferation there are all kinds of entertainment choices readily available through numerous outlets. So, a choice is revealing and perhaps a little disturbing.

A submissive is often simply a beta dominant or a dominant who is not in the preeminent position of authority to some other dominant. While all of this may be intellectually interesting it really doesn't speak to how the dominant role plays out in a kink setting.

Within kink the issues with the most amount of energy in mainstream culture are played out using the exaggeration of roles within a tight frame of a one-on-one relationship. Humans are working on domination and submission issues. Humans are working on the proliferation of bully-wealth celebrity culture asking serious questions about what is really happening and should it continue or change course.

It is already changing course. Expanding rights for women, persons of color and persons of different than normal sexual orientation are transforming the American patriarchy even as we speak.

Within kink individual couples are using the energetic charge of sexism, objectification, power abuses and more to explore both their own bodies and how they want to experience their relationships. Domination and submission are treacherous waters. This is why they are exciting. It is easy for a role to go to the head of the person inhabiting the role. It is also easy for a person to lose a good relationship due to an inflated head.

Is Kink A Community?

Many people in kink want to organize like a community. But, we really share very little in common. An interest in the exploration and removal of authority over sex is not a big base. It may feel important but there are only a few actual points where a majority of the people who participate in kink actually agree.

From the outside the opposite appears to be the case. When you visit a fetish website you see millions of people engaged in sexually kinky acts or interests. But, if you get just a little bit closer you discover that they agree on almost nothing else. We are a little like a herd of cats, impossible to move in any particular direction for any length of time. It's okay. We don't really need or want to create new governing measures for sexual expression and experiences. Such would negate the vitality of kink.

The reality is that kink is composed of the diversity of the mainstream culture. Perhaps the defining marker of a participant in kink is his or her discomfort and unwillingness to accept the overt rule and controls imposed by external governing bodies such as governments or religions regarding sexual interactions between consenting adults. Kinky people value sexual potentials. That's it, that's the community or lack thereof.

Not everyone will agree with me. You will find all of the typical signs of organization that you might expect with any group. Some people form non-profits or event groups and others just get kinky in the bedroom. Many people try to establish rules, agreements and categories to identify and quantify everything. It's okay. The bottom line is that sex is between individuals, it isn't received by listening to someone talk about it. At the end of the day who is paying attention to the rush of organization when they are in their bedroom with their partner?

Most of the people in kink are interested in the tools of control, perhaps more so than in mainstream society. Exploring those tools is at the core of power exchange.

So, what's really happening here? Why do we seek these things out? Why do we need them? What are we and who are we? Who are you and why are you exploring kink?

Emergence

Emergence: The act of coming forth, emerging, rising into view or the recovery of consciousness.

We sometimes use the term to describe the process that many people experience when they *'find'* the kink side of themselves. In its more profound philosophical context emergence suggests an awakening or epiphany-type moment, a transition from a state of being unaware to a state of sudden sharp awareness. Inside our body it feels a lot like the awakening of the self. In many cases the discovery of kink begins when the individual is in their late teens to early 20's *(this is more common today with the popularity of kinky erotic novels),* mid 30's *(for most men and women),* to late 40's *(for virtually everyone else).*

More women are attracted to kink (numbers responding to surveys) than men. Only a small percentage of women respond to surveys with an interest or preference in domination. It is important to note that surveys can only measure those who are willing to participate and they may not accurately reflect the composition of kink. One good way to look at this issue is to note if you have responded to a survey and how many of your friends have responded. In my case, I've done many surveys but the demographic being measured was 'college participants' so the demographic was primarily between the ages of 20-24 years old.

You may be wondering why demographics are not simply drawn from membership on a kink website. This sounds like a good idea until you understand that many people create multiple identities on such websites. In addition, many people create an identity and leave, never to return (obviously their interest in kink is questionable if the metric used is participation online).

Is online participation the interest measure you want to use as a metric? What if the person with the profile has no interest in meeting another person to do anything, they just like to interact online? Does the person creating the profile have any personal interest in kink or are they joining for professional reasons such as psychology or law enforcement? What portion of the kink population isn't online?

> *Are the people on kink websites an accurate reflection of kink demographics?*

In general, the online environment favors younger participants simply because the technology became available later in life for older people and many have not felt comfortable using the Internet. This means they may not be adequately represented. Online participation also favors specific personality types – people who prefer distant, anonymous interaction. As you can see, there are many factors that challenge the creation of good, factual numbers representing the kink demographic.

But, people are being attracted to kink. You are here

reading this book so it means you are attracted. This doesn't mean you feel connected like this is something you really want to explore yet. You might be there. If not, here is what might happen to you. Some people equate the experience of emergence to a sense of living their life in a partially asleep mode until one day they encounter a thought, idea or concept which suddenly wakens the self.

Many people begin a process of self seeking near the end of their twenties, trying to discover the source of a sense of restlessness within themselves, a gap or void which despite their best efforts remains unfulfilled. Often this process will include spiritual examination or exploration.

This sense of restlessness may propel them toward new relationships in the belief that what is lacking may be filled by interaction with a new person. Generally they will find that while their needs might be met for the moment, the void eventually returns, often with greater intensity. This presses the individual to seek again, generally while not really knowing what they seek. Sometimes a person will recount that this process is very much like looking for hidden part or secret knowledge held inside of themselves. Strangest of all there exists a sense that the gatekeeper of this mysterious secret is their own mind. This is a puzzle where one part of the mind knows something but is reluctant to reveal the nature of the secret to the conscious awareness of the person. They can sense the existence of the secret but are unable to directly pinpoint its nature or how they might reveal what it is.

Within a historical context this inner search may be expressed as the desire for the individual to find the second half of their soul (ref. Plato) based upon the idea that the soul was sundered or split in half at birth and that somewhere out there is the vastness of humanity the other half of the soul also seeks-each seeking the other half. And, when you find the other half of your soul you would then feel a sense of completeness. From a religious context this search may be equated to a search for enlightenment or a desire to fill the void within the self with the 'god presence' so that the individual will no longer feel alone.

It is perhaps this sense of loneliness which is the most difficult feeling to deal with. As a human being we seem to have a sense that we are not supposed to feel alone, but to feel connected to at least one other being and perhaps to all other beings by extension.

To continue this discussion within the religious context, a person who experiences a moment of wakened enlightenment might then identify that moment as the exact point where they were reborn or more commonly, born again.

It does become important to ask yourself why your own mind would keep hidden information or thoughts which would result in such a profound moment. Wouldn't reaching that moment be a positive thing?

I will deal with only one of the possible reasons here, the concept of the forbidden. To hold, believe or intuitively know that ideas, concepts and thought which are identified to you as being those you are forbidden to think, such thoughts resonate with meaning to you. If you possess such thoughts and know they are forbidden or will result in societal or community punishment then how will your mind deal with this conflict? There is a sense that if you acknowledge these forbidden thoughts within you that they will change you forever, that you will no longer be fully party to the society which emphatically holds such thoughts to be forbidden.

Many people want equate the concepts held within the idea of domination and submission to be inherently sinful. Sin here is an act that is censured under the idea that it is morally repugnant based on a moral standard created by (usually a religion) and sometimes by a community. The sinful act isn't one person dominating another, it is having sex outside of the missionary position for reproduction purposes (the only type of sex advocated under many religious morality concepts). When a person willfully embraces the sin of sex for pleasure then they move into conflict with their religious understandings or it places them outside of the religious community. A consequence of kink involvement may include shunning, censure and social rejection.

If you are isolated it means you are alone and often this created isolation is used as a means of punishment with the underlying message being, if you do wrong you will be alone. To be alone and lonely means that you 'are' wrong.

Yet sometimes we know that we will never feel a sense of fulfillment unless we allow ourselves to think forbidden thoughts and begin in truth this journey toward our inner self and towards uninhibited sexual exploration.

The first blast of emergence can feel exactly like entering a new relationship, exciting and scary. The actual process of coming to terms with your kink choices will take years. It has been my experience that there are several phases that seem to be consistent during this emerging process.

At the onset many people are uncertain where they might fall in this new world. They often have fantasies that conflict with what is acceptable in their mundane world yet seem to fit in with the images, descriptions, and ideologies they find on a kink website or by talking with other people interested in kink. The most common way to make contact with kink is through interactions online.

There are several problems with discovering kink in this way. One of the most significant is the case of the new telling the new what to do. This is the blind leading the blind. The cyber kink world online is composed of all of the types of people you find in any group of human beings. There are those who are cyber only who find the Internet a way to have safe quasi-kink experience interactively, with total anonymity and safety. There are those who are into naughty sex that doesn't quite rise to the level I a mostly talking about in this book. These tend to be people looking for quick, easy, cheap sexual contacts and affairs with that edge of kinky that they cannot find in their vanilla life.

There are those seeking to prey upon the new and innocent by promoting themselves as something they are not. These can be sociopaths who enjoy injuring and

> *How can you tell if your kinky online friend has the experience they claim to have?*
>
> *Is the advice you receive accurate?*

even killing people. They are beginning to use the Internet successfully as a hunting ground. Then we have people who are more active and a bit more honest. These people often enjoy making friends and contacts on the Internet for it is truly an excellent resource and way to connect with people who will share your sexual interests. For an emergent or newcomer this makes the discovery process rather complicated and sometimes dangerous.

Sorting out how things really are often requires experiences that are painful, ugly and even dangerous. You can't invest or trust anyone based on what they say online. As a newcomer you also shouldn't feel pressured to attach a role label to yourself until after you have experienced several or many real life interactions.

Just because you have realized you like the idea of kink and because you have fantasies of spanking someone on the butt doesn't mean you are a born dominant.

The fantasy may actually represent a desire to receive a spanking but in your imagination you can't spank yourself or maybe you feel your gender precludes receiving a spanking (will it make you a girly man?) so your fantasy is one directional, at the moment. The factors that create fantasies are psychologically complex.

The individual should consider the process one of growth and inevitable change. It is impossible to fully embrace one's dominance without tasting submission as well. You might wonder why. If you intend or want to give another person direction you need to 'know' the process from the inside out. Your only direct experience of submission or dependency occurred in childhood when you were in development.

The person you hope to dominate will not be a child

and probably they won't be dependent. The area of domination will be sexual which is usually beyond the experiences of childhood. These two factors radically alter the experience of adult submission. To understand these changes and the challenges of adult submission you have to submit sexually as an adult. You have to feel it, struggle with it and comprehend your own emotional and psychological state.

The other issue is baggage. Many people exploring kink have unpleasant relationship experiences in their past. Often they haven't dealt with these issues, they've stuffed them. That stuff is fuel. It means that it *will* inform your next interactions. Since it was unpleasant stuff, it will leak out into your next interactions as unpleasant stuff.

For a dominant that can mean wanting to punish the current person for stuff done by the person in your life before. This is a type of revenge upon the generic substitute, the submissive in front of you. You might tell yourself that you are *training* the new person but really you are venting or abusing them because you have unprocessed crap inside of you.

It is also common to view the abundance of available sexual partners on a kink website like a buffet. If you just exited a broken relationship you may be ready for casual sexual encounters that include a bit of that venting I spoke about. You may also think that you want a harem of female slaves because…why? What exactly is your fantasy telling you? Lots of sex? Women groveling at your feet and begging you for attention? Your every need met merely by ordering it on a gold platter?

Guess what, you are normal.

Are you even remotely ready, competent or capable of giving an adult direction? You think you are. Can you prevent yourself from causing harm and suffering? If you think you can, how did you fare in your last relationship? Did you cause hurt and suffering to your last relationship partner? Did you end up feeling hurt? What have you done in the intervening time to correct your behavior mistakes? Classes? Workshops? Therapy? Beer?

If you did nothing but drink beer and bitch to your friends then you will go into your next relationship with the same dysfunctional relationship skills that grew weeds in your last relationship. You didn't fix anything. Kink isn't a magic wand. Just because (in theory) you can order a submissive to serve you and give you sex and (in theory) that submissive won't call you on your shit, doesn't mean you will magically have a successful relationship. In fact, if your relationship skills are sucky, the submissive will simply stop submitting, call you an asshat and leave. It won't matter one bit if you have a paper contract promising eternal genital sucking. You can use the paper to masturbate in the shower, alone.

The same can be said for many submissives, though in general, I find that more submissives actively educate themselves than dominants, at least in the beginning. Many people will make a contact or engage in a cyber relationship that fairly quickly progresses into a real life meeting. For a new dominant this is a terrifying thing. They have no experience in what is really safe or not safe, how to act, behave or respond. Some attempt to bluff their way through by selecting a submissive who is just as much a BDSM virgin as they are. Again this is the blind leading the blind. This new dominant, if they have not become active in the local community, may adopt or pattern their behavior upon what they have noted in porn, the online cyber chat rooms or forums. This can be absolutely disastrous as many of the role playing rituals so common online simply do not work in real life.

A new submissive may make the same mistake. I have had several submissives tell me they are trained (experienced) and then I discover that this training was exclusively online, not in real life. Please note that you can become educated online, you can engage in private scenes that can be meaningful and challenging to you, but you cannot experience tactile reality without being physically with another person.

> *How long will it take you to unlearn all of your bad relationship habits?*

Note for men who want a submissive experience. It is bad form to place an image of your penis as your profile picture and then claim two years of submissive experience. Really.

Fem doms, like most humans, can't have a relationship with a dick. Females guess that you have a penis and that you really, really think your penis is important. But, the female isn't going to admire or covet your penis like you do. She probably won't give it a cute name and talk to it by itself (after muffling your ears). Really. Dicks don't talk, they dribble and make messes.

It becomes especially dangerous when a new submissive creates fabrications of safety based on 'how wonderful' an online dominant is. Many feel it is unseemly to question someone too closely and can even feel that such questioning may appear to be a lack of trust. Many are afraid to attend local events alone, fearing they will be pounced upon by lurking dominants. *Yes, they live in the bushes outside restaurants! Not.* Because of this, they may develop a skewed understanding of the real life gatherings and people.

There are numerous safe ways to attend events and demonstrations that do not require for either a new dominant or submissive to be attached. Many real life BDSM people will voluntarily and willingly host newcomers and invite them to attend events as part of a 'group' of people so that they will feel more comfortable. Investigating these options is something a new dominant and submissive should actively do as soon as possible when they recognize they have kink interests.

In the 3-5 years after initial emergence the dominant will generally slow down from their initial frenzied state. Previous habits will often begin to be dropped. Many of these are long term vanilla habits of interrelating. This takes time and hard work. It requires accepting difficult aspects of the inner self and an acknowledgement of the levels of personal responsibility that are necessary in actively living in a kink relationship. Many people in this stage will form longer term consistent relationships though seldom will they successfully transition to a full time kink relationship at this point.

This is where many dominants learn how to be honest (with relationship partners), often for the first time in their life. They tend to learn that honesty is no longer optional but necessary. They also may begin to become intolerant of deceit, machinations, and all kind of underhanded antics (including their own). In the later stages of this phase the dominant will often begin to consider seeking out one or more special persons to share their life with.

A submissive will endure some of the same experiences in the 3-5 year range. Often they will become quite discriminating on whom they will interact with. Many become locally active in community groups and volunteer to help other newcomers in their learning processes. Some submissives will spend a portion of these years exploring their dominant side, either as a switch, top or as a full out dominant often while still submitting to their favorite dominants. Newcomers often find this confusing.

Another feature of personal growth is an increased focus on health. Often kink people seek to become more centered and healthy. It's pretty simple, as your health declines so does your libido and your ability to participate in kink. In the later stages of the 5-7 year period the experienced submissive will often reach a stage of peaceful acceptance of themselves. Their desire to be combative will have faded during the process of removing the habits they had developed from childhood. It is at this point that they find they can reach out, perhaps for the first time, to offer themselves fully and without fear as a person who enjoys submitting, service or masochism.

It has been my experience that for a vast majority of people from the first contact with the BDSM community to the point of peacefully embracing their inner self is a process that takes from seven to fourteen years. For some this is much shorter and for some this never fully occurs. Many people do find that they have lived with aspects of kink, in its vanilla form, for the majority of their lives and the transition for them can occur much faster! There are no rights and wrongs to the process itself although education will help reduce the risks and bad experiences. There is no rush to 'be' anything and no right or wrong to any orientation or the absence of role. In the end you will find that you will continue to change and grow long beyond the initial stages. What is natural will eventually be the strongest and in that you will find the most satisfaction. Try not to obsess on any role or on kink itself, keep other interests and hobbies open and active. Being well rounded is mentally healthy and allows you to make better choices.

IDENTITY

Sometimes it feels like humans have an overwhelming need for labels. Everything should fit into neat little categories as if the world or the universe is a gigantic jigsaw puzzle and everything had its rightful place, if we look hard enough. The lack of a label or classification makes many people nervous.

There is a longing to fit in, to find that perfect place where everything will make sense and we can belong at last. We tend to believe that such a place is external to us, maybe existing inside of other people. We look for that acceptance and in the search for belonging we uneasily take on the descriptions and labels that others offer to us as proper.

The existence of self-applied labels tends to make us feel more comfortable, more in control. If I know what you are then somehow I can manage you inside my mind. You become an it, a totally understandable something. Compartmentalized, homogenized, categorized and invisible! Guess what, you are not an object!

None of us is the perfect, it! None of us is the containment of just the traits or characteristics that get that oh so important label stuck on us. When we accept a label, an external identity, we are acknowledging only part of our potentials. All labels fail. Any label can only describe a broad category at best. The limitations of placing too much weight or importance on the label cannot be ignored. To be whole as a person we need to acknowledge and accept all of our traits, characteristics and sides. This means you can't be an it!

> *Labels are limitations you accept on your potentials!*
>
> *Giving up labels is like telling the person who gave you the label that they are wrong – will you lose your connections to them by rejecting their labels?*

The existence of all of our quirks is what makes us unique, different, beautiful and strong. At some point it becomes important to release the desires to fit into any role, label or identity. The only true label that fits is that of a human being. At any given moment in our life we manifest some combination of all that is within us. All roles will fail. All!

Some people believe that those attributes or traits which are different should be pounded out, eliminated or abolished. Differences mean that things don't fit exactly. If something is different then it takes on a level of unpredictability. That unpredictability makes control of it more difficult, harder to manage. Control is important. Right? Labels are used to control or manage chaos. If you can identify something then you will probably believe that the existence of a name makes it less frightening, more manageable. Are you chaos? Yes!

As broad terms or labels the identity of dominant and submissive can be considered useful in a temporary and fun kind of way. It's fun and sexually *hot* to call a person submissive or slave in the midst of a juicy interaction. Fun. But, it isn't the person. It's fetish, a tool, not an identity. As personal identities the need to utilize such a label can be harmful and misleading. Most often the individual will note where a majority of their feelings or attributes tend to place them within the sphere of a given label. This leaves a minority yet viable percentage of the individual, unaddressed. In addition people like to harden labels. Force fit. If the individual admits to any variation in the acceptable label then they are not admitted into the club. Again the individual is made to feel outside or unacceptable. This is the threat of being alone, lonely and punished.

People create labels. They are artificial. Labels are an expression of a viewpoint at a precise moment in time. That moment passes, moves into the past instantly. The label cannot persist because in the next moment the person is likely to be displaying other aspects and features that have nothing to do with the collection previously labeled. People are relieved that labels exist and they seek comfort in being recognized. But, only a part of the person is actually being recognized or acknowledged, other parts are being ignored. That first label, so long ago in the past, created by a parent or doctor at birth, still clings, trying to inform you about you. When you cast off labels you also cast off your connections to the people who want you to accept the label as a description of your limitations. You will make them wrong, you will make yourself wrong. The opposite of labels is potential. That's who you are – mysterious and unconfined potential.

Participants of kink are diverse. You will find all colors, shades, orientations, sexualities, genders, desires and persuasions. No one is excluded. There is no unified model that is the attainable perfection of any role that every individual should strive for. There is nothing which says that one interpretation is any less valid than another. It is not mandatory to enjoy pain, it is not mandatory to need humiliation, it is not necessary to vacate any part of yourself to belong here. It is in our variety and differences that we truly reach our fruition, our individual and collective strength. Being unique and whole is the core of the true self. Be willing to stand outside of the acceptable labels, groups, clusters, organizations, and rhetoric. It's necessary. Your strength and the strength of humanity is in the open expression of our individual truths and full chaotic potentials. If our differences make us more uncomfortable to others, harder to control and contain, then that is a problem for those who wish to control and contain us. If we allow ourselves to become trapped within the created labels of others we are essentially accepting an external level of control or entrapment.

Know that how you express your domination or submission or lack thereof, will be unlike any other human being. You will do it like you do it. Becoming comfortable and accepting of yourself is when you will find your personal strength and internal peace.

Dominant vs Master
Dominatrix vs Mistress

These titles are abundantly used in kink, but they are especially popular online. This is primarily due to the rapid growth of kink via Internet accessibility and the assumption, by newcomers, that they clearly understand such role labels prior to actually doing anything beyond read a little bit online. Up until the 1980s the BDSM world was a tightly closed, fairly secretive network. Due to laws, public censure and mental health perspectives participants frequently kept quite private and hid their interests with significant effort.

Within kink the most active and populated groups or networks were homosexual males. Heterosexual activities and conduct was often through veiled personals ads, shady pulp sex newspapers and hidden clubs. For a clear understanding and exploration of kink history I recommend you visit the Leather Archives and Museum in person or online at http://www.leatherarchives.org/.

A dominant is a person with an ability to guide and direct or inspire the actions of others. Within many online venues the role of dominant is expanded (by individuals) to include other features. I encourage caution in investing belief in any of these descriptions. Most dominants are persons who selected the title, label and role by checking the dominant box on an online website in order to attract potential sexual partners. The skill of checking a box has no relation to interpersonal management capabilities. The choice of the label dominant versus some other authority role label is an indication that the individual believes they are interested in the D/s relationship style.

A master is a person with an ability to guide and direct or inspire the actions of others. However, instead of selecting dominant in the online check box, they selected master, in order to attract potential sexual partners. They are showing a preference for the M/s relationship style.

> *Does your potential dominant partner moonlight as a submissive using another screen name?*

The role selection is identical except that one will expect their partner to be a submissive and for that partner to call them one of the many dom associated titles like: sir, lord, daddy, etc., or ma'am, lady, mommy, etc.

The role selection of M/s expects their partner to be a slave and to call them master or mistress.

Persons selecting dominant roles range across a spectrum. Some might be called dominant-light persons who favor a minimal application of D/s, just enough to have some fun kinky sex and to feel like they are kinky. Some will have a stronger interest and fall somewhere in the middle and then you will find some who range all the way out to extreme that want what they perceive is the full measure of the D/s relationship style. Most people fall somewhere in the middle. Everyone starts with no experience. Some manufacture a personal history that doesn't hold up to the sniff test. You will find exactly the same variety of personalities, characteristics, behaviors, issues and problems that you find in mainstream society. The only difference is that these people intentionally sought out kink, a kinky website and a box labeled dominant something.

The moderate dominant is the most common dominant and will characteristically be interested in a relationship at some point, though often they many not desire a full time relationship when they are fairly new to the community. They tend to have a broader range and more committed style than the light dominant and the submissive will find them to be more stable in terms of activity levels and participation.

All kink participants have a more active interest in exploring sexuality. Over time they are more likely to become sexually educated and knowledgeable. This tends to attract persons who are moving away from a strongly conservative background although many people in kink are traditional and conservative. Where they break with conventional conservative viewpoints is centered on sexuality and sexual issues. This may not translate into other areas of their beliefs.

Mid-range dominants often try to control through the accentuating of traditional type disciplines and by creating or trying to maintain patriarchal sexist role positions that they believe are proper or suitable. They will attract submissives or slaves who are working on the same issues, who want to step back in time (to a time that never actually existed) and role-play the historically skewed modern take on behaviors of an earlier era. The challenges of this choice are simply that both dominant and submissive are living in a modern era and regardless of their desire to dial-back history, they will continue to live in a modern era and they will face ongoing challenges to their choices.

The heavy dominant can be distinguished primarily by a compelling desire to live in a 24/7 relationship with at least one submissive (sometimes a harem). They are likely to want contracts, strict rules, heavy participation and may be working towards an in-home dungeon and a house full of kink.

I only describe any of these as light-to-heavy based on how active their interests in kink are showing up in their behaviors. None of this makes them good or bad at giving direction, it's merely an interest level.

One of the unusual traits found in a lot of kinky people is the basic desire to provide some kind of service to another person (for personal gain). When in scene the dominant is serving the needs of the submissive by scening them. In those terms the dominant is the giver, the submissive the receiver. In a good or well rounded relationship this flows back and forth between both dominant and submissive. The submissive is giving the substance of obedience and consent to the dominant, the dominant is giving the appearance of direction and control to the submissive.

Another role commonly found in kink is called a top. A top is generally an individual who enjoys scening from the top position (with no D/s or M/s aspect, role or relationship style in place). They will still meet the basic description of a person giving direction over another. Many tops will openly indicate that they do not consider themselves to be a dominant, they generally have little desire to be in a controlling position of another person's life.

Many view their interests as more fluid and less fixed and less attached to role-playing concepts. They simply want to interact in a scene from the top position. This doesn't connote a relationship with their scene partner beyond the extent of the scene, even though many are also good friends with their scene partners. In some instances they will identify that they are a service top, or interested in the activities of topping as a service to the person receiving (the bottom). Sexual benefits may not be part of this exchange which is frequently a difference from a dominant role.

The other role that needs to be looked at is the sadist. A sadist may or may not be a dominant, in much the same way as a top. Often sadists will openly identify themselves as a sadist. They scene because the inflicting of pain upon another being brings them pleasure, period. In many cases the sadist has no desire to live in a controlling position over another person. Also most sadists are very attuned to scene limits, they can and may be a stickler for very precise identification of what is permissible and what is not. In general terms they are not oriented toward serving the pleasure of the person they scene with, though often they are very skilled, very intelligent and very careful. Some are very interested in their masochists enjoyment and they will work hard to achieve such results. Each will likely be very specific and very clear about how their orientation towards sadism works. It behooves the masochistic submissive or slave to listen carefully and to only engage in activities where they have experience of their own limitations.

Many dominants, masters, tops (and other titles) are sadistic and they will enjoy including sadism into their relationships or interactions with their partners.

Many persons who enjoy domination also seek multiple partners. The individual's ability to manage complex multiple intimate relationships can best be judged by the duration of those poly relationships. If the relationships are of short duration or if the dominant doesn't allow the new submissive to talk to those who have left the relationship, it is likely that it isn't a successful poly environment. In general, all parties to a poly relationship should be well read about poly, should attend five or more local poly gatherings and speak with other poly people, and they should encourage their submissives to have additional relationships outside of the relationship with the dominant. Otherwise, the dominant is in a fantasy and the multiple relationships are not polyamory but polygamy or one directional.

In most cases this is a fantasy wish fulfillment type of ego stroking. Functionally, the more people within a relationship the harder it is to manage. It is quite difficult to manage a single relationship well. Every division of time, energy and focus reduces the overall quality to everyone within the framework of the relationship.

There are a few dominants who can and do manage and maintain several intimate relationships at the same time. Most often these relationships are one primary relationship and numerous satellite relationships. Sometimes the secondary relationships are essentially friends with benefits. To participate in poly relationships (that are successful) requires poly education, support, constant open communication, luck and for every person involved to be giving 100% of their effort to making it work.

The Alpha Dominant

Some people have the characteristics, background and experience of leadership. Sometimes this stems from inheritance compounded by parenting and education that placed a high demand on performance. Sometimes it comes from a particularly good set of genes that creates physical attributes that allow the individual to become competitive and successful in a physical arena like sports. Occasionally a person will be gifted with a strong intellect paired with good access to education and a caring upbringing.

This can create a person who is open, has good self esteem, who is socially competent and materially competent. It can also encourage spiritual interests that develop into a fairly well-rounded, well educated, physically fit individual. This doesn't mean they will also possess good judgment and caring for others but when it does, this person can legitimately earn the recognition by others as an alpha dominant.

I carefully noted here that such an identification would not emerge from the individual and would probably be dismissed out of hand by the individual. If all of the components are present and if the individual is interested in kink then they are likely to excel at kink just like they excel in other areas of life. The reality is that they will apply the same techniques for mastery of D/s that they apply to other areas of life and this application to figure it out along with intentional and focused practice will produce a level of mastery. Kink and the various aspects of it are not spontaneously gifted by some accident of birth. No one has a free ride.

The most common problem with a person inhabiting any role in kink is the lack of experience, the inflation of ego and the inability to know when they are wrong and to act quickly to remedy or grow from their experience.

All humans have alpha characteristics and most people have expertise in at least one area of life. You cannot be an expert in kink and be sucky at everything else. Your entire life and behavior inform what you do, say, think and imagine in kink. You have to fix and work on the mundane issues first and continuously or your kink will suck.

Many people gain expertise in whips or needles or receiving humiliation or some other 'skill' that others notice in kink, particularly at public venues. People often equate time and such expertise with elevated status. This is a terrible error. How long any person has practiced wielding a flogger has absolutely nothing to do with their ability to give direction to another person in a non-hurtful way. When a person focuses on the toys or tools instead of the individual and spiritual health you end up with someone that is not balanced.

Be careful to understand this about yourself first and about the people you are attracted towards. While becoming competent with toys and tools is part of kink, it isn't all that important. Many times a lot of kink isn't about caning a person until their ass looks like raw meat. That isn't a great accomplishment. Any robotic arm can accomplish this feat. In fact the destruction of physical tissues is questionable on many levels, whether you *want* it or not. What you want isn't the criteria you use to understand competency.

A few other misconceptions to address. The term lady is often seen. Lady can be an indicator of either dominant or submissive. Many dominants and submissives call themselves ladies. Lady, lord, Ma'am, madame, etc., are merely some of the numerous honorific self-anointed titles commonly found everywhere you look at people involved in kink. They don't mean anything special. I can call my dog Lord Poo and it doesn't mean his poo is elevated above my cat.

Many dominants like to inform potential submissives or slaves that they aren't allowed to address them as Sir or Ma'am unless they are formally connected to that person such as through a collaring process. There aren't any rules here. Your best option is to ask your potential partner how their fantasy rules are structured. Or, they will tell you and possibly make you think you made some huge protocol error with your supposed *mistake!*

Uhmmm, no.

Again, there are NO rules, no common guidelines, no protocols, no old established governing system. This is the Wild West folks, everyone has a gun and their own idea about what is going to work in their personal town. So, when you are told you screwed up or you don't know the rules. There is one rule, there are NO rules.

Remember that you are welcome to adopt the rules of any potential partner you are interested in. You can make up any rules that suit your fancy. But, they are your choices, not mine, not the next person, not the munch groups, not the convention participants, no one's rules but yours.

In public, be courteous. Use the name any person offers as their 'handle'. Be polite. That's just good common sense. Online is in public. If someone is rude to you online, they will be rude in person. If they sound like an expert, it doesn't mean they are. Ask around.

SUBMISSIVE VS. SLAVE

This distinction appears muddled, misunderstood and generalized by a great number of the people that I converse with. First I would like to make a point. Language at its best shifts from area to area. Within this one continent we have many variations or dialects of usage. This can be seen in terms like sweeper meaning vacuum cleaner etc. So, many words within any large community can mean different things to different people based on the 'age' of the person, their background and the common usage in the area they live in.

The submissive is a person who prefers to receive direction from within a D/s style relationship.
The slave is a person who prefers to receive direction from within a M/s style relationship.

A submissive is any person who wants to receive and comply with direction for any length of time towards a person recognized by the submissive as a dominant. A slave is the same as a submissive except that they will tend to frame their behavior in terms of absolutes such as desiring a total power exchange or a relationship without specified limits or safewords. Many articulate a desire to experience a situation as close to nonconsensual enslavement as possible. This tends to be the general differences between how these two roles are conceived by most people in kink.

You will find endless varieties of descriptions of how these roles are formed, how a person is natural or real, how they can only comply, etc. The truth is that the process of submerging your ego for any period of time to the direction of another person can be quite challenging. As the time period increases, the challenge increases. Conversely, many of the behaviors can be stored as habits and become an adaptive process if the person is in a relationship they enjoy or feel unable to change. It is unfair to try to cover or explain the many variations of ideas and possibilities that any two people experience as they are drawn towards kink and the submissive aspect or role in kink.

> *Why do you feel more attracted to one role label versus another role label if they are essentially quite similar or perhaps even identical?*

It is helpful to know that more than 60% of the women attracted to kink select the submissive box on the kink websites. Women outnumber men in kink but submissive females are the most sought after kink role type.

In a general way it appears that most people who are

exploring submission may share some feature of their childhood that felt incomplete. This concept suggests that attraction towards submission is likely to change over time and many people find that this is true, even if at first they cannot conceptualize ever choosing any other role besides submission. I mention this because an incomplete childhood experience positions a person on a path (intentional or otherwise) to attempt to complete this aspect of development.

Sometimes what a person seeks to complete is an experience during childhood that has become stuck or fixed. These experiences do not need to be traumatic, they can be confusing from the perspective of a child. However, this 'delayed' completion process has a finite finish point where the ego attains an autonomous status with authority figures. This means that some people will transition from a focused orientation on submission to a less focused continuing interest in kink that may include role changes.

Some submissives select dual roles with one partner as their dominant and another partner as their submissive. I mention this because many people fear that they will lose their attraction towards kink if they don't isolate themselves within a single role. In fact, the reverse is true. When role is viewed as less of a fixture and more of a temporary choice, the ego isn't as likely to feel trapped inside the role when their satisfaction with the activities of the role begin to change.

This role has the same range of interest or attraction that I described for the dominant. In fact, they are essentially the same in terms of how the roles are experienced for a newcomer. You may only be interested in being submissive in the bedroom on Friday nights. Or, you may want to be submissive inside your home with your husband. Or, you may feel like you want a really dominant person micro-managing every detail of your life twenty-four hours a day, seven days a week, forever.

The feeling isn't the reality.

The feeling isn't your capacity or ability.

The feeling is *charge*.

The passion you feel is directly related to how much energy is fueling your experiences. In general, if you have had a lot of challenges in your past and if you haven't really processed or dealt with everything, then you will have a lot of passion.

The urgent need you feel will show up as a desire to submit. This urge is actually a desire to deal with your passion or unresolved internal issues and stuff. It's a bit like anxiety, like an itch that needs to be scratched. Your fantasies give you clues as to the area that is the center of your interests. These clues will be coached in the language and imagery you have found in novels, reading websites, seeing images, watching movies, porn and more. They will not actually represent the exact things you are excited by in a direct reflection. They will simply be in the area of the energy or passion.

Most people have some understanding of their past and some knowledge of the source of their fantasies. But, for whatever reason the person often hasn't worked through all of the triggers of the situation. By placing themselves into the trustworthy hands of another person in some way that mimics some aspect of the original issue, they can re-experience fragments from a safer perspective and allow their adult brain to process what their younger brain had trouble figuring out.

Your submissive interests can also disappear one minute after a scene. Some people call this phenomenon *buyers regret*. As the body and brain reach a point of culmination, the anxiety-like passion is dissipated or drained off. Often the individual will feel satisfied and sometimes they will feel disgusted with themselves. This can last a short time or for many days until the passion rebuilds to the same level of need that existed before.

All of this is normal.

You won't know how you will experience any interaction until the exact moment of the interaction. You may think you can predict your responses based on your own knowledge of self, but this is part of your fantasy, not part of your actual reality.

In this way your fantasy is likely to conflict with your real life experiences and this can disturb, disrupt or even end a potential relationship because it will not consistently conform to your fantasy ideal of how you think you expect to feel.

THE SLAVE

Most people are attracted to the idea of the slave because the word suggests a higher level of intensity and in the individual's experience of their own body they believe their level of intensity is very strong and can only be explained or described as a slave.

In the idea of the slave the person gives up all limitations on their interactions. Great fantasy. Not particularly a good indicator of good mental health (essential to provide reasoned consent).

Let's be really clear here, it is illegal to own a human being. Period. Fantasy ownership is legal but has no legal merit. It's a fantasy. Why does the person want to vacate their rights? Why does the person want to subject themselves to the potential of mental and physical damage?

These are questions that must be considered in any situation between partners regardless of how little or how much they wish to experiment. The label *slave* has a continuing historical charge from American involvement in the black slave trade, to involvement in indentured servitude, to enslavement behaviors towards most persons of color for centuries. In addition, slavery aspects continue backwards through colonization and throughout history.

> *Does kink slavery have anything to do with historical slavery in the United States?*
>
> *If so, what is the attraction and why are so many people exploring kink slavery today?*

The first logical thought is to say that no one alive actually experienced any of these historical events. This is essentially true. But, most Americans have some historical connection to all of these events if they had family members in the United States prior to the Civil Rights Act of the late 1960s. The past is very close. If a person came from other countries, it is equally certain that their country of origin also had its experiences of slavery. Slavery is a continuing present trauma on the psyche of humanity.

All of this means that each person attracted towards the master or slave role play persona, has a connection to the charge still remaining in the concept or reality of human slavery. It is this charge that resonates in the mind and body causing a sensation of increased interest.

On a practical level, each person is only dealing with their own fantasies. Most don't give a hooey about my historical comments. What is active and present is what is happening in their body and brain at this exact moment. This is the essence of the kink potential.

The reality of enslavement is anything but sexy. It is harsh, violent, traumatic and a horror.

The reality of kink enslavement is sexy or at least this is how it shows up for most people, with some association with sex and sexual activity. They don't imagine themselves scrubbing a stone floor with a toothbrush while clad in filthy rags, with sores on their body and being fed hard bread and dirty water from a bowl on the floor. That isn't the slavery of their imagined fantasy.

In kink, you cannot give ownership of your body to another human being. Ever. You and other people can role play situations in real life that are closely similar to slavery. But, your rights continue to exist and are completely enforceable. Forever!

This means that kink slavery is a fantasy shared among people for their own entertainment and pleasure. When it ceases to meet the needs or expectations of any person, it ends.

This is kink slavery.

The Alpha Submissive

There is a category which I call the alpha submissive. This is the submissive who is auto-responsive. When in top space they can and may appear to be a dominant. This is any person who enters an altered mental state easily and quickly. Upon entering this state they hyper focus and listen for directions with an intensity that can be unnerving. This is a nearly automatic response.

As an individual they may have difficulty controlling this response. Usually this auto-response is accompanied by hyper-alert states or the trance-like states common to people who are easy to hypnotize. There are several factors that can create this type of response. With some people there is a natural affinity to 'shift' towards altered mental states. This can be enhanced by a meditation practice or by participation in many kinds of drumming or musical events.

Hyper alertness tends to come from some event in a persons past where it was necessary to look for danger or risk. Many people think that this must emerge from an abusive background because this is the common source for some hyper-alert behaviors. However, a person who, as a child, was asleep in a car seat when the car was in an accident that was sufficiently serious to thrust the child out of a safe space and into a traumatic or chaotic space, can experience the conditions of hyper-alertness.

The most common source for hyper-alert responses is based in a childhood environment that was unsafe. Often this stems from a parent or adult who has mental illness, poor behavior management, erratic temperament or behaviors or addiction problems that manifest in similar ways. A hyper-alert state is used to assist the recipient individual in responding quickly when the out-of-control person is present.

Some altered mental states can develop during childhood to allow a child to escape experiences mentally and emotionally. Sometimes the individual is not really aware that they use altered mental states in this way until they discover kink and discover that they are listening differently and responding differently.

Calling this set of features an 'alpha' is somewhat a misnomer. Alpha generally means a beginning or elevated form of something. In this case my label is suggesting that a person with these features is somehow more important or desirable than someone without these features. This isn't true.

However, when a dominant encounters a person who responds in this way the experience of the encounter is often potent and the dominant may be likely to favor a repeat of the experience potentially believing that the responses they have encountered mean that the submissive is particularly keyed toward that particular dominant in a powerful way.

This is both true and false at the same time.

There is a survival characteristic that will surface more easily with a person with these features to align with the person whom they identify as potentially dangerous. For the duration of contact they are likely to perform with both auto-response and to all appearances a deep immersion in the experience. But, be warned here, things are not exactly as they seem. These are survival traits. While the person is genuinely experiencing submission, there is a wary observer calculating the situation at all times.

It is likely that the individual has developed strategies for removing themselves from situations that activate these responses. In a sense, these responses are a warning that similarities to past events are present.

A person's responsiveness can also lead a dominant to believe that their personal behaviors and techniques are superior in some way that is reflected by the excellent performance of their new partner. This is a delusion.

If a person is vulnerable to 'suggestion' they may also be vulnerable to obsession or fixating on their partner almost from the moment they meet either online or in person. This places additional responsibility on the dominant to both understand and protect the interests of that submissive as they may lose the capability to adequately protect their own interests once they fix their attention on the dominant. Many people who select dominant roles are not competent to interact with people who have vulnerable mental states. Know thyself!

One final note. There is what is loosely called a 'submissive network'. This network is a system which has existed probably since the origination of the SSC credo *(Safe, Sane and Consensual)*, wherein submissives share information. This becomes important if you are a new person. A dominant is only as good as the reputation they maintain. There are persons within this community who use the label dominant, top and even sadist to cover their activities of non-consensual abuse. Consent is the most commonly violated aspect of kink. Often this violation is associated with sex with a partner while they are unable to escape. This is rape, regardless if you gain consent during the act while the submissive is in an altered mental state. This is like raping someone when they are drunk.

The good reputation of a well-known person is no protection from consent violations. As a newcomer you are unlikely to properly check out the person by talking with their former play mates. You are likely to rely on their prominence at events or in comments from others. Don't.

If your consent is violated and you are raped, contact law enforcement. This is in real life. By the same token, before you agree to scene a submissive talk to the dominants they have seen before. If a person has 'abuse' issues with every person they play with then they will have those same problems with you.

There are some persons who will experience profound regret and denial after a scene and accuse the dominant of abuse, assault or rape. You are not required to medically diagnose, just be open and honest. Do your due diligence and talk to former relationship partners for a full picture. Submissives also live by their local reputation. When encountering or beginning a new relationship, be honest about any occurrences which may reflect poorly on your reputation. Establishment of trust requires this. A dominant may be accused of abuse and a submissive accused of being a habitual drama queen or liar. Gather the information and take the time to get to know the individual before making a judgment!

The Sexual Submissive

A sexual submissive is a person who inhabits the submissive or slave role only in direct connection with sexual arousal and release. In all other aspects of their life this person will probably comport themselves in a manner that is neutral or indistinguishable from a non-scene related vanilla person.

This brief description accurately positions most submissives as sexual fetishers. This means their interest is really centered on improved sexual experiences and less on improved relationships. However, it is also important to remember that on a whole, we are culturally conditioned to judge a person with a sexual interest as a person in a 'lower' state. Our conditioning tells us that the only 'good' or 'higher' state is for sexuality to be associated with relationship and when possible for that relationship to be heterosexual and monogamous.

This means that sexually focused people often experience discrimination in kink just as often as they do in mainstream culture. A fetish is an object or part of the body that arouses sexual or libidinal interest generally to the conclusion of genital or orgasmic release.

There is a lot of rhetoric that positions roles as distinct from fetishes but I believe that may be an effort to bolster a viewpoint rather than to look closely at the realities of both. For many people 'thinking' about submitting arouses sexual and libidinal interest in exactly the same way 'thinking' about shoes or licking a toilet might trigger a person with those specific fetishes.

By viewing sexual submission as a fetish it becomes easier to understand how acquisition of the sexualized state can temporarily satisfy the sexual need. If submission was truly a facet of personality then this wouldn't be true. Since I believe it is likely that both situations are operational it becomes easier to see how submission or domination (for the same reasons) is less a state of being and more a response to information.

Since the mind is obviously part of the body, this thought process can then be viewed as potentially a fetish even though the thought process itself might be relatively broad and appear to be unfocused *(in terms of fetish type focus or obsessions)*. When the entire mental process become obsessive the specialization seen or noted in traditional fetish behavior becomes inclusive or not easy to note.

> *What is the BDSM versus sex issue all about and why does this division appear to be growing inside the kink groups?*
>
> *Why are many submissives unhappy with the removal of sex?*

It is interesting to consider that within the framework of 'scening' or the theater of the sexual arena the sexual submissive presents identical aspects of submissive behavior found in persons who don't identify as sexual submissives.

I've suggested here that duration is a distinguishing factor. But, this is less true than it appears. It is important to realize that people tell stories to themselves to explain their feelings about any subject. In the case of the submissive (as a role) many submissives are in the business of establishing how submission is a pervasive condition of their personality and character.

Any deviation or fluctuation in their submissive presentation is subject to dismissal, stuffing, denial or some other personal explanation. To be a part-time submissive appears to violate the romantic ideals that form the foundation of so many relationship attempts. Frequently people try to infuse sexuality with relational importance. This is particularly common for women.

It is common to hear someone say they will only submit for that special dominant person who can control the submissives 'strength' etc.

Really? Submission comes from inside a person not from the imposition of external control. If strength is needed it is internal strength to negotiate the many inhibitions provided by the very active ego. You control your behavior and choices in the world. You. No dominant can ever control the inside of your skull. Ever.

You are carrying around your cultural conditioning. You may think that by showing up on a kink website that you have somehow vacated your conditioning into a new state of sexual liberalism but you haven't. At every turn you will discover that the 'rules' you create for yourself to establish what you want to experience are usually near mirrors to the rules you were raised with.

Are you looking for the *one* special person? Why one? Do you have one friend who is supposed to meet all of your needs, forever? Do you have one friend who likes to read books, another who watches sports, another who likes to shop, another who talks gossip about everyone you mutually know, etc? You don't have a single discrete box of satisfaction. You have a multitude of interests and most commonly you share mutual interests with other persons who have similar interests.

Why do you believe your intimate relationships should be different, that there must be a single fully dimensional person who fits all of the boxes? Conditioning. Escaping your cultural conditioning means you need to throw out the template of romantic assumptions completely.

If you think about submission and immediately picture yourself having hot sex. Own it. Recognize that your response is about a lifetime of suckworthy sex based on inhibitions created by a shared sexually-constrained culture. You don't fix your sex life by simply re-framing your sexual problems with a new additive of kink.

You have to fix your entire orientation toward sexual expression and sexual activities. It begins by admitting your interest *is* sexual, not a devotion to service.

If your fetish was truly a devotion to serving someone you would be at another website that is devoted to serving the needs of the homeless, the displaced, catastrophe responses etc. You are here. In kink. It's about SEX here. Specifically, it is about your issues related to experiencing crappy sex and trying to make it better.

If you don't feel submissive all the time, guess what, you are normal. A person whose sexual triggers are so linked to submissive behavior may have great difficulty understanding their 'lack' of submissive feelings, desires or thoughts outside of the sexual arena. Some might even consider themselves to be flawed or stuck, as if they have reached a type of submissive plateau when in actuality they are not submissive in the narrow definition of submission that tends to be popular on websites and chat groups.

It is common for a sexual submissive to have strong mental submissive or 'force' imagery within their mind at any time they are in a sexually 'interested' state. This would be any time the body is desirous of physical genital release. This long obsessive state leads many sexual submissives to erroneously believe that they must 'be' submissive since they have a strong desire to experience the submissive 'condition' during sex.

The sexual submissive often finds that they are experiencing many conflicting mental messages when they attempt to adopt submissive behaviors outside of the sexual arena. They might note that they don't automatically rush to help out other people. They usually tell themselves that this is because the other people are not the *special* person they reserve their submission for, as a gift.

Actually, they are not in service. They are in denial of self authenticity. They might also note that their submissive sexual thoughts revolve around sexual specific submissive behaviors are not inclusive to all submissive behaviors. These internal limits may feel peculiar and may elicit challenge and lack of understanding of self. Are they a brat? They really don't like to comply unless it's sexual and hot. Who wants to clean the floor when no one is around to notice?

Most people inhabit a role for the show. This means they only inhabit any role fully when they are being observed. Otherwise the dominant would be handling all of their thorny issues like their personal health, their weight, their finances, their relationships with their parents, and more. Otherwise the submissive would be serving at every level. What does a submissives home look like? Take a look at the background in most kink images on most kink websites. In particular look at the background when people are taking photos of themselves in a mirror. See a mess? What is that about? If the person is in service why doesn't it extend to basic cleanliness? Don't submissives long to do chores? If you look up the word submissive in any dictionary and follow the words you will eventually reach words like drudge. But, what is the submissive in the photo really eager to show you? A hot shot of their body.

Take a look around your home at this minute. What does it say about your actual personality and normal behaviors? There, what you see is what you do. That is what is actually true.

In most cases you are willing to be submissive to someone else to get your needs met. You may describe those needs as someone telling you what to do. You remember being a kid. When your parents told you what to do, such as clean up your room, it got you so excited and eager to race around doing it, right? What actually happened?

If your parent's couldn't dominate your behaviors with 18 years of practice and a deep personal relationship with you what makes you think that your behavior will magically be transformed by a sexual dominant? The reality is that each submissive must manage their own behaviors. If you want to correct issues in your personal life you cannot displace the responsibility for those issues onto a person as your special gift.

Who wants that kind of gift? That is tantamount to

inheriting a rebellious teenager. Sure, the trade you offer is hot sex, with you and more attention, for you and even then will you perform as you promise? Take another look around your room. When do you actually perform, such as by cleaning it up? Is someone coming over? Do you want to present a certain image to that person because you value their attention? Is your cleaning up a temporary behavior when you fear loss? If you are a slob will they like you less?

These are a few of the issues at the core of submission and truthfully at the core of domination.

One of the indicators or identifiable traits of a sexual submissive occurs in the aftermath of a sexual scene where they have performed as a submissive. After the sexual 'scene' has reached its natural conclusion the sexual submissive may in fact feel strong feelings of remorse, chagrin and confusion over the nature of their nature. Many do not really understand why they need to relate to their intimate partners from a truly submissive framework, why this arouses them so strongly and why the aftermath is so challenging and difficult.

Some sexual submissives feel a sense of revulsion for their actions or behaviors and have great difficulty returning to a state of wellbeing sometimes for hours after the sexual scene has concluded in genital orgasmic release. This sense of revulsion can appear almost instantly once orgasm has occurred.

From a dominant's perspective the revulsion post scene can be shocking if they haven't experienced it before. The withdrawal of approval, appreciation, and other positive relational interactions can be like a slap on the face. What happened? What did they do wrong? On the other hand, being with a sexual submissive can be enormously enjoyable too, primarily if the two are sexually compatible within the framework of the fetish type triggers that the sexual submissive displays. It may allow the dominant to dominate during this type of very erotic scene and be able to be with their partner in a neutral, almost vanilla type relationship in all other areas of their life. This can be a relief for many dominants.

Not all sexual submissives have the emotional response I've described. Some hit space and come down to their normal mental state in a gradual way. Some experience old and troubling traumas from their childhood and need a lot of emotional support. All of these responses are common.

If you experience great difficulty presenting yourself as a submissive outside of the sexual arena then it is likely that your submissive response is tied to specific triggers. If you believe yourself to be a sexual submissive then I urge you to become comfortable with who you are and not try to force yourself to fit into any other person's idea of what you must be.

SWITCHES

The Switch (also known as being versatile) is a person who enjoys scening from both a dominant and submissive perspective. Adding this component into the understanding of roles is often similar to adding a dose of confusion or chaos if you are strongly attached to the idea that a role is the manifestation of your true personality.

There is a persistent attitude of dismissive censure

when a newcomer comes across an online profile with the word 'Switch' prominently displayed.

Obviously, this means that the person isn't real or true or authentic or something. This is the typical reaction. Saying you are switch is a great way to attract almost no sexual interest. It's the big heterosexual D/s turnoff. The only thing worse (from a submissive female perspective) is for a guy to be a submissive male. How gross! How can any self-respecting guy wear a dress and grovel at the feet of a female?

Many people hide their disdain but then they avoid the person, never considering the remote possibility that this could be *the one*. The common female submissive perspective is that they want a strong man who takes charge of the sexual situation and who makes *them* feel sexy, wanted and important. What can a submissive man do for them? You may have noticed here that in the submissive female's perspective a switch is the same as a submissive man.

> *Why do supposedly sexually open people engage in shaming behavior towards individuals who self-identify as a Switch?*

You may also have noticed that my account of the dismissive sub-fem internal dialogue is also a problem. If a submissive female is 'in service' then why can't they serve the vanilla needs of their current husband who is unlikely to be expressing dominance?

The existence of the switch or submissive male poses serious issues for most submissive females. He challenges their romantic perspective of submission.

It is fairly common for male switches or submissives to contact *all* kink females. They would like to find a fem dom but females who self-identify as dominant are less than 15% of the females on most fetish websites. This means the submissive male needs to expand their options. They have two choices, make contact with more open male dominants or make contact with submissive females and hope they can *turn* them into reciprocal dominants.

While many men are open to same sex—sex, many men aren't open to that degree of intimacy with another man. But, their kink options are limited.

Since everyone's first love experiences involve being told what to do and being corrected for behavior problems, there is no mystery to the allure of submission. People want to *feel* more in their adult relationships.

People are attracted to kink websites for sex and sexual access, not to be truthful about themselves or to show their true nature.

If you attempt to force yourself into performing as just one side or the other then a part of your self will remain unaddressed. Eventually this can lead to bursts of energy release which can be enormously destructive. In other words roles are not sustainable.

Place any dominant in a hospital and they become submissive. You may want to argue that this isn't a good argument, how can a person be dominant when they are ill. Exactly. If this role is actually a feature of the self then it wouldn't cease based on environment and circumstances.

In some cases the individual may be with a person who believes that their non-conforming aspects need to be destroyed. This can lead to language such as breaking.

Attempting to rid a submissive/switch of their dominant aspect through breaking is gross assault against the integrity of the individual. Mental and emotional battery designed to destroy a part of another human is absolutely wrong, cruel, non-consensual and most often reveals weaknesses within the perpetrator more than anything else. The need to break someone is usually driven by fear or dislike of people with good self esteem.

A dominant/switch who attempts to hide or mask their desire and need to occasionally experience the opposite of their dominant role may actually transfer personal frustration onto the submissive they are with. This can manifest as momentary episodes of lack of control, verbal abuse, emotional abuse and even physical non-consensual abuse or battery.

Maintenance of good mental and physical health are essential in preventing these types of destructive events. This is done through healthy choices. It is all about keeping a balance, addressing all sides and attempting to neglect or ignore nothing. Being honest about your needs is essential.

Switching from one role to another can be fun and easy. After all, you were designed to enjoy all sides of yourself.

Learning how to move easily and comfortably between both roles takes time, a sense of personal understanding, emotional security, and a lack of fear in how either side will be viewed and interacted with by those who are important in the individual's life. Anything which impairs this sense of personal security can make the switch aspect feel threatened and defensive. It is my personal opinion that all humans have contradictory sides which in most cases they attempt to hide through a fear of appearing weak or too strong. Failure to be open and honest about these sides leads to secrets, closed communication and feelings of personal frustration. This can, in turn, lead to destruction of relationships.

There are no rights or wrongs to roles. You are not diminished by being open to all sides of yourself. You may attract less interest but do you want to stuff the parts of yourself that don't fit into some easy role concept? Moving from one aspect to another is common and many believe that full range of experience is the best way to learn about yourself. Living as a switch offers an individual the opportunity to fully experience the challenges and joys of any role. Expect to struggle, expect to change more. Enjoy!

SSC: Safe, Sane and Consensual

SSC is the acronym used to represent the slogan "Safe, Sane and Consensual." This slogan is the cornerstone credo used the D/s BDSM community to identify and separate the community from the appearance of or common language used to identify actions of abuse and assault. This slogan was developed within the community (attributed to David Stein) to distinguish kink from assault and to encourage participants in kink to recognize the inherent risks involved in these choices.

Safe

Safe is defined as secure from threat or danger, harm or loss.

Except, there is no such security. Within all human activities and kink in particular, safety is tenuous at best. Assurances of complete safety cannot be given. The idea of safety, however, should always be at the forefront of any activity with a heightened risk factor. A considerable amount of information is available on tool and toy safety so I will not cover that aspect here and I actively suggest that you purchase a variety of BDSM safety books and tool oriented texts to independently augment your working knowledge of safety issues.

It is also important to remember that while such texts can offer good general advice, no book can anticipate the individual environment or applications of such objects so additional common sense must also be in place each time you use objects on a person.

There are also many people who invent brand new things, environments, behaviors and rules that can all negatively impact safety. For this reason it is important to view safety as an issue that needs to be continuously re-evaluated and possibly updated regularly.

It is also critical to understand that experience doesn't equate to safety. No two humans are the same. You can use exactly the same techniques on two different people and your experience with one person is a situation of safety and with the second person it can be an unsafe situation.

I urge you to remember that safety issues do not remain stable or the same from year to year. New information becomes available and participants of kink are aging, with all of the typical increasing health problems of the aging process.

Tool or scene safety is the easiest and most visible interpretation of the safe concept within kink. It is important but in many ways overly considered when people think about what is safe or what isn't safe. It is much easier to cause significant injury emotionally or psychologically than it is to cause long-term physical injury if you are well-educated around physical injury issues and you are adhering to those parameters.

Danger within D/s comes in all of the same forms that it exists throughout life and within relationships. There is the obvious physical risk to a submissive who engages in a scene with a dominant. All relationships begin between strangers. This increases risks. The responses and behaviors of both people are unknown. When a stranger (or any person) is untrustworthy, the sub may be injured or even die. However, there is a significant amount of psychological danger too. A submissive must give over trust psychologically, which places them in a position of mental and emotional vulnerability as well.

There is a less obvious physical danger to a dominant. Most dominants are not in physically vulnerable conditions during a scene. But, creating and managing a scene is also physically taxing and many dominants are subject to erratic blood-sugar levels that can result in passing out and falling, leaving their submissive partner in potentially high-risk bondage or stressed conditions. When engaging in a new relationship everyone places themselves in positions of intimacy with strangers. Mental problems often go unseen in the excitement of pending play.

You can't know how a person will react to any stimulation, even those that appear innocent and low risk. Each person is a product of their own history and that history can be a map with many hidden holes. Reactions may be triggered which set off irrational behavior. In such cases submissives occasionally act out against their dominant, sometimes with fatal results. Again, this risk can be managed or minimized by taking the time to get to know your partner slowly, not succumbing to fast scening when you do not know their mental triggers.

And, if you like volatile partners, use your own safe

call or scene in semi-public so that other people are around to accurately observe the interaction for your safety as well as the safety of the sub.

As a submissive, the foreknowledge that the scene partner (dominant's) name and location are known to someone external to the scene offers some protections. It isn't a good idea to meet at a hotel. It isn't a good idea to meet at a café and then go to an unknown play location. Use your common sense. There are sociopaths in kink just like in real life. Just because a person is smooth, charismatic and funny before you get tied up, doesn't mean they aren't bat-shit crazy.

Request and check references. Ask for the name and contact info of former play partners. Ask those partners about any negative rumors or experiences with your potential new play partner. This goes both ways. Submissives can be equally unstable or they may enjoy victimizing others. Be careful. Be thoughtful. Go slowly.

> *When you negotiate a scene with a new person what are the essential elements you need to know and check before you scene with them?*

The presence of repercussions often operates like a good check and balance and if you are told that there are reasons for denial of information by a person you intend to scene with then you should become immediately wary! It is understood that some people participating in the S/m lifestyle are violating aspects of their relationship or marriage promises and they might be reluctant to divulge information which could be used against them to directly damage that relationship.

This may all sound legit and maybe in your specific case it is legit. However, I feel it is essential to point out here that the person who is actively violating their marital or relationship agreements with one person will actively violate their agreements with you too.

Consent is the most common violation in relationships both vanilla and kinky. A consent violation is any violation of agreed upon behaviors within a relationship. If a person says their primary sexual partner knows of their kink involvement, ask to speak directly to that person. If it's legit, it's legit. If not, it's someone violating consent.

Most people think of violating consent as in 'being raped' but this is short sighted. Cheating is simply another version of violated consent. When a person cheats they know that the discovery of their behavior will cause suffering to another person. This is why I call it a violation.

If you want your primary relationship and other kinky relationships, be open, otherwise your level of trustworthiness is questionable. Your word is not worth much.

You probably don't want to divulge sexual and relationship secrets to a stranger. It's called shared risk. If you elect to scene without real life knowledge of whom your scene partner is then you are increasing the risks to your life enormously. To some degree the mutual risk exposure is part of the 'given' exchange making each person vulnerable to the knowledge their partner possesses, this becomes an important safety issue. However, even with comprehensive knowledge of your partner you do not become risk free.

A violation of boundaries is all too easy to do, especially when a relationship is new. Your partner cannot know the details of your life, events in your past and the residuals of abuse that may exist. Some of the same triggers which stimulate a person can be gateways to abuse. There are no fast ways to learn these things. Every individual is unique and their past is unique. This is true for both the dominant and the submissive. It is possible for a submissive to behave in a manner which triggers a dominant into negative actions based on past events.

People can be threatened from any role. A dominant may try using threats in order to control a submissive. *(This is a very poor technique and ultimately will lead to total failure of the relationship.)* A submissive may try using threats in order to control the dominant. *(This is equally poor, generally reflecting poor mental health, selfishness, and a failure to release control.)* An example of this is the submissive who might threaten to out a dominant publicly *(thereby ruining their reputation and may even destroy careers and family)*, or a person may threaten to commit suicide if their relationship ends. All of these types of actions within a relationship are examples of poor self esteem, poor mental health, inferior understanding of how to direct action, and a demonstration of personal fear.

A relationship which uses threats for control is in trouble. This is an expression of fear of loss. That loss may be of control, respect, trust or of the relationship. Fear can destroy everything. It makes people irrational and subject to making choices they might never consider at other times. It can drive them to injure, abuse and destroy. Safety suggests we should be free from threat, that the actions we take should not driven by an underlying fear.

Danger is exposing or involving anything likely to inflict injury. When considered in this way it is easy to see that D/s and BDSM are dangerous. It is virtually impossible to be secure from anything that is likely to inflict injury. From the physical standpoint the dominant is in the position of stressing and extending the submissive both mentally and physically. This is dangerous. It becomes an issue of risk management such as through attempts to reduce aspects that are known to be life threatening or potentially so, including mental damage. This can be fairly easily done in the physical aspect by the dominant and the submissive learning the straightforward dangers of various tools, toys, techniques and apparatus that they wish to use in scene.

It is very hard to predict or prevent danger in the mental aspects. The application of mental pressure can easily damage, diminish the self-esteem and even thrust the submissive into reactionary modes if they perceive their internal survival to be threatened. The signs that this may be occurring are not always easy to recognize or identify. In addition, the dominant cannot truly know where that edge is. If their submissive has a past with strong abuse issues, it can be an accidental usage of a word or phrase that has severe implications to the submissive. Finding a way through the delicate psyche takes lots of time, effort and care. Conversation and the open exchange of information becomes even more crucial in handling issues when they do arise in order to maintain trust and respect.

I am sometimes asked what is the one thing I would tell someone who is exploring this lifestyle. My single and best piece of advice. My answer is this, *Do No Harm*! This goes for both dominant and submissive. If your relationship is in any form injurious to the other persons involved *(or yourself)* step back and consider why. It is just as easy for a submissive to injure a dominant through lies, deceit and a cavalier attitude as it is for a dominant who makes similar behavior choices. No one is invulnerable, invincible or impervious to damage. Keeping your partner as safe as possible is an action of cherishment and value. Taking the time to go slowly is an expression of worth. For those that want to speed down the track of instant scening with strangers and express window delivery, you are toying with a much higher risk of creating suffering in yourself and others.

It becomes important to remember that a large number of relationships will fail and within those failures people will sometimes have difficulty managing their behaviors. Since not all human beings are taught how to manage their negative emotions in healthy ways, it is even more important to learn and practice these skills in your kink relationships. There will be relationship failures. Persons with immature emotional management skills are likely to act out, threaten, try to intimidate, shame or cause injury to others. Develop a good exit plan. Practice good communication. You should act intelligently and have a good exit plan if you believe your relationship partner may be unstable. If either person in the relationships has threatened actions of self damage should the relationship partner desire to leave, such as language threatening suicide, this is a clear and direct signal that the individual threatening the behavior is currently or actively mentally or emotionally unstable. Professional advice from a licensed therapist should be sought immediately and all activities including scening with that person should immediately cease. The unhealthy individual needs to return to a mentally healthy state in order to return to any type of active D/s relationship.

Sanity

How sane are you? Mental health isn't discussed much in kink overall even though everyone wants everyone to be healthy enough to play. Have you ever asked a potential play partner if they have any history of mental illness themselves or in their family? Funny how that question usually isn't part of negotiations. How about what mental health drugs do you take? This sounds pretty basic, right?

Most of my potential play partners never ask me anything like this. The assumption of mental health is a big error. In general, approximately 18% of the population of Americans are currently taking medications for mental health problems. That is one out of every 5-7 people you meet. Do you think that is important?

It is important. The basic concept of consent hinges on mental health. Mental health affects competency. Each person has to be able to comprehend and actively act to protect their own mental and physical health in order to offer reasoned consent.

A dominant and submissive must carefully evaluate

the apparent mental state of any person they are considering entering into a relationship with or even scening with on a one-time basis. This is far more difficult than it appears. Not only do people find it difficult to ask the 'rude' questions about mental health, most don't want to know the answers either. Few of us are psychological experts and the simple truth is that sometimes persons who are the least competent mentally can mask themselves sufficiently to appear sane to those they are interacting with.

Evaluating sanity in the best of times is very difficult. Most often we offer people allowances based on circumstance, prior events, crisis, stress, etc., in our effort to find that perfect someone. We tend to quiet our intuition when it raises questions as to the veracity of the individuals word or suggestions that perhaps all is not right with someone. This is exactly the opposite of what should be happening here. BDSM is not innocent, nor without significant risk and danger. That risk transcends many levels of life.

> *Does engaging in kink place your competence to manage your own health and welfare in question? Does kink participation negate competence making BDSM abusive?*

From a dominant's perspective, if the submissive they are communicating with, is in any way demonstrating a lack of competence or diminished mental state, then that dominant must consider that individual submissive potentially incapable of making consensual reasoned choices regarding engaging in activities which can and may be seriously dangerous to their health, both mentally and physically. A person demonstrating a lack of care for their personal health is not mentally competent *(in my opinion)*.

What cues should a non-professional look for in the behavior and lifestyle of the potential partner? Addictions are an easy clue. Excessive drinking, drugs, gambling, hoarding, sex, dangerous activities, food, exercise, drama, all of these and any obsessive actions or behaviors are clues to behavior management problems.

I already recommended looking in the background of photos to see how a person behaves when they are not staging circumstances to impress others. This is a peek behind the scenes into everyday life. Evidence of addiction problems may suggest self destructive behaviors or be an indication of a less than healthy mental state.

Some people are attracted towards kink hoping for support around their inability to manage life in a constructive and productive way. You are not their therapist or savior.

You do not want to be their maid and drudge. If you want to do a lot of floor scrubbing on your knees then volunteer with a dog shelter or homeless shelter. Seriously, how people manage their life and its stresses are a good indication of how they will respond and behave with you.

Mental distress and disorder can also be displayed as excessive cleanliness and order. Excessive washing, concern with bacteria, excessive shopping, excessive unpaid bills, inability to maintain a job, inability to maintain family relationships, these are all clues. If a person has lots of stories about why things around them are in the state that they are and why they cannot fix things, these aren't good signs. A person in reasonable mental health will care about all areas of their lives. They will look to their personal physical health, maintain good relations with people they care for *(such as extended family)*, have a moderate number of friends and activities outside of the BDSM world and more. A well rounded and non-fixated life with richness and depth in many different areas are all good signs of reasonable self esteem and care of self.

The risks and dangers or level of danger is not the same for a dominant as it is for a submissive when BDSM is also a factor. The exploration of BDSM will position the submissive in greater danger both physically and emotionally. The first exchange in a D/s relationship is trust. Placed poorly that trust can and does at times cost a submissive their life. However, other issues exist here too. If either person selects someone who is very compulsive, jealous, or subject to sudden outbursts of extreme rage or violence they can find themselves in a nightmare situation compounded by kink.

People, regardless of their BDSM orientation, live socially in wider society. Most hold jobs, have children, go to PTA and Scout meetings, attend church and generally must live a fully integrated life. They have reputations to protect. The threat of exposure can be very real and turn voluntary submission or domination into forced submission or imposed role. This can force a dominant to continue in a relationship they know is flawed and unsafe. Behaviors to look for include: any usage of personal threats, fear, embarrassment, shame, guilt or duress trying to compel the actions or behaviors of others. If a person attempts to control someone else using any of these tools then it is a huge warning sign and they should be avoided. I say a person here because manipulation can come from both sides and does. Sometimes I talk with people who threaten to commit suicide *(as noted earlier)* if their Dom/sub leaves them. They forcibly impose a power exchange in an effort to control the actions of the other person. In some cases they cannot distinguish a lie from the truth and will use any form of deceit in order to attain or attempt to attain the goal they seek. These signs are indicative of significant problem and professional help should be quickly sought.

Then we have people who routinely vacate personal responsibility for anything negative that occurs in or around their life. We each have the ability to make choices that can place us in positions of compromise. If we choose to get drunk and engage in a sex orgy, explanations after the fact are simply not good enough. Each person should be expected to possess basic competence to make valid decisions in their life or you shouldn't be dealing with them. Lack of basic competence is a sign of poor mental health and makes that individual inappropriate to engage in a S/m relationship with. No action is completely accidental. Something within the individual encourages the choices they make, regardless or in spite of potential consequences. Bad judgment isn't good. Shifting responsibility or finding justifications or excuses for obvious behavior and choice problems is a good indication that the person has some work to do to be a stable state. In order for the terms Safe, Sane and

Consensual to mean anything both people need to be mentally competent and stable. Otherwise, engaging in scene with someone incompetent does violate all three of the aspects of SSC. An incompetent submissive may or may not express the truth about their limitations, may or may not be able to make choices that are healthy for them mentally, and with the mental state impaired cannot be fully considered to be able to offer their reasoned consent! An incompetent dominant may become obsessed to the point of destroying their submissive either mentally or physically!

CONSENSUALITY

Consent: Compliance with or in approval of what is done or proposed by another.

There is nothing more important in kink than the idea and practice of consent between adults. We talk about consent a lot. There is a very good reason for this, the line between D/s and abuse is consent. Non-consensual control, manipulation, application of pain or direction is abuse/assault.

However, as with most things the meaning of consent is far from simple. When a submissive is new in their exploration of the D/s

> *If consent is inherently unstable, why do so many people rely on its durability?*

and BDSM worlds consent seems easy and basic. They have no personal experience of consent as a complex agreement that is acted on by intense mental, emotional and physical states. What they do have are ideas, thoughts, hopes, dreams, feelings, beliefs and desires. These often conflict or add to the difficulty of establishing consent. A person can think they will enjoy something only to find that in reality they do not. So, we are immediately faced with a dilemma.

It is impossible to truthfully consent to something you have never experienced. You can consent to trying something, but you cannot accurately state that you will enjoy or like it until after it occurs. This means that in some ways the consent offered is a blanket approval that covers actions that may not be approved of in actual experience. In many cases it really means that the submissive will consider trying something to see if they enjoy it. From the dominant's standpoint this is treading on shaky ground. If you scene someone and really get it wrong, the consequences can be pretty stiff. As I noted earlier, consent violations are the most common issue in kink.

Many new dominants and submissives spend a great deal of time looking for and searching out potential partners *(frequently and increasingly on the Internet community)*. Often people find potential partners who live at some distance where they cannot meet easily. This can lead to protracted long distance cyber and phone relationships. These types of communication can foster the building up of scenarios, ideas and expectations. The problem with Internet evaluation is that humans establish attraction and interest from multiple cues and many of these cues are physical or present only in person.

When the two manage to arrange a meeting, they

bring with them all of the expectations and the baggage that has accumulated before and up to their meeting. Often a long-distance build-up encourages many people to vacate simple safety issues based on their romantic illusion that this is the perfect partner. They are so eager to jump in that they want to play within hours of a first meeting. Sometimes they go so far as to pre-scene this meeting based on the idea that the first meeting should be spectacular and a clear example of their future roles together. It is not terribly uncommon for a new submissive to agree to a first meeting that places her in a foreign state, in a motel room, naked, kneeling and waiting for her master to show up. Really.

In addition the new dominant arrives prepared with their expectations that this novice submissive will perform in some introductory scene and love every second of it because the dominant has convinced themselves that the gushing admiration they have been receiving from the submissive online and on the phone means that they really are the extra special one. In many cases this may be the very first scene the dominant has ever tried and they may have or feel extreme pressure to meet the submissive's expectations. How hard can BDSM be, really? There are millions of profiles online so it just can't be that important if one or neither have any experience. But, this can be a setup for true disaster.

This week *(spring 1998)* the news was filed with an ongoing court case in NY wherein a woman is suing a man whom she claims raped her. She made contact with him on the Internet and engaged in extensive correspondence *(some of which is included in court records)*, and phone conversations. After 5-6 months they arrange such a meeting. They engaged in-scene for nearly 20 hours. Afterwards she accused him of rape, rough sex, forcible sodomy, assault, battery, various kinds of bondage and torture and a few other things. She agreed that she talked to him about her interest in BDSM but she claims that she was interested in him and played along because she liked him. She acknowledges voluntarily meeting him.

This is important. Early, heavy scening with an unknown person forces assumptions of consent on both people. A submissive can and may feel pressured to go quite far in order not to displease their new dominant. They may agree to things under duress or contact pressure. A dominant can and may feel pressured to perform to the ideas they have fostered through prior communication. They can be total novices doing things they are not really prepared for. It is simply impossible to know a person you have just met. You cannot know their body language, the suggestions and subtle signals necessary to truly read their responses. This type of pre-scene creation can and does kill people. It can create situations much like I described that are becoming much more common as participation in kink becomes more popular, especially through poorly researched pulp novels.

Many people believe that consent in a license, that it gives them a blanket permission to do what they want to do. This is simply not true. Consent at the beginning of a relationship is more the option to explore further. It offers no guarantee to the dominant or submissive that they will be held blameless for what occurs. Those that engage in sudden intense scening willfully place their reputations, careers, family and life on the line. When you are dealing with a stranger, you cannot guess how they will react three days after a scene when they bottom out and you are not there to discuss or comfort them. Remorse, pain, regret, embarrassment, shame, anger, feelings of diminished self respect and outright rage can and will drive people to take actions against the person they have previously consented to scene with.

An action may include: outing the person's behavior to other kinky people in their local area: outing the person to friends, family, co-workers, employers, children, neighborhoods and law enforcement. This was supposed to be all about sex and fun, right?

Initial limits are just that, initial. They should be expected to change, evolve and alter over years and experiences. They are merely a way of offering an idea of the range of interests that the individual believes they are interested in pursuing. Consent can, at best, be considered to be fluid. In addition to the above, it should be noted that everyone is not the same every day. There are days when consent to the range of play will be much wider than on other days. These variables can be affected by mood, health, stress and many other things. Assumptions that consent is constant can and will lead to problems.

CONTRACTS

A contract is a written agreement signed by one or more persons and used to define the characteristics and behaviors all parties to the contract are agreeing to support. Kink relationship contracts are FAKE! They can exist in real life on paper and signed in blood but they continue to be FAKE! These contracts may be entered into seriously by all parties with every intention to abide by the terms of the contract but they are simply fantasy contracts applicable only as long as consent remains constant within the relationship by the people of the relationship. American law trumps all other contracts.

As an American citizen you do not lose your rights no matter how much you want to give them away to someone else. The action to try to give your self away legally means you are legally considered to be incompetent. The court and legal system act on behalf of this potential and real incompetence by ignoring any and all written contracts limiting your rights as a citizen. You can't enter the contract legally.

Contracts which are often labeled as submissive or slave contracts are becoming far more common today. They are very popular devices. People want to use a contract to validate the intensity of their commitment to the kinky premises of their D/s relationship. Some people erroneously believe that the existence of a contract in some way legalizes the 'idea' of enslavement or acts of submission between human beings. In the United States of America enslavement of human beings is illegal. Period. I am repeating this because people who are in the thrall of new relationship energy can be obtuse about these things.

A judge will not care if you have a contract that was notarized and witnessed by a hundred people. The fact remains the same, slavery is illegal. So what in truth does the existence of a slave contract mean? Nothing. A slave contract has no legal standing and no means of enforcement of the agreement stated upon it. It cannot show 'consent' of the individuals agreeing to participate in a consensual relationship. It can show that some type of relationship existed at the moment the agreement was signed but it cannot identify if either partner to the agreement was feeling duress during the signing of the contract.

Further, regardless of the language included in a contract *(such as 'forever')* a relationship lasts only as long as it lasts. The existence of a paper stating that at one moment in time either or both partners believed and hoped that what they were embarking on *(their relationship)* would last forever doesn't make 'forever' actionable. When either partner no longer believes in the relationship then the relationship ends. The contract cannot maintain the relationship and cannot be used as a means of forcing compliance where none voluntarily exists. Further, a contract is positioned in finite reality or it describes thoughts and ideas attached to a specific point in time. A relationship is positioned against infinite reality and is not attached to a specific point in time. As the relationship evolves any finite instrument or promise may become void of any substantive meaning since the finite instrument *(contract)* cannot evolve with the relationship but remains fixed or trapped by its own language.

One final note, if you are with a human being who has signed a slave contract with you stating you may do what you want with them, this does not mean that you now have permission to assault and abuse them such as to whip them until they are bloody believing that you are to be held blameless for such damage. You aren't. You are governed by the laws against assault and violence just like every other human being and you should know that your 'slave' need not contribute to your arrest in any way for you to be charged with assault and violence.

It is assumed that no 'sane' person will allow damage to occur to their body *(mind/spirit)* which will alter their ability to enjoy their life and pursue happiness. This means that the state will become to some degree 'guardian' over the inability of your 'slave' to escape or evade placement of themselves in such a position of permanent damage. The state will act on behalf of your slave's 'silence' to end the unreasoned battery upon them and may go so far as to solicit professional therapy for your slave to aide them in mentally escaping the idea that their death or permanent damage is acceptable within the context of any relationship.

So, if you are a predatory assaulter you should recognize that you cannot engage in assault against any human being without being subject to the full measure of the law against you.

Hard Limits

One of the first questions asked of a new submissive is "What are your limits?" To some extent this is a meaningless question because a new submissive doesn't know the answer to this question. They have never had those limits tested or challenged. Because of this, it is common for a submissive to state that "They have no limits!"

The statement of no limits can mean only two things. Either the submissive is a new or they are incompetent. No person should ever make a statement of no limits.

All sane human beings have limits. There are or should be fundamental boundaries across which the human mind should not cross. These are called hard limits. A hard limit is an issue or belief that must remain inviolate for the individual to retain a belief in themselves and the world around them. These are beliefs that will never change. They are a part of the core or inner self.

Here is a list of the basic minimums.

- No children (they cannot consent)
- No dead people (they cannot consent)
- No animals (they cannot consent)

Once you read this basic list you probably think that these items are a no-brainer. But, there are people who will actively cross these lines. It is best to always state them so that there isn't any question about where you stand.

Unfortunately, I would love to tell you that everyone in kink has pure interests and they would never cross these boundaries but if I tell you that it would be a lie. You will find people looking for mother/daughter combinations and people who become more interested in making contact with you when they realize you are a parent of young children.

Yes, they may like young children and may intend to pressure you, over time, to include your children in your sexual activities. This may sound ludicrous at the onset but you are unaware of your vulnerability to suggestion within the D/s framework until you experience it in real life.

Yes, there are people who fantasize about dead people. Some like the vampire mythos and others are simply 'into' having sex with a human who cannot challenge them. Access to dead bodies is difficult but not impossible and people with this interest can find ways to acquire bodies. In addition, there are kinky items that are made from dead bodies. This is only illegal in some vicinities, not everywhere.

And yes, there are unfortunately a lot of people who are interested in sexual acts with animals. Many state that the animals really like it and show obvious enthusiasm. Really? Gross! Say no and keep saying no. These are the basic three hard limits. None of the above can consent. Ever. People who actively choose to violate any of these limits violate Federal, State and Local law as well as International laws and they violate the basic parameters of what is Safe, Sane and Consensual. They violate and abuse the rights and freedoms of those they interact with as well as taking actions which are morally repugnant and ethically corrupt! Those who prey on the weak, the young, the animals or the dead are not part of my perspectives of kink. I will not accept them or their actions and choices as just another kink. Non-consensual usage is abuse, assault, rape, wrongful imprisonment and torture.

Some people believe that these limits are so fundamental that they are simply understood. I disagree. One should never assume that the person you are interacting with understands something or believes something they have never actually stated to you. There are people within this community who will accept a statement of no limits as an invitation and expressed voluntary consent to damage, injure or destroy another human being or to engage in activities that are illegal, immoral and wrong. It is crucially important when seeking a partner within kink to find someone whose baseline hard limits match yours. Be specific, direct and pointed when asking about these limits. If you don't then you may be placing yourself in a position of vulnerability where you may be forced into a situation which you are unable to evade behaviors and acts you don't want.

> *How do you build trust with strangers so that you can explore your fantasies safely?*

Hard limits are called hard limits because they never change, they are not subject to stretching, extending or expanding and the violation of any of them is sufficient by itself to totally sever the relationship and probably extend criminal charges against the perpetrator. It should be noted that you may have differing hard limits than those stated above. There may be additional issues which you mandate as inviolate within your own life. Look carefully into yourself and try to clearly evaluate where those fundamental lines are within yourself. There is no right or wrong to having a longer list of hard limits. Each person is an individual and unique. Identifying and expressing that individuality clearly is important.

It is also essential here to look at a dominant who asks or demands that a submissive have no limits. This can mean at least two things. Either the person *(note I do not identify them as a dominant)* considers the submissive to be without value and desires to use, injure, mentally or physically damage or destroy them. Or, the dominant requires that their submissive have no limits beyond mutually shared hard limits. Ask! If the person you are interacting with clearly states that the submissive/slave should have no limits at all, leave! This person is not a dominant.

They may attempt to coerce you into continued communication using charisma and claims of being misunderstood or of joking – or they can go the other way and use guilt, shame, need and intimidation to convince you that this is what you really desire. Do not stay! Expect such a predator to be charming, intelligent, smooth and very able to skew things into something you may agree to. This is not D/s. One of the best ways to identify someone with problems is if they attempt to limit or control your access to information and limit your contact with other persons involved in kink. If you have met a dominant who tries to isolate you from information or contact with others-BEWARE! Remember that a dominant should not be afraid of you having information, it is part of informed consent. In addition, the forming of real life friendships within kink is considered healthy. This is a place where people share information and support each other.

However, a dominant may ask a submissive to withdraw from a friendship relationship if the dominant believes that the individual friendship is negative or unhealthy for their submissive. As long as this is done based on the merits of the situation then it should not be construed as an attempt to isolate the submissive unless each friend is deemed to be a problem. The dominant should ensure that the submissive has other acceptable friendships who also are participants in kink. A dominant should never be a submissive's sole resource for information and support, no matter how romantic that sounds at the beginning of a relationship.

A limit is the word used to identify the range of play acceptable to the individual within the D/s or BDSM framework. This is a way for each individual to state their kink preferences and taboos prior to entering a relationship. This is done to ensure to the best of one's ability that the issues, beliefs, rights, needs and desires unique to that individual are clearly understood. Some people go so far as to engage in written contracts identifying these limits so that there can be no later misunderstanding.

It is assumed that within a play scene or session that the dominant will not violate a submissive's stated preferences or limits. It is further assumed that within a play scene or session that the dominant will test, extend or stretch certain of that individual submissive's stated limits. This appears to be two statements in total conflict. The language of pushing limits is sometimes code for violating consent. Be careful. If you feel violated or deceived, then you have been violated or deceived no matter how the dominant explains it to you. Trust your feelings.

Part of the complexity of the BDSM world revolves around its constant contradictions. It is frequently paradoxical. Limits are those things which the submissive is most sensitive to. Within those limits hide fear, embarrassment, shame, guilt and especially pains or wounds from the past. It is common for a submissive to state a limit knowing, wanting and desiring for their dominant to take them into that place where they are unable to go alone. This is called a soft limit. A soft limit is where the boundary means danger, not stop. Soft limits are things which challenge the mind, the body, the spirit and the past. A new submissive should not agree to these until they have numerous experiences with one or more dominants and until they feel confident that they can attempt something with some degree of safety.

When a dominant and a submissive are first exploring each other to see if a relationship is possible they will engage in intense conversations. Within these conversations they will discuss the range of limits and play that each hopes or feels a need to engage in. Also, within these conversations will be a discussion of forbidden or hard limits. Areas that are never to be challenged, stretched or extended by the dominant. It is important for both people to communicate clearly and openly and listen clearly and openly to what the other person is saying here. If a submissive can identify and state their hard limits then the dominant will have a means to clearly understand where the submissive is coming from. After establishing these hard limits then the conversation will often move further into soft limits.

When you are new your soft limits are everything except what is basic or simple. Think kink 101. Don't guess at tricky stuff no matter how much you like the other person and feel they are trustworthy.

When you are ready, here is a common list of soft limits:

- No blood sports (these are any activities that penetrate the skin such as guns, knives, needles and piercings)
- No water/scat sports (these are urine, feces play – both of these pose substantial health risks)
- No air sports (these are any activities that block air or oxygen to the body – asphyxia includes choking, strangulation, bags, smothering and similar)
- No broken bones, mutilation or permanent body marks.
- No mental edge play such as humiliation, shaming or difficult mental challenges.

Note: There are numerous other aspects of play which the individual submissive may consider to be limits, some of the most common are gags, blindfolds, confined spaces, heights, suspension, multiple scening, bisexual scening, homosexual scening, overt humiliation, public scening, as well as a full range of limitations on certain types of specific equipment or toys. As you can see the variations and options regarding soft limits are virtually limitless.

A submissive may state any number of things as a limit with the knowledge that many of these limits will be challenged and changed over time. Nothing remains constant except hard limits. All other limits evolve, harden or disappear over the course of time and experience.

Playing against these soft or fluid limit boundaries is the dangerous and tenuous challenge of the dominant. It is often part of the dominant's desire to take a submissive beyond the point where that submissive believes they can go. To soar, to fly and to transcend those thresholds is sometimes a huge part of the allure of kink.

Often, in edge play, a submissive is challenged to confront issues from the past in a controlled and dramatically changed way. This is a fragile exploration. It is easy to err in edge play and to go further than you should. This is the area where good communication between a dominant and submissive becomes essential. It is not the desire of a dominant to injure or damage their submissive, it is their desire to meet their submissive's true needs. Playing along the lines of the contradiction is where both will find the greatest dangers and sometimes the greatest rewards.

BEYOND LIMITS

The Illusions of Safety.

Sometimes it seems that people want and need the security they feel by putting rules in writing. Contracts, restrictions, and regulations create the illusion of safety. Yet each of these is a way of limiting the free expression of ourselves and others. This is a trade-off many people aren't willing to accept. These are the familiar tools that created seriously inhibited and sexually dysfunctional generations of people. This is how we control societies.

We have lots of reasons why such rules are healthy, necessary and even promote the good of all. The truth is that these rules are artificial and what they create is an artificial suggestion of control and safety. Rules are simply an agreement between two or more people to abide within certain constraints for a given length of time. What we believe to be healthy, necessary and good are individual perceptions based on our culture of origin, our environment, our life experiences and our personal desires.

In situations of extreme events these well-crafted limitations disappear, especially if your fundamental belief in their worth is not sincere. It is quite easy to mouth the words of acceptable, common social behavior while internally you carry beliefs that are at odds with them. In addition we generally learn to trot out what we believe another person desires to hear if we wish to manipulate that person into a situation that is of benefit or desirous to ourselves. The capacities to lie, cheat, steal, injure, damage and destroy are all part of our human nature. In a sense we will or may take the actions we believe will attain our desired goal.

The only true limitations are those fundamental values that you carry at your core. These are the inviolate lines that you will not cross, for to do so you believe would compromise who you believe yourself to be. These are the final line in the sand.

Some people enter the BDSM world and immediately collect a nice assortment of rules. They exchange the rules of the vanilla world eagerly for these new rules and becomes rule enforcement persons, strongly vocal about why such rules are needed by everyone. They tell you that if you do not conform to these rules then you are doing something wrong and sometimes this leads to being ostracized. Rules make us feel more comfortable and in control. We like to feel safe. Rules suggest structure, reasons, rational justifications and agreement between many people, like a community. This is what you may hear being called kink orthodoxy. You will hear that there are commonly shared rules to just about everything in kink. The only problem is that these rules are only shared by some people, for the rest, they don't exist.

If you are truly exploring the potentials within yourself then one of the first things that you have discovered is the simple fact that you probably know little or nothing about yourself. In many ways you are virgin territory. It is likely that you have had mostly typical experiences in mostly typical ways and that you haven't been sorely tested except by random accident and then, only briefly. The cautious part of you probably fears such a testing. The adventuresome side relishes the concept, the challenge, but realizes you may not and probably are not nearly as adventurous in real life as you are inside the safety of your head.

The collection of rules and limits is your cautious side setting up the rules of the game. It is a way to pre-control the boundaries by which this exploratory game will be played. If you trust too much in the value or worth of these limits then you set yourself up for potential problems. There is the person inside whom we want to be and the person inside who we are. They are seldom the same. In many ways we tend to avoid looking at whom we are in favor of whom we wish to present to the world. In this way we can buy into a grouping of limits that are not truly ours. It makes us acceptable to others to offer acceptable limits to maintain the illusion of our normalcy among our new peers. The problem is that this is a veil. Behind that veil we hide.

The unexplored limit has as much real substance as cobwebs in the corners of the room. It is essentially an idea of a boundary. Limits identify unsafe areas. Things that make us uncomfortable, embarrassed, terrified, disgusted, repulsed and excited. Within everything a contradiction exists. Things that horrify us to the greatest degree often enthrall or captivate our imagination with the same intensity. An example might be the fascination we feel upon observing a horrendous accident, especially when someone dies in a gruesome way. There is something exciting in the testing of our horror, to be suddenly exposed to violence and terror. In that excruciating moment we are truly alive. We feel our blood. We taste our superstitious fears and our primal nature wakens. We feel exposed, vulnerable, profane, out of control and sexual. Death wakens our sexual urges. The primary response to such a shocking incident is a blast of primal energy and our desire to reproduce, to survive into the future is centered in that primal energy.

You might say that identified limits reveal areas of the strongest emotional responses. Within those responses lay the path of our personal history. To participate in some of the practices in our fantasies would leave us morally bankrupt or without any respect for ourselves as humans. But, the fantasies persist, telling us something important.

Conventional society tells us to deny and resist such impulses because they are demons of some kind. Well, demons don't magically vanish by hiding them in our internal closet. Instead, they fester in the darkness to peek out at any moment when our control of the closet door is weak, such as in moments of vulnerability or intense stress.

Do you want to harbor demons? If denial doesn't protect you from the spontaneous eruption of what's hidden what should you do?

When talking about limits, I try to express to people that they should actively avoid anything which may damage their ego, morality or fundamental image of themselves. For me that line is the non-consensual violation of the self. If you can't protect the integrity of your inner self then you can't pretend to protect others. You have to start with self value and a desire to deal with your demons on real terms. This is partly why you are attracted to kink. Kink will give you an opportunity of controlled access to the door that hides your demons.

Over the coarse of my life I have found that I have the capacity to explore far beyond what I considered a limit in virtually all areas. When I adapted mentally or conceptually to the idea within something my mind, in some way, found the way to solve the handling of that idea. I do not believe that I am in any way unique in this. I do believe that in the beginning I knew little and understood less. To learn, I had to touch, taste, feel and experience. Otherwise, I was only making assumptions about what I thought I felt or knew. In addition I have found myself to be in constant evolution. Things I enjoyed 20 years ago, I may have no interest in today. Limits, desires, wishes have all shifted, altered or changed.

Within a D/s relationship only one person's limits actually count. That is the person in power. This is the dominant. A submissive should realize that they live within the barriers or inviolate limits of the dominant they choose to be with. Many dominants try to adapt to the brandished listing of limits that a submissive will carry around with them. They attempt to sincerely promise not to cross those lines. However, this promise is only really functional in the clear head-space prior to doing anything. When you animate kink, the demon doors of both persons will be activated.

> *After a scene where your limits have been violated, what do you do when other kinky people tell you just to learn from it and go on?*
> *Is this some kind of group sheltering behavior that devalues the rights of submissives?*

You can't negotiate with the demons hidden inside the past of the person you are thinking about hooking up with, particularly when you don't know about them.

Newcomers are particularly vulnerable to this failure of control however, violations are common. It is fair to look at kink participation in the same way you look at how a person behaves on drugs or while drunk. Kink is a dis-inhibitor. What a person is like when they are sober is not a good measure of what a person is like when they are subjected to the influences of kink.

Many people use their sober nature to disguise the duplicity of their kink nature. This can be a lot like Dr. Jekyll and Mr. Hyde. Over time both people will learn the nature of their inner demons and they also learn if they are predatory beneath the veneer of acceptable behavior. In general terms most dominants, after going through several years of experiences, become quite graphic or blunt about the nature of their interests. It becomes incumbent upon any submissive interacting with them to listen very carefully and hear what that dominant is telling them. If a dominant has found their true limits or edges to be very extreme, they will often tell the submissive that their range is quite extreme. It is imperative for the submissive to truly hear what that extreme edge can or may mean. Under the influence of kink each person will attempt to go as far as they can in order to address the intensity of their hidden stuff, seeking relief from that intensity or satiation.

You will hear about submissives who only express satisfaction when they experience physical damage and you will hear about dominants who only express satisfaction when they cause physical damage. This is what happens when the inner demon has full reign or when a person cannot control their inhibitions.

The alignment of core limits is the only true safety that can adequately protect the dominant and the submissive. A dominant does not desire to violate another person's limits or rights. Nor does a dominant wish to restrain themselves in an effort to be with someone. As much as a submissive wants to be free to express themselves completely, so does a dominant. Be careful who you select. Take the time to get to know the person. Go slow in scening. Leave before you injure. Do not place your trust in untested limits!

One way to view this inner demon is by recognizing that it is composed of the wounding you sustained over the course of your life. It is what happens when you don't process traumas fully out of yourself. When you get drunk, those traumas, which feel like intense energy, will become exposed and raw. You should never allow these issues to overwhelm your reasoning. But, kink is a way to intentionally release small chunks of the demons inside to confront and work on a little bit of this stuff.

The trick here is to only allow as much of your demons out as you can manage while you are in a disinhibited state. As you can see, this is dangerous. Your stuff is emotional, mental, psychological and physical. This means the danger is in all of these areas at once.

Predation

Opportunity + Access = Consent

This formula is familiar to any woman who has been sexually assaulted. If a woman appears sexually accessible, if there is an opportunity such as the woman being in an isolated environment, these two factors are components of rape.

When you are thinking about kink and about offering trust to a virtual stranger and when you intend to create a situation of isolation and bondage where the genitals are exposed, it is quite likely you will be sexually violated.

Violations, however, are not limited to sex. In a dis-inhibited state the formula works for any type of fetish. In this case a fetish is any act, belief, object or behavior that any person experiences intense attraction towards that frequently sets up as 'sexual'. Kink encompasses all fetishes.

Take a good look at the fetishes listed on your potential partner's profile. This is likely to be the area where you may discover yourself during kink if your partner becomes strongly dis-inhibited during kink. How do you know if this is how they will respond to you? You don't. Each person reacts to other people differently so you can't even base your decision on how that person behaved in the past. But, checking their behavior provides good clues into how deep into uninhibited 'space' that person is likely to go during kink.

What happens in kink doesn't stay in kink.

Bad cliché, I know. However, what you do in your mundane life informs kink and what you do in kink informs your mundane life. Exploration of kink is likely to change you. How you change and in what direction you change is complicated. If you want kink to be like masturbation, you can approach it from the whack-off position. Some people call this being a 'do-me' person. In this regard the person is all about their specific experience no matter how much they tell the other person that the other person is important. If a person is all about getting 'things' for themselves, you will see this across the entirety of their life, not just in the bedroom.

To some extent all people are in this for themselves first. But, even if people believe they are an island independent of others, this isn't true. The experiences you share with other people affect you. You may want to think that when you masturbate in the shower, it doesn't affect others. But it does. Your act changes you. How you behave after an orgasm is different from how you behave before an orgasm. Your levels of anxiety or agitation are different. Your mood changes. Your needs change. Your mental focus changes.

When you violate limits, big or small, the violation is registered and experienced by two people or by all of the people present. It is internalized and it feeds into how you are being changed and how your changes act upon others who experience your presence.

> *Why are consent violations so common in kink and how do you come to terms with the prevalence and how you want to manage your own experiences?*

Limits are about your perspective of self. An absence of caring equates to low self esteem. An excess of caring can also indicate low self esteem.

We create limits to shelter the aspects of our self that we believe are critical to our maintenance of identity, of person-ness. We all endure violations of aspects of self we hold dear. It is within our struggle with these violations that we develop a clearer sense of self knowledge and it is within this struggle that we gain visibility of how our own violations of other people's known limits negatively impact their perspectives of self. When you experience something that you respond strongly against, look carefully, because it is likely or certain that you have committed this offence in parallel with someone else. This doesn't mean you have raped someone. This means you have intentionally violated opportunity and access to do or say something to other people without their consent. This is why it feels so hurtful because some of the hurt is inside of you, created by you and acted upon towards others. You know what you know what you have done.

Additional energy increases the likelihood of consent violations and limit violations.

If you enjoy scening in public, it is more likely that you will play to the crowd watching rather than be tightly focused on your partner and their limits. The encouragement of exterior voices drives behaviors. To some extent you may attempt to comply with external directions while you are in a dis-inhibited state. This is true for both a dominant and a submissive in a scene.

Safewords – No Safety

One of the most talked about features of BDSM scening is the existence and usage of the safeword or safe call or safe sign. For a new dominant and new submissive this seems easy, convenient, and essential to the creation and sustaining of free will, consent, personal integrity etc. There are lots of reasons and issues that propelled the existence of the safeword in kink. Many are quite valid and useful to distinguish kink from physical abuse with the issue of consent being the bottom line.

During the early stages of emergence or that part of your life where you are just learning about adding kink into your lifestyle you may elect to incorporate the safeword as a good rule. It looks like a natural component with no down side, to be followed and seldom thought about. There is so much to learn, so many other issues to explore that it fades backward into the obscurity to lay there dormant and untouched for sometimes years.

For the new submissive it is the golden key, held as the ultimate last word. It allows that submissive to retain their personal vision of equity within the standards of societal norms. It blends in quite nicely with all the other assorted rules of engagement, contracts of conduct, and definition of limits.

For many this key remains intact. Both dominant and submissives often agree that this is a necessary ingredient, like a check and balance system to hold people accountable for their actions and to halt problems before they become serious.

The existence of this key is a limit. It gives the submissive an out. While you may be saying "Yes, exactly as it should!" the mere existence of the key alters the event. From the submissive's perspective, especially when new, this seems no problem. If things get too hard I will just yell out my word, and I will be safe, and everything will stop. And, for that submissive this is possible. But, safewords don't account for space. Space is simply an altered state of consciousness that every human can access depending on their inhibitions and susceptibility to trance-like conditions. There is some variation in how any two people acquire space. But, if you sleep, nap, daydream, get drunk, high or otherwise respond to things like music, drumming, chanting or rhythmic sounds, then you are experiencing space.

Space in kink is associated with many of the identical triggers of space in other situations. Space includes energy conservation, dis-inhibition, altered perceptions and more. Scening places pressure on the individuals and challenges them to adapt to new circumstances that will in some way be difficult. This requires a heightened focus (heightened focus is one of the entry points into altered states), often it requires heightened listening (heightened listening is one of the entry points into altered states), it causes the deployment of drugs into the blood stream (drugs are one of the entry points into altered states), it causes increased energy use (energy use is part of energy conservation and related to sleep which is an altered state). As you can see, these compounding factors will alter the mental state of any person involved in kink to some degree.

If you are strongly susceptible to altered states you can enter such states merely by thinking about kink. When you are profoundly involved in space and when you are a submissive and when you are in a scene you can lose the ability to articulate speech, you can lose the ability to remember code words, you can become so detached from mundane reality that it becomes impossible for you to evaluate your physical, mental or emotional condition. This is why safewords don't work. Additionally, as a submissive attaches or bonds to their chosen dominant, they begin to desire not to fail their dominant. In the process of this their desire to use the safeword decreases to the point of utter refusal.

The dominant may not realize this. As the submissive gains experience they become more dangerous for the dominant they scene with if the dominant relies on a safeword. The deeper into space that the submissive can go, the higher the level of physical intensity they are able to endure, the more euphoric they become *(the more irrational)*. The dominant who has come to rely on the safeword as the final stop can, may and will exceed that submissive's limits. A dominant can also get euphoric in scene as easily as the submissive and be equally incapable of clear evaluation of consequences.

If you've ever been with friends or family and someone gets drunk, you know that most drunk people believe they are sober enough to be safe, to drive safely and to think clearly. All of these operate the same way for both a dominant and submissive in scene.

Many dominants maintain the safeword as a way of reducing their personal responsibility for the safety of the submissive. That responsibility is a weight that many do not desire to carry. If they can get the submissive to carry it then they are off the hook if something bad happens. They can say, "No safeword was used. I am no mind reader, I didn't know the submissive was in trouble." Wrong. The submissive must relinquish all responsibility during scene. The dominant must be required to remain sufficiently in control to be fully responsible for their actions.

Responsibility

You are responsible for yourself.

Your potential partner is responsible for themselves.

While you may scene a power exchange and you may temporarily accept responsibility for other people within a relationship framework, this is typically bordered by physical limitations such as bondage and only lasts during the actual time the person is in bondage.

You can sell yourself into abject slavery and I'm still going to tell you that you are responsible for yourself. How you feel, what you experience, who you choose to interact with, all of these are consensual choices that you must make from a responsible position. If you are not responsible for yourself then you are unable to offer reasoned consent and unable to participate in kink.

When another person is dependent on you physically, you and you alone become responsible for their continued well being. No safeword can be used to explain injury.

But, responsibility goes further. Both or all people in a relationship are responsible for helping to shape and maintain the relationship and the wellbeing of each person in the relationship.

There is a pervasive belief that because you are now oriented toward a different lifestyle that it is permissive to break all the rules of good conduct, ethics, morality, sexual responsibility and basic human dignity. It is not permissible. I get it that you want to be seriously objectified or seriously worshipped. But, if you indulge your whims to the exclusion of the wellbeing of both the unified relationship and the wellbeing of each person in the relationship then your interaction will fail.

Fantasy is fantasy. What you enjoy in your fantasies for a short period of time may never translate into every day all day. Trust me, you aren't sexual all day long. And, you are responsible for the non-kinky, non-sexual parts too. Someone has to feed kids, go to PTA, go to a job, tend to elderly parents, and go out with friends. Your life is part of many relationships and all of them are important in many ways.

Responsibility includes managing kink at a level that isn't destructive of other necessary aspects of life. You may want to be a slave all the time, to live in skimpy outfits or be naked every day. But, this desire or need is that demon talking, all that wounding from out of the past is fueling your thinking. If you give in to such thoughts you may not be competent.

Most people who go towards a dyad kink relationship with D/s features develop strategies to allow themselves to feel the kink around their sexual intimacy while preserving most of the elements of mundane life. It's important to be able to function happily in both spheres and to move seamlessly between these spheres with friends, family, children and people who are otherwise important in your life.

Responsibility needs to be shared evenly across a relationship. You can decide which person does what but expect that to change if your circumstances change. If you get fixed in the idea that the submissive is or must be the person doing the dishes then when that submissive is ill the dishes will be filthy. You cannot divvy up roles by traditional standards and miraculously expect them to work when half such relationships with identical standards fail in mainstream culture.

Responsibility goes beyond the easy ideas of role and promises, you have to remain flexible and adaptable and you must know that you will change. What you are so eager for today will not be the same in 2 years or 20 years. You need to grow as much as you need to explore, the more fixed in the role idea you become, the less satisfied you will be over time.

Abuse

The shadow of abuse is a constant presence in kink, just as it is in mainstream culture and across the world. The importance of sexual assault against mostly women has been magnified in the past twenty years but it isn't the only type of abuse or even the most prolific type of abuse. It is common for both men and women to endure all kinds of assaults on themselves on a daily basis. Attacks come from media, culture, family, friends, peers and strangers. Every aspect of behavior is judged and assigned a value, often monetary. With judgment comes censure and sometimes physical assaults along with the verbal and emotional assaults. No one escapes.

We bring all of this stuff to kink, to an environment where it is even easier to abuse others. It is easier to use derogatory language, diminishing behaviors and physically damaging interactions. This doesn't mean you will be abused or that you will abuse others, but, if you have been abused and have abused others in your past and if you have not worked very hard to correct the worst of your habits, then you will repeat them while you participate in kink.

It is quite easy to move from sexualizing degrading comments in a positive way to inflicted them with the intention to cause suffering and injury. Often this can emerge simply from habit. Often this habit is driven by poor interpersonal relationship skills and bad communication. Usually these bad habits are associated with inadequate skills at managing your own emotions and feelings. Instead of working through your emotions you use the energy of the emotion to strike out at another person or you try to cause that person to feel responsible for your pain.

This is a lot of bad stuff. When you add this volatility to a kink environment it is likely that you are going to have additional injury and increased suffering.

The only savior here is that most participants in kink are acutely aware of abuse and many are in the process of dismantling old abuse mechanisms through intentional confrontation by using kink.

It's important to mention here that almost everyone in kink is not a professional psychologist. These are ordinary people struggling to improve their life experiences and sexual experiences by moving their intention, communication and consent processes.

This means that everyone's an amateur and you and your partners are going to make big mistakes, you are going to experience failures, arguments, bitter disputes and lots and lots of relationship drama. In the process you will also confront the very demons that torment your life and you will probably discover that you and you alone control your inner demons. Other people don't make us feel things. We feel things because we assign meaning to the behaviors of other people. We assign meaning in our thinking process and the meaning we give triggers the hormones that manipulate our senses into the feelings we experience.

I can say this in literal terms but even if you agree

with me intellectually, you will still experience feelings in this way until you actively confront how you create meaning and until you are willing to let go of the meanings that you have created. Letting go is very difficult because the meanings you give are connected with the story you create about how the world operates and what is happening in your life.

When you let go of meaning, you also let go of personal story and your explanation for why you aren't doing what you say you want to do in life.

People abuse other people as a mechanism of control. By 'sharing' meaning other people can intentionally trigger responses in others. Usually the abusive person will believe and even say that they are doing or saying something hurtful because of something good. It isn't received as 'good'.

> *Is abuse in kink growing or are people becoming more educated on abuse and simply calling it out more today than historically?*

This is the magical intention defense. My intention when I called you fat was to help you gain visibility of the issue so that you can be more healthy. Lie. The intention in this excuse is merely an attempt to abdicate responsibility under the idea of 'good intentions cause good results'. What is actually happening is that the abusive person is feeling 'charge' from seeing a person non-conforming to the cultural mandate to be a specific size and appearance. In order to maintain their agreement that there is a preferred size and appearance and that it has value to them, showing they conform with culture, they abuse others. This alignment with cultural metric is designed to show their elevated cultural value based on their agreement and defense of culture. There isn't anything good about it. At the root of this abuse is a fear that the abuser has of not being valued by others. The abuser is always in fear of being othered and in fear of losing connections with everyone around them.

Abuse is epidemic. People are often attracted to kink because it allows the individual to explore the very triggers that are hurtful, the same memories, the same physical experiences, the only difference is that the actions and behaviors aren't showing up because one person is trying to cause suffering for the other person. In fact, in most cases one person is trying to have fun with the other person.

Taking ownership of hurtful experiences is part of the healing process so in this very limited way it is fair to say that all people who explore kink are partially moved by some aspect of healing. Often, people don't experience kink in this way, at all. Most focus on the immediacy of the experience and that is perfectly okay.

What you need to know is that the person you interact with has similar crap in their past. As much as you may think your past is more important, this is just perspective. As much as you might want support and sympathy around your past, you have to reciprocate in kind. You aren't special. You are just like everyone else.

Abuse doesn't define you as a person unless you devote your energy to creating that reality for yourself. Otherwise, it can inform you, trigger you and amplify your feelings but you are not eternally damaged unless you intentionally prevent yourself from seeking out healing and acting towards healing for yourself.

Many people worry that participating in kink means that they are defiled, that their spirit or soul is somehow twisted toward some manifestation of darkness. This can be particularly troubling for people with religious backgrounds or who are actively religious.

Let's be clear, kink isn't a religion. Kink isn't about religion. You don't arrive at kink by falling from grace. Sexuality isn't a sin. Your body has enormous capacities that are barely tapped in regular life. You are simply tapping in to what exists. How you view or use kink can impact your perceptions of faith but I suggest you align your practices with your belief structures if that feels essential to you. Try to stay open to changes in yourself and in how you view the world. Abuse tends to skew our perceptions of our world and of other people.

If something you are doing (in kink) is feeling wrong or abusive to you, stop. You are the best evaluator for what works and doesn't work for you personally. Don't allow anyone to convince you that your feelings are wrong. It is also important not to judge others by your feelings of any acts. Each person is on their own path regardless of how similar it may seem to your path.

DAMAGE CONTROL

Most people will encounter someone who becomes deeply triggered in scene. Like I said, you aren't a professional therapist and for sure you aren't your partner's therapist. Don't pretend to be a therapist.

Cease your scene immediately. Stop all role play. Ask

the person what they need. If they tell you to leave them alone, leave them alone. If they tell you they need to cuddle, cuddle. Don't try to compel them into performing like they are okay. They aren't okay.

Scening with elements from past traumas can evoke the trauma much like Post Traumatic Stress Disorder. Your job is not to make things worse. Your second job is not to make things worse. Your third job is to be prepared in advance of any scene with knowledge of medical history, knowledge of doctors (if they are having medical care for continuing medical issues), knowledge of when to contact those doctors if your partner is unable to function.

It is up to each person to request good information from their partner so that they can respond properly and promptly if a medical emergency occurs.

Know the KAP members in your local vicinity. KAP is Kink Aware Professionals. There is a main list on the National Coalition for Sexual Freedom website. Look up your area, note the various doctors and keep the list with your kit. If your partner doesn't have their own doctors in your area, you will be able to use the list to locate professional help quickly.

Most people can tell you when they are feeling like there is a problem. You need to be able to listen and completely let go of role play concerns. If you 'play' that your submissive cannot voice their opinion without permission you can create a situation where you don't hear when there is a real problem.

Most people know what is in their history and many can give potential partners an overview of areas that are dangerous. Listen. Don't think you can explore these areas because you are special and you have lots of experience. You don't. Don't try it. You are not supposed to be messing around with another person's responses to trauma.

If you think I'm talking about just submissives here then you are wrong. Your dominant partner can be equally triggered during a scene although it tends to be more rare. You should have the same information on them that they have on you and you should know enough about their past to know when things aren't going as planned. You need to know what to do if you are alone with your partner and there is a problem.

If you like scening alone then you must make sure that any person in bondage can escape under their own power within a time frame that will not compromise their health.

There are devices like keys that you freeze that will melt and allow someone to unlock things. There are also quick-release restraints. Buy them and use them. Damage control is all about preparing to be safe, sane and able to survive when things go wrong.

RESPECT

(To consider worthy of high regard, the state or quality of being esteemed of expressions of deference.)

Worthy. Deserving. Respect is something many dominants expect and receive for no particular attribute, deed or behavior. We tell ourselves it is earned and inspired by consistent actions but it isn't. Most people expect respect one minute into an online conversation. You might think that casual expressions of verbal respect are not real respect but again, this is a story.

Courtesy is a form of respect. It is part of our common social structure to trot out phrases and words with an ease born of a lifetime of training, particularly for women towards men or older people.

A role isn't respect-worthy when it is self-given. Period. Courtesy needs to be mutually offered and consistent regardless of role otherwise there is probably a problem happening with someone's ego.

Courtesy is a form of communication designed to reduce conflict between strangers or persons of culturally perceived different status.

Within kink and within our mainstream culture conditioned courtesy is also used as a tool to manipulate others. If you are conditioned to respond with courtesy then you are likely to be giving up some of your critical thinking and evaluation tools in order to be a 'peacemaker'. This is particularly true around persons with 'acting out' behaviors where courtesy shifts into a form of coerced compliance for relationship gain. Women tend to placate the eruptions of others. This is both instinctive and learned. When a woman becomes a mother part of her instinct is to soothe infants. This soothing behavior possibly reflects an ancient need to quiet the most vulnerable from the attention of passing predators.

How it shows up in D/s relationships is a mixture of relating to a peer-age relationship partner with 'mothering' or soothing comments coupled to conditioned behaviors to present yourself as courteous and possibly pleasing to potential authority figures, particularly men.

This leads women into difficulties with self advocacy and agency. Many women and some men have strong negative reactions towards conflict and they are so triggered that they become conflict avoidant. This means they would rather produce a peace-keeping behavior that complies with others rather than deal with the elevated energy of other people who wish to impose their wants, rules and desires non-consensually on others.

This is the state of many women and some men when they enter kink. A lot of the online and in print BDSM rhetoric talks about the expectation of submissives to behave respectfully towards their potential partner. Most encourage only common courtesy until a person otherwise 'earns' additional respect and that sounds great on paper but it just isn't what happens in real life.

It's important to realize here that a person seeking out a dominant or master is looking for that particular role in order to experience domination. That domination idea includes worshipful respect at the feet of the dominant or master. This means they have already crossed the bridge and when a dominant messages with them online a part of them is already engaging in the presenting themselves as 'submitting' even when they believe they are being discriminating and looking carefully for trolls.

Now, when the dominant communicating with them is well-known in any way, that perceived celebrity creates a condition of 'already worthy of respect' to any person who values that celebrity. In a sense most people are hard-wired to seek out and align with perceived authority, that's why people listen to some news channels that produce information that is ludicrous and people still believe in it because it's on television therefore it must be true.

Within the BDSM community it is common to find large numbers of people who believe that by merely self-labeling themselves as a dominant, this ensures them the right to expressions of respect. It doesn't.

It's very difficult to combat behaviors that date into your infancy. It is even more difficult when you are unaware that these behaviors or conditioning are influencing your critical thinking in detrimental ways.

I've mentioned several times how kink attracts people with consent violation issues. Now you can see that it also attracts people with critical thinking deficits around their ability to accurately evaluate the qualities and characteristics of potential relationship partners.

It doesn't really matter here that I'm telling you how this works because you can't intellectually overcome conditioning merely by knowing what's happening. Being rude isn't overcoming conditioning, it's being rude.

A submissive is caught between two walls, the need they feel to submit to someone and their pre-existing conditioning that encourages them to 'feel' respect without evidence of respect-worthy behavior.

> *Why is respect a real problem when you don't really know enough about a person to determine if they are worthy of respect?*

You don't have to go far on any fetish website to encounter someone identifying as a submissive who will be snarky or flame anyone who says anything they don't like particularly if that person has also self-identified as a dominant. It is almost as if the submissive is 'hunting' dominants in order to embarrass or shame them online.

You will see a proclamation of how the dominant is obviously a troll, a fake dominant and any of a host of other derogatory names. If you follow the threads that this submissive visits you will quickly see that their analysis and response is consistent everywhere. Apparently every dominant on every fetish site is full of shit, or they are an asshat, a predator, a rapist, and an overall despicable human being.

Is this submissive wrong?

Not really. By their standards of evaluation no person is worthy of respect and that is why they have some challenges finding their dominant.

My point is that your personal standards are your tools of evaluation. The behavior to offer courtesy and respect too easily are just as problematic as the behavior to disparage others for not saying things you agree with. The behaviors are related.

People explore kink because of issues they are dealing with. If your primary wound is centered around respect and consent violations, all of your energy will be directed towards looking for and punishing others for what you perceive to be examples of respect and consent violations. You may view yourself as a champion of rights and like a knight you must race in to defend all other submissives from the evil dominants who are plotting to do hurtful things to every vulnerable submissive.

In this way this submissive is successful in finding a medium to express their outrage at what was done to them sometime in the past by someone not present. However, they are transferring their unprocessed pain onto others by projecting their analysis, judgment and punishment on strangers. It is like saying, "I'm in pain here and you *must* share my pain because you didn't agree with my thoughts about X and that made my pain feel fresh all over again and it is your fault." So they commit verbal assault. As I noted, being rude and committing assault in the name of protecting others from assault is not only illogical, it's a delusion. You have become exactly what you believe you are fighting against, someone who wounds others non-consensually. This type of consent violation is your kink, your fetish. What you show everyone is your wound and how you keep it open, fresh and oozing puss.

Respect is a component of trust. If you are unable to

invest minimal trust in your potential partner then you will never get out from behind the computer screen and into a real life meeting.

As I noted, you are most likely already compromised by your upbringing and conditioning. This will skew your ability to use your critical thinking skills. It will offer you mediating thoughts that may compromise your ability to act on your own behalf. This is simply the truth you need to deal with.

If you are going to place your life and your trust in an individual, it becomes increasingly important to make the best choices possible.

One tool for newcomers is to ask another dominant, someone who will not be interested in you for themselves, to read your (online) interactions with someone you think you are interested in meeting. Put outside eyes on the discussion, the communication. A third party who is not directly involved can often offer a clear perspective on the relative merits disclosed in the conversations. Listen to that person.

Exercise due diligence. This means you want to examine the received information for authenticity and you want to externally validate the dominant's story for accuracy.

From a dominant's perspective it is necessary to avoid manipulating submissives based on their pre-existing conditioning. You aren't worthy. You won't be worthy unless you can demonstrate respect-worthy behavior over time. It doesn't matter how you look, how long you've played and with how many people. It doesn't matter if you are successful financially, if you are a kink celebrity, if your kids love you. None of this makes you worthy of the respect and trust of your next partner.

The appearance of respectability is one of the easiest masks to wear because the conditioning to believe a person in apparent authority is so deep that it takes obvious failures for people to realize they have made a mistake and often that comes too late. Think about how prevalent it is for clergy who protest sinful behavior strongly from the pulpit and media, to be discovered to be participants in the very sins they speak about.

Remember that it is easier to lie over the Internet than it is in person. In person you can more easily read the physical cues of deceit. If you intend to meet someone, make it at a public restaurant. Have a friend go separately to the same restaurant and sit in an adjacent booth so that they can overhear and watch the conversation of the first meeting.

After you meet, stay after the potential dominant leaves and get together with your friend to discuss what each of you saw, heard and felt during the meeting. You probably think this is duplicitous or a lie. It isn't. The submissive is in the position of greater vulnerability here and should be the one taking more precautions.

Note in your online profile that you will 'check out' any potential dominant thoroughly before you move towards any relationship. If someone is interested in you they should stand up to your scrutiny and it is up to them to actually read your profile. If they don't bother to read your profile how much do they care about your interests or limits? Not enough.

Trust

Trust is critically important for a kink relationship or even a casual scene. To try anything you have to be able to tolerate a certain about of risk. You are probably not going to know the person you scene with well enough to trust them completely the first time you trust them completely.

Some people are lucky enough to scene with a husband or wife where the trust has been built over time. Most people will scene with a relative stranger. I've already talked about some basic safety measures, the problems with respect and what you should be wary of inside yourself.

Trust is finite. Once you betray trust, you can never recover the loss of trust that you have caused. Ever. Many people like to test this out by cheating in relationships rather than being honest about liking to fuck more than one person at a time. They believe they can risk potential loss of trust. Often they have tested loss of trust in minor ways in the relationship over time and the relationship continued so they feel some degree of safety in the idea that the risk is fairly low.

What actually happens is that trust in a new relationship is like a cup full of sugar. When you tell your partner something that later turns out to be a lie, a little bit of sugar is spilled. You may not notice the reduction of sweetness in the relationship but it's there. Trust affects how each person views themselves. If they accept the bad behavior of their partner it opens a wound in their heart about their own value to themselves. This wound may heal over time if no other violations occur.

If there are numerous small violations the wound remains open and it grows because each violation will spill more sugar. In the relationship the spilled sugar creates tension and hurt. This will change the way each person relates to the other. Over time tension and hurt corrode the relationship more. It's like a bacteria eating at the soul of the person. At some point it becomes an intolerable pain and the person will withdraw and attempt to find means to heal themselves from their action of allowing behaviors that were known by both persons to corrode and destroy the foundations of the relationship.

This is a failure of the self to advocate for the true needs of the self which is to be in a relationship where both persons are actively working to prevent causing suffering to their partner and especially to themselves. It is by valuing yourself that you reduce suffering not by trying to change others to suit your ideas and beliefs.

If a person is violating minor issues of trust, it is a good indication that the parameters of trust expected in the relationship are wrong for the relationship. A person can only violate trust if trust is expected. If you know that you want multiple sexual partners along with a primary partner, you negotiate this up front so that you don't need to commit a violation of trust in order to be authentic.

People also violate trust in passive aggressive behaviors when they want to break the relationship but they don't want to overtly break the relationship. In this way they push back by making themselves less sweet to their partner so that at some point their partner will let go and withdraw. Most people don't want to own this type of behavior, they want to internally believe that they are honorable and that they live up to their oaths, even when they don't. They will create ways to reframe the oath in their mind to escape personal knowledge that they have trouble advocating for their needs and being truthful with others.

Diminished trust in a kink relationship can pose additional dangers and problems than in a vanilla relationship. How a submissive responds physically is connected with their head space. As trust diminishes they will bring these issues into their interactions both consciously and unconsciously. They may tell their dominant that they forgive them and everything is forgotten but this isn't how the brain operates.

Part of the brain is designed to respond to survival issues. Trust violations elevate risk of physical and emotional damage and reduce the boundaries of survival. This means that you remember everything that has to do with challenges to your possible survival. A person can intellectually forgive, but the memory and elevated risk of further damage will not be erased. The brain is not film.

In scene, this means that the mental state of the submissive is forever changed by the knowledge that you might intentionally hurt them. As they hold that knowledge in the back of their brain it will affect their body and how their body responds. At the very least they will not have the same tissue recovery and safe space to experience. A part of their mind will always be watching and will always have tension which produces chemicals that change the experience potentials of any scene and interaction. How it changes isn't likely to be favorable for the long-term health of the relationship.

Submissives cheat too. Submissives engage in trust violations just as often as dominants will. The same factors are at play here. The dominant cannot forget the violations either and how they respond to their submissive will also be altered. The pain they feel for not advocating for their real needs and allowing themselves to engage in agreements that are not stable that will cause them to experience suffering can play out in hurtful interactions with their submissives.

Both people are human and given to poor management of their emotional and mental states. A small trust violation wound can and often does grow into a large nasty wound that results in additional bad behaviors from both people often blaming each other for what happened.

The only way to address this is to not create expectations and rules that offer easy targets for trust violations. Then, tell the truth. If you don't know the real truth from the-way-you-want-to-see-yourself-truth, then avoid specific agreements and pay attention to your actual behaviors to discover how you really are versus how you want to think you are.

Space

Space is a spectrum of altered mental states commonly experienced by the combination of physical, energetic and mental components triggered by features of many kink interactions. Altered mental states are the magic, the pathway and ultimately the secret that flourishes within kink.

It is important to consider the history of humankind when you seek to understand not only its nature but how this exquisite potentials of space can be accessed through behaviors that would appear to stand in opposition to all other traditional pathways into this place.

Space has always been the guarded treasure of the devout or deeply religious individual. To access this treasure, an initiate was told they needed to dedicate their lives to austerity, the denial of temptation, and to the application of tightly focused religious devotionals in order to achieve a clear enough mind to experience space. This was a lie. Denial can be a tool used to prevent average human beings from attempting to experience transcended or evolved spiritual states.

Denial is one way to avoid some of the more flagrant interactions that produce emotional wounding. But, denial also creates its own form of wounding. This isn't a book based on the virtues of religious devotionals but it is necessary to observe parallels between spirituality and kink to understand how the mind engages in space. If you are involved in kink you will encounter or experience altered mental states. Your experience of space will alter how you perceive reality, your relationships and the universe itself.

It is curious that altered mental states have been held apart from Americans and other peoples who live inside constrictive religious cultures. The message of most religions is that you must 'receive' altered mental states from indoctrination and participation in the religion.

But, this isn't how your body works. This isn't how your spirit works. The very mystics at the center of organized religions didn't 'receive' their experiences from a religious organization. They experienced mysticism directly, in the body, in the brain, from behaviors and practices they thought up and tried upon themselves.

> *What do you do when your kinky experiences turn spiritual?*
>
> *Why is space so important in kink?*

Other people witnessed the 'flight' of mystics and they wrote down what the mystic did and may have said about their practices and some of this became the dogma of the resulting religion. But, there's a problem with received information. If you have ever played the telephone game you know what I mean.

If you line up 10 people in a row and tell them that you are going to give a message to the first person in line and that person is going to whisper it to the person next to them and so on and so on. When the message reaches the last person it is unrecognizable as the same message.

Each person alters the message before 'giving' it to the next person. You may think this doesn't happen with words that are written down but again you are wrong. Once a person writes words and releases the copy to someone else the words pass out of the first person's control.

Up until a few hundred years ago humans had to hand-write every copy of every book. They used scribes. These were people who copied out pages individually, often doing only some of the pages in a work. Several scribes might work on one book all at the same time.

If you study medieval book making, you quickly learn that making mistakes was quite common. Because writing materials were pricey you didn't just throw away a sheet if you forgot a few words. Then you have translation issues and editing issues. After a few thousand years, hundreds of scribes, hundreds of editors, dozens of translators and a much later standardization of word spelling and meaning (the first dictionaries), what you end up with is not recognizable as the same document or book that originated during the actual life of the mystic.

Yet, people are told every word is exactly correct and that no errors could possibly have been made because they are the words of god. When actually they are the words of countless men and women with their own agendas and motivations.

I only mention all of this because the outcome of religious austerity hasn't been creating 'mystical' people. Instead people have been led away from direct experience and told that direct experience is sinful. Essentially this message is that the mystic they worship was totally sinful because they experienced mysticism directly.

To overcome this logical failure the person is told that the mystic received their experience from god and to receive god the person shouldn't follow what the mystic actually did by exploring everything around them, instead the idea is that you have to receive the 'correct' path from the religion, as if the direct from god path has magically dried up.

Space is not the idealized restricted gift of the devout. It is possessed by all human beings and access to it is readily available if you unify the three sides within yourself.

These three sides are:
- Body
- Mind
- Spirit

I know you've seen this list before and you may be having a dismissive reaction right now. All you want to do is kink, right? Why am I making it complicated with religion and now new-age stuff?

I get it. The only problem is that when you do some really hot kink you are going to end up flailing around right here, in the middle of mystical new-age world. It doesn't make a bit of difference if you are an atheist and detest the whole new-age 'thing'. Your brain doesn't care the least bit about your opinions. Your body doesn't ask you how it should or shouldn't respond based on your beliefs. And your spirit, do you really think your consciousness doesn't experience stuff because you don't believe in anything about or related to mystical states?

When I talk about unification I mean that you have to embrace all of these aspects at the same time to bring your experience into its greatest potential. Achieving an altered mental state requires no religious, spiritual or mystical devotion. None. After all, if you sleep you enter an altered state and it doesn't require prayer to sleep.

Accessing your body using stimulation is the first the of the three elements in my list. But, all stimulation isn't the same. When you trip off a curb and fall to your knees and wrists hard, scuffing skin and creating deep bruises, you will launch into an altered state. Your body's immediate response is to prevent you from dying. Back before humans direct memory it was necessary to immediately prevent the appearance of physical vulnerability and falling to the ground might make a person a target for a predator. So the brain does a thing. You feel pain but this pain is often metered by your surrounding environment and circumstances. In today's society it is not likely that you will be eaten by some randomly prowling large predator. But, you may be targeted by a mugger. Perhaps your fall to the ground was caused by a mugger.

Depending on the external circumstances it is likely that you will attempt to rise up and move away from your position of vulnerability. To accomplish this your brain adjusts your level of pain by dumping lots of chemicals into your body and by jolting you with your own body's equivalent of shock paddles. Energy will leap up your spine, you will flush with heat, you may interpret this shock of heat on your skin as embarrassment (learned meaning response) and you may attempt to indicate to anyone present that the injury was minor or negligible.

Did any of this require spiritual thinking? Nope. This was all back brain self-preservation stuff trying to keep you in one piece. So this is what your body normally does.

Before I talk about what the body does on kink, let's look at the mind question. Most people believe that they feel emotions based upon their experiences. But, during a trauma or crisis they are sometimes shocked by feeling or doing things that are contrary to the gravity of the situation. Sometimes they even laugh at really horrid things. Often they experience a host of emotions that shouldn't exactly be the emotions they think they should have in the situation. It is almost as if the mind is responding to different information or to the situation from a different perspective.

Let's go back to the falling-down example for a moment. Often the first thing you think when you hit the ground is how stupid you feel for _____. This self-judgment seems to show up even before the 'are you hurt evaluation'. Why would such a thought show up first? What does the thought do *for* you? If you follow the logic of the behavior being part of your survival response then the first thought bypasses your 'thinking' part of the brain and is simply responsive. This means that thinking you made a mistake is somehow helpful to your continued survival. How?

Unfortunately you have just demonstrated vulnerability. If you were 100,000 years ago the tiger would already be lunching on your scuffed knees. If you were mugged then the other human is moving in, generally not intending to kill you but certainly intending to seriously ruin your day. By showing vulnerability you have indicated where the power lays in that exact moment and it isn't with you because you just called yourself 'stupid'. There are a whole host of mental behaviors that relate to response to authority and you just set them off. You have exactly two choices, demonstrate authority or broadcast submission and try to out-think the perpetrator in order to survive.

Something else happens, you start having emotions. Remember that jolt of heat from the shock to your body? That jolt is virtually identical to the flush of embarrassment. All of the same body responses are triggered and you 'feel' embarrassed because you have a habit of interpreting this complex mixture of responses as embarrassment. You might laugh. Laughter is another reaction to shock and uncertainty combined with physical stimulation.

Your interpretations are now skewed. In that initial blast of chemicals and energy, along with pain, your body flooded with stuff. Some of the chemicals are designed to muffle the pain to allow you to run or fight, and the energy is to give you the juice to act.

All of this happened in a split second, you couldn't control any of it. None of what happened in those first seconds has anything to do with you as an individual, your opinions on politics, your preferences in food choices or your religious or spiritual choices.

But, what happens next has everything to do with you as an individual. After the first acute seconds all of your unprocessed wounding comes into play both physically, mentally and spiritually. How you think, as an individual, is a direct product of your life experiences and your conditioning. Most people are not given good instruction on how to manage their emotions. Men are often taught to 'show no emotion', women are often taught to 'stuff their emotion'. This means that it is very common for most people to be full of unprocessed emotions.

During a trauma the energy you use to manage all of your old unprocessed stuff is suddenly needed to react to the situation. This means all of your 'stuff' will be informing your thinking. Since you didn't handle 'past traumas' this is the overwhelming message that will permeate your current trauma. Unprocessed stuff also skews your thinking. So even if your body wasn't being fueled by this old stuff energetically, your thinking is full of thinking errors that are likely to replicate the same type of wounds you've experienced in the past by repeating the same thinking.

> *If even small traumas are important how can you develop the management skills to process current small traumas so that they don't get stored as future wounds?*

Religious people don't get off the hook here. Many religions suggest that their members should give their wounds to god instead of process them directly. This means that the religious person is likely to give over agency in a sort of abandonment to authority. Making your experiences the responsibility of others, even god, is a way to avoid doing your processing. It places the actions of 'god' in the hands of the perpetrator who doesn't seem to have your interests at heart if they are attacking you. If you don't have any responsibility it means that your god is going around causing assaults, murders, and terrible heinous crimes.

The other option is for the religious person to say that god gives them strength. If you look closely you see this is the exact same response choices I noted earlier, submit or re-establish authority. This is assuming that flight isn't possible in that exact moment. Flight is an action trying to re-establish authority over self. In this way you can see that the religious 'thinking' is simply a frame for the same choices.

But, there is a spiritual component at work here. You may have noticed the emphasis I placed on unprocessed wounding. For most people the concept of wellness centers on removing the obstacles that impede your direct experiences. In general these obstacles are learned behaviors associated with unprocessed wounds and the clinging to thinking errors that cause suffering.

At the beginning of this chapter I talked about how the mystic experiences directly. The religions that document the life of the mystic attempt to replicate the steps the mystic took to remove their obstacles to achieving an elevated or transcended state. The problem with the religions is that the dogma doesn't change yet no two people have the same experiences. Yes, there are commonalities but each person grapples with unique issues. Applying a universal ointment will not produce universal results.

Back to our falling down scenario, if a person has done the work of processing out their issues to a large degree, they will have fewer thinking errors, they will have less 'garbage energy' informing their thoughts or manifesting as emotions. That means that after the initial shock of the trauma their thinking will be more clear and that the systems in their body will function better. It ups the potential of survival. This is where kink comes in.

So far my scenario has centered on a non-consensual random physical trauma and the way you, as an individual, are most likely to react to that trauma.

What changes when you are preparing and participating in stimulation for the express purpose of creating the faux-trauma experience?

First, let's take a look at your objectives. You may think that scening or even being in a relationship interaction with power exchange behaviors is the objective but it isn't. What is your objective?

For a couple engaging in a D/s or M/s relationship it is likely that they have allocated specific areas where they will engage in role and power exchange. This varies widely from once a month physical encounters coupled with daily online interactions to people who interact daily, say at all times where they are in private at home or in play spaces where their interactions will not cause them other problems.

The objective in most relationships is to experience intimacy, connection, acceptance and support. It is likely that in addition to these basic desires each person wants to experience other things like specific fetishes. People also want to experience specific emotions, feelings or physical sensations. All of these things are part of the objective of relating through a kink focus.

For other people the objectives may center on types of sexual interactions as the short-term goal of a scene. Some simply want the satisfaction of the acts and reactions of themselves and their partners. But, everyone has a goal.

It is a good idea to work out the type of objectives

that interest you the most and pay attention to how you and your partner might achieve your objectives either immediately or over time.

It is also a good idea to take a look at how you will change over time based on your experience either in a relationship or by scening. You won't stay the same.

People alter their reactions to trauma in several ways. The most common is through training such as with military personnel, police and fire fighters and people in similar occupations where sudden violent changes are common. In this instance people are trained to maintain focus during the trauma and to modify or overcome some of their instinctive responses. This allows the trained person to shape their mind-bending chemical reactions during an actual event.

In many traumatic events the mind shifts into a hyper-alert state that is tightly focused on the exact area likely to possess the greatest danger. This focus occurs at the same time that chemicals are washing through the body and brain. So, while one part of the brain is hyper-alert, other parts are displaying characteristics of intoxication such as reduced sensitivity to sensation, dis-inhibition, increased impulsivity and decreased ability to accurately evaluate the situation.

When a person is trained for trauma response the hyper-alert state is encouraged and habitual training is used to replace impulsivity and dis-inhibition as much as possible. The objective is to overcome behaviors that are counter to the objectives of the person or group that is training the individual.

This means that the person is desensitized to trauma in some ways so that they can respond according to their training rather than based on their personal inner messages. This allows people to shoot and kill other people in the moment with less second-guessing of the behavior. There is a big price that the same person will often pay for this reduction in empathy once the trauma is over. But, usually the consequences for the individual are less important for the trainers than the trainer's objectives.

To achieve this type of head space it is common for a person to displace their emotional processing during the event. After the trauma and after their body/brain return to a more normal state, it is common for the individual to begin to display emotional problems.

In a military-type situation routines are implemented to counter the chaotic emotional state of the individuals. In addition, many individuals seek out intoxification in the form of alcohol or drugs to return themselves to as close as possible to the mental state they experienced during the event when they felt 'able' to distance themselves from the emotional reality of the experience.

Other ways that the person may use to cope is through return to the theater of violence (such as the battlefield) or to engage in other acts of violence with others (such as physical fighting). Reactions can display as emotional violence, attempts at suicide, attempts to run into enemy fire or other violent behaviors.

The events I'm talking about here are those that expose the person to empathetic conflict. A firefighter is unlikely to be exposed to this type of trauma except where he may have to leave a fire when someone is still in danger in order to preserve his own life. Frequently, people who share danger, such a firefighters, bond from the shared experiences and spend time talking to each other about the details as they work through them as best they can.

I've offered these examples to give some visibility to how head-space operates and how it can be modified and some of the consequences of altered states after events.

In kink the most common head-space is called:
Subspace
This term is used to describe the altered mental state of a person in the receiving, submissive, bottom or masochist side of a kink interaction. While it is true that this head-space happens to submissives and it is true that it is a head-space, the identification of this space as subspace is not correct.

Sometimes I'm approached by submissives, bottoms or masochists who tell me that they never achieve subspace.

From my discussion thus far you can probably see how this simply isn't likely to be true. What is true is that altered mental states are a spectrum and each person has a different level of vulnerability and responsiveness to entering any altered mental state. This means it is easier for one person to fall asleep versus another person. However, except in very rare cases, everyone falls asleep. The same is true for other altered mental states including subspace.

The issue tends to be that people have no idea what it feels like. Some believe they should feel drunk, some think they should feel detached or alert or all of the above. Some feel they shouldn't feel any of the pain of stimulation.

Well, that isn't how it works. Unless there is something wrong with your nervous system you will feel sensation. What is true is that how you interpret sensation is informed by how you think and by how you've trained your mind and body. Most people haven't ever tried to train their mind beyond stuffing it with school stuff. Few actually examine and shape their thinking directly. For this reason, many people don't know how their mind thinks or feels or works.

For some people, moving into an altered state is very easy and quite familiar. These same people are likely to find it easier to shift the sensory signals of pain into pleasure and shift their experience of a scene dramatically. For other people this is very challenging because the altered states they are familiar with appear to simply happen rather than to occur through intention.

It's true, as I described in my falling scenario, that the first effects of a rapid trauma are instinctual for most people. But, kink is an intentional process often known in advance and planned for by both persons.

This adds another component to physical responses. Your brain is responsible for triggering chemicals, energy and responses in your body. With intentional processes some of the automatic reactions of a random trauma are changed. In a sense the individual has some control over what they experience.

My recommendation for persons who believe they aren't experiencing subspace is to practice. The best form of practice is simple meditation performed for 30 minutes a day, everyday. When you meditate pay attention to how your mental state changes. You can find free videos online to help you learn to meditate.

Top Space

Everybody experiences top space. This is your normal head space when you are active and awake during every day.

Marginally Down Space

From a kink perspective this space occurs when the dominant in the relationship directs attention at the submissive. This may be a glance, a light touch, a small sound or any combination of these triggers. This can even occur from a distance when an interaction is planned. This marginal appearing contact drops the submissive out of top space into a state of waiting and/or listening for command. This waiting aspect has some of the features of being hyper-alert and directionally focused towards a single person. Sometimes they will cease talking even in the midst of a comment. They may stop moving. They will attempt direct eye contact with their dominant to see if they have a direction or command for them. If nothing further occurs they will most likely re-top. Or, go back to full functional top space. If the dominant mentally presses they will generally descend further into space.

Although I am using the word submissive here, this is incorrect and incomplete. A bottom, masochist or vulnerable person may also display the same responses to a strongly emoting person whether they are in a relationship or not. Some of this is instinctive and the individual is evaluating to see what may occur and how they will respond to whatever is presented.

Sprite Space or SAM (Smart Ass Masochists)

Some submissives will squirm and utterly deny that this space exists. They will swear to you that they don't have it, that it doesn't exist and they would never perpetrate mischief. Hmmm. Essentially just under or into down space there is a level where the submissive will test the dominant's attention, desire and will to control them. They may unclip cuffs, slide out of assigned position. All in total innocence. They didn't hear that command. The blindfold muffled their ears, etc. If they note that the dominant doesn't catch their action they will fear their dominant isn't paying attention. This belief can cause all kinds of issues and problems. So, pay attention when you should be paying attention. This doesn't mean you should reward acting out behaviors with your attention unless that is a fun part of your dynamic and how you want to interact with each other.

Down Space

As I noted earlier in the progression into an altered state some of the features of intoxication can appear. If this occurs before any stimulation you may wonder how a person can release the chemicals necessary to produce this effect. Remember that most altered mental states do not require trauma. Many submissives intentionally move towards a state of mental relaxation similar to sleep. This is part of how they relax control over their autonomy and shift towards the behaviors expected of a submissive.

To some extent they have decided in advance not to struggle against receiving direction from another person. To achieve this they need to relinquish control and they need to pull back their ego. This process often looks and feels like a detachment. Some submissives feel like their IQ drops as they step back from self-management. This isn't true but what is shutting down is critical thinking and skepticism.

Many submissives will tell you that their up person is off to the side watching everything. They will feel themselves getting slower mentally. In down space the submissive has trouble with rational thought. If you ask them if something is uncomfortable they are likely to say, "I dunno". The truth is, they don't know. At this point they are not capable of distinguishing danger to themselves, and they may not utilize any safeword. Portions of their earlier negotiated agreements become incomprehensible to them. In their mind, they have you, the dominant, they love and trust you, you won't let anything happen to them.

Sub-Vocal or Primal Space

Expect a struggle. Many people want to suggest that they are continuously submissive. It just isn't true. In fact the supposedly submerged ego is constantly squirreling around finding ways to establish a beachhead, even during the midst of a scene. See, the whole of the individual doesn't agree with scening. All of the aspects of self that you suppress in your effort to 'be' the perfect submissive are not agreeing to scene at all. In fact, what you have is a reluctant majority submissive. This means that other parts of the person are in constant struggle with authority and their annoying submissive sides. When I talked about 'Sprite Space' I was talking about the beginning of this behavior.

The non-agreeing sides of the individual are in the

business of getting away from the trauma. They don't think that kink scening is innocent, fun or anything they should be allowing to happen. So, they work against the situation trying to demonstrate to the parts that are submitting that they are wrong in their evaluation of the situation.

As the individual takes on more chemicals and energy these aspects are also fueled. Dis-inhibition can release a person from their desire to be submissive. This doesn't mean they stop wanting to scene, although some do want to stop, but it does mean that the inner conflicts between the person's aspects can show up in the scene as a person struggling. Many people enjoy struggling against bondage (in particular) or they enjoy yelling and experiencing their emotions without the restraints imposed by culture. I often hear requests that a person wants to cry.

Sometimes the submissive will penetrate what I call the sub-vocal barrier. As they drop through into this deep space they can struggle violently so any bondage should be safe and secure if that is the objective of the scene. Their voice may become deeper and very assertive, their eyes may alter towards a hyper-sensitivity to sound, light and movement. They will be fast and sometimes pose a danger to themselves or other people within range. They can and will claw you, bite you or toss you into a wall if you are a small person. In a sense they are tapping into ancient responses. If they sense any weakness in your control (or your construction of the scene) they may attempt to take you out. Most won't ever utilize safewords here. Some forget modern speech and prefer grunts or just sounds.

These are the most common and basic levels of space. Prior to beginning an exploration of kink the dominant and submissive should have intensive conversations about what the submissive may expect and how the submissive may feel. If you intend to use safewords you should practice using them in minor scenes so that the submissive feels safe and comfortable using them. Many submissives believe that using a safeword is a slap in the face to the dominant. You need to practice the behavior if you expect it to operate correctly in a more intense scene.

Some basic information: Never ever leave your submissive alone in space unless you wish to risk severe potential problems. You are their sole connection to reality. If you leave your submissive alone they are likely to stop having any fun and to immediately shift into evaluating and judging the situation and they will find your absence very wrong.

Remember what I said about how a submissive is only a temporary majority agreement. The rest of the person isn't the least bit submissive and they won't have any problems making that clear. Always keep any in-scene commands simple and direct. In space a submissive will obey but thinking can be slow. Never impose responsibility on your submissive for any aspect of the play. Most people can communicate quite well during a minor scene. As you increase intensity that communication can change. At no point should the scene be re-negotiated during the scene.

Talk to your submissive in a reassuring fashion, if penetration of subspace is new, they may be frightened. The further into space your submissive goes the higher the chemicals pump into their blood stream, and generally more intense the play can become. For a first timer, you need to tell your submissive that subspace exists, what it is and how it may feel to them. Many people will desire to please you, and they will try to be open to seek this space.

Many people want to include crude language during a scene, this may be an essential part of the scene. Before you launch into this type of verbal stimulation explore in minor scenes to see what the aftermath is for that individual. People tend to internalize verbally degrading comments. What sounds sexy pre-scene may be damaging after a scene. Before you go too far, really examine the self esteem of the individual.

Dominant Space

A dominant is exactly the same as a submissive, both are human beings subject to the same forces and responses.

The behavior of a dominant during a scene is necessarily different from the submissive. The dominant doesn't have the same privilege of letting go that the submissive has as they detach from responsibility for the scene. Instead the dominant is more like the fire fighter. They get just as excited, but they need to use their hyper-alert state to manage the agreed-to scene. Their focus is likely to be the elements of the scene and the submissive. Unfortunately the same dis-inhibitors are present that I described earlier.

This means that the dominant experiences some level of intoxication during a scene. When the submissive is in a position of sexual vulnerability, some dominants act upon this access and violate their agreements with the submissive, particularly around having sex.

A person doesn't function the same when they are intoxicated. You may know and like a person while they are sober and dislike them intensely when they are not sober. The submissive needs to understand this prior to scening with a dominant. Who are they when their inner constraints are turned down or off?

A dominant in dominant space is more alert and anything that is not directly involved in what has triggered their attention, will be set aside or discarded. Usually the acceleration of energy will make the dominant feel like a switch has been turned 'ON'.

If a dominant is triggered on and the stimuli continues for a period of time then that dominant will progress. In this stage a dominant will often feel an upswing of energy. They are actively prepared to react or respond quite literally to anything. They may find themselves almost hyperactive from this sudden energy boost and at times they will scramble mentally to adjust to the dis-inhibition process. They will note that their perceptions alter, vision acuity will tighten, hearing will intensify, and adrenaline will flow through them offering a rush of sudden strength. There is a sensation of increased awareness and details will magnify.

If a scene has been initiated then the dominant will often note a sensation of alert mental detachment. This is a separation of their normal emotional responses to everything that is around them. This becomes easier to achieve with practice. Some dominants will also note a sensation of energy flow, this appear or sometimes feels like it is emanating from the submissive they are scening.

With some dominant there will be the distinct feeling that they are inside of the submissive. A part of the dominant will experience the scene from within the submissive's perspective at the same time they enjoy their own experience. Some dominants will report hearing the mind of their submissive. There is a sensation of accelerating excitement, these sensations may be so intense as to produce a physical quiver in the body. A differing set of responses will seem to replace those they would consider to be normal. These responses are often keyed directly to the person or scene they are involved in. The emotional detachment and altered responses allow the dominant to take actions or play with their submissive in ways they would have difficulty with during normal space. It is important to note here that scening excites a dominant, that excitement and the attached levels of danger pump chemicals into the dominant's blood stream exactly the same as with the submissive.

The further down that the submissive goes in scene, the further down the dominant goes. The submissive's responses to the dominant's actions trigger and retrigger the dominant. That dominant in turn does more and the escalating spiraling cycle of energy exchange begins to spin. This energy is as euphoric for the dominant as it is for the submissive with one profound difference, part of the intensity that the dominant feels is because of the mental compression necessary to maintain tight physical and mental control throughout the scene, until it builds into a final crescendo.

If a dominant is strongly effected by dis-inhibition they can reach a point where they violate the submissive or even hurt them. They may lose their ability to maintain clear thought. Some dominants will discover a level of personal cruelty within themselves that they never imagined existed. Any dominant noting total detachment within themselves from the welfare of the submissive they are scening should immediately recognize that they have gone too far and exit the scene. Even a momentary step aside can bring a dominant out of this danger zone. From that point forward the dominant should work toward ending the scene as quickly as possible to prevent a recurrence of entry into this type of head space. If this sounds like you, set an appointment with a KAP (Kink Aware Professional) member and get some help and insight into the situation.

After a scene has ended both the dominant and the submissive will need aftercare. The need for intense bonding is common as is the desire for immediate sexual release. Many couples enjoy wrapping themselves around each other and coming down together. There is simple safety in this type of intimate contact. Expect to feel energy depleted or energy enervated for a period of time until your body adjusts and returns you to a more normal state.

ACCESSING SPACE

For the purposes of this section I will assume that the submissive is new to the lifestyle and that the dominant directing them has limited or no experience with this aspect of BDSM.

It helps to practice. Most people are conditioned to resist the exploration of altered mental states. If, as a child, you liked to daydream (an altered mental state), it is likely the people around you told you to pay attention and stop. The message here is that an altered state is negative and inappropriate. Because of this many people resist entering altered states intentionally, instead their experiences are passive such as falling asleep or spacing out while doing housework.

Control of your mind is up to you. You are the operator of your body and brain and your mind is part of that system. If you never engage in direct interaction with your mind it is like any muscle, it becomes quite flabby and not particularly responsive.

Many people think their mind can only operate on automatic. The very idea of paying attention to how your mind works may seem ridiculous and what does it matter if, as I noted earlier, your responses will trigger space anyway, right?

Most people never attempt to guide their dreams when their brain is in REM (rapid eye movement periods during sleep). Again, there is a cultural concept that dreams 'happen' passively and that you as an individual are captive to some mysterious film-like dream experience. The most frequent cultural message around altered states is that they are something that happens to you and there is nothing you can do about it.

Except that none of this is true. Basically your brain is a lot like a computer and most of the time your mind (your thinking aspect) runs along on auto. You tell your mind that you need to study a math problem or memorize a book passage but most of the time your mind is busy chattering away in a constant conversation with itself. Most of the time you don't give your thinking any structure, you just allow it to happen.

This is a lot like having a computer and no keyboard or mouse to operate the computer. You stare at the screen while content flows along. You occasionally see a cute cat picture and you 'think' *I like those* and your mental fingers toggle some cat picture resource to help you out. Was your act deliberate and intentional or reactive?

Practicing moving in and out of space doesn't require kink at all. As I noted earlier a basic meditation practice is a good place to start. This will allow you to notice your mental state and it will allow you to create an intention of going in and out of space without any chemicals or energy components.

A second way to practice is by noticing your entry into sleep behaviors. Most people have a sleeping routine that assists them in informing their brain that it is time to shift into sleep. This may include bathing, a period of watching television, the application of moisturizers on their feet, maybe sexual activity or many other similar sleep rituals.

First, note your routine. Jot it down on a notepad. Look for the 'language' you use to inform your brain that you are ready for sleep. Usually this is a combination of factors including body position, sound, a reduction in light and mental habits you use to shift your mental state. All of these have developed over time and often from childhood when you were 'told' to go to sleep.

After you note how you tell yourself to actually go to sleep next tell yourself to pay attention to what happens while you are asleep. This may sound contradictory, if you are asleep how can you notice what happens? Well, the truth is that when you are asleep your brain is actually quite busy doing stuff, keeping an eye on how you sleep is not impossible. Many people find that it is easier to tell themselves to remember their dreams.

To recall a dream you only have a few seconds after you leave your dream state where the information remains in your short term memory. Have your notebook handy and jot down what you remember of your dream. Later, when you try to read it you will discover that your notes aren't particularly coherent. That is normal and common. As you 'practice' recall you will get better at it.

At some point you can give yourself direction while you are dreaming. Again, this is an intention that you form while awake and reinforce into a direct message to your brain so that it obeys. Your in-dream action may be as simple as to look at your in-dream hand or you may decide to shift dreams if your current dream is not satisfying and it is bugging you.

Many dreams are composed of fragments of memories from the day or week prior to the dream. Often they are not linear and don't make a lot of sense. Some are from childhood, some are scary, some recall actual events and replay them. In many cases a dream is helping you process something. This is your brain giving you clues about something that you experienced that remains incomplete. But, the objective in this text isn't to analyze your dreams but to practice control features that you have during experiences that are inside altered mental states.

What you want to achieve is not only a better recognition of altered states, it is also an increased ability to intentionally shift in to and out of such states and while in such states an increased ability to guide your experience.

Basically, you want to recognize that your altered state has a steering wheel and you have the ability to accelerate or decelerate your perceptions while in the state.

After you practice these basic techniques alone you can augment your techniques by incorporating your partner.

If you don't live together you can have the dominant create a meditation CD that follows the same meditation script of the submissive's favorite meditation CD. Keep the script the same. Replicate the tone used by the expert and use a similar background music.

The submissive using this type of CD will begin to associate the sound of their new dominant's voice with their practice of meditating and of following the direction of the voice. Over time and as the submissive becomes more expert at meditating daily a second CD can be made to include more personal or meaningful meditations. I am not suggesting you include sexual stuff in the meditation as this will negate the non-chemical and non-energetic aspects of meditating or to be blunt it will defeat the purpose.

A more personal or meaningful CD would describe a landscape that is more on point for the submissive. If you like waterfalls and your test CD from the expert uses a

> *Some people have trouble being sadistic if they feel close emotionally to their partner – this can lead to avoidance of intimacy bonding exercises.*

visual of a blooming flower, this is the kind of change you would make in the more personal CD.

The objective of most meditations isn't to think, it is to release the aspect of your mind that is used to automatic mental chatter.

When a couple lives together they can meditate together and learn joint meditation practices that will allow them to feel more connected during experiences of altered states. Again, don't be sexual and kinky during such practices. The area and time of meditation should be 'safe from' any other demands of focus.

A dominant who has substantial training in hypnosis can also incorporate hypnosis sessions into the regular life of themselves and their partners.

Other types of bonding that encourage shared altered mental state experiences should also be practiced. Place yourselves in a non-sexual context, while dressed and comfortable. Set a mutual intention for the submissive to be open to receiving silent mental guidance from their partner. This may include the submissive closing their eyes to reduce distractions. Some submissives also wear ear muffs. The dominant should caress the submissive such as to gently brush back small tendrils of their hair *(This is a pattern)*. Retain physical contact. We are all electrical beings to some extent and part of what we feel from or radiate to each other is the movement of energy. This flow of energy can be best directed by touch during the entirety of the practice session.

When a dominant touches a submissive and directs thought at that submissive, that dominant is actually directing their own physical and mental energy at the submissive. Practice improves this ability. When the relationship is new, the maintenance of this physical conduit is very important as both people are learning how to feel each other. At some later stages a dominant and a submissive can often feel each other without the need for this physical contact. The dominant may have an experience which can best be described as empathic or feeling through their submissive. Learning how to find this space from both directions takes time, patience, natural aptitude and a strong desire and intention.

This practice goes beyond simple recognition of space and allows both partners to engage in deep listening. After the session where the submissive practices receiving silent mental messages the two should reverse roles.

The dominant should close their eyes, muffle their ears and relax. The objective of the submissive is shifted towards conveying their feelings and experience towards the dominant. Information passed silently is only as good as the recipients practiced ability to 'hear' what is being communicated. Both people need the same practice. Silent listening doesn't magically appear, it is a skill that is learned and practiced between partners.

To achieve good silent communication both people need to practice silencing their own inner mental chatter and intentionally listening for the communications from their partner.

This skill is made more difficult by people who have less control over their ego. To some extent you need to realize that your ego doesn't need to answer for everyone around you. Often we allow our ego to tell us what we want to think other people are saying and thinking and meaning about everything. We give our ego this permission and then we seldom call it back and allow others to fully communicate on their own.

With this shared mental communication will come increasing awareness of the 'state' of the other person. This type of skill practice also improves trust and investment in the individual's experience during scening or interactions.

The submissive with this skill may feel themselves to be flowing along their dominant's energy stream. This connection is important. Once a submissive has entered space the dominant should maintain physical and verbal contact with them at all times. The submissive may feel that their connection to reality is through the dominant so abandonment in space can be terribly frightening and almost certain to cause a serious loss of trust when the submissive re-tops. Some submissives actually visualize this conduit or connection to their dominant as being similar to a cord of luminescent light that connects them together. Their dominant is their safety. By vacating perceptible reality the submissive is releasing themselves to a level of personal vulnerability *(should children wander in to see them zoning, etc.)* The submissive trusts that their dominant will protect them mentally, physically, emotionally and even spiritually when they are in an altered state.

Space enhances awareness of the subtle sense array that each person possesses. By limiting the brain's input to a few tightly controlled or monitored sensations and sounds the brain moves away from the cacophony of mental sound and within that movement becomes capable of highly enhanced potentials. To some extent it may be considered that space is a higher level of brain functioning or the individual is selectively using specific parts of the brain in a more efficient way. Space allows the brain the ability to view and experience incoming data in totally different ways, which inevitably alters how the spacing individual will view reality after they have exited space.

When space is achieved during a scene for the first time it is crucial for the dominant to realize that the effects of space will linger inside of their submissive for a long time. This makes aftercare vital. Your submissive will need comfort, reassurance and what can best be described as cuddling. Do not limit this aftercare to when you *(the dominant)* believe that enough has been given, but allow your submissive to cuddle or maintain physical contact for as long as they feel the need. If this exercise was done after dinner then it is an excellent idea to cuddle for a while then climb into bed together where physical contact can be maintained.

The dominant should be aware that at this point their submissive may be too close to space and that sensory contact *(such as sex)* may be difficult on them mentally. The scening event may be more than enough for them to process that night. Other submissives will become extremely aroused by the event and need the completion of intimate relations if sex didn't occur during a scene. If your submissive appears to only want to cuddle, let that be enough. You will or may see variations from one extreme to another as you explore space further with the same submissive.

The dominant may have minimal desire for sex after a scene. In many cases a dominant may not live with their submissive and the relationship may not be one of sexual intimacy. This doesn't mean the aftercare shouldn't include physical cuddling. However, in many cases the two people may wish to cuddle their intimate partners who may not be involved in kink at all.

Many people require food immediately after intense scenes. Proteins, carbs, water and electrolytes are commonly provided immediately after a scene to replenish the body. These may feel more immediate and important to some people rather than making physical contact with their scene partner.

Unexpected Problems

It's important to mention here that altered mental states are not always safe. Some people, in childhood, develop a strategy for escaping danger by 'going away' in their mind. Most people with this rare disorder know about it and will talk about it prior to engaging in kink. A few people are not aware that they have used this strategy to escape from extreme forms of abuse.

When such a person encounters an altered state, even sleep, they can feel very frightened. In addition, the altered state may allow past experiences to come into awareness or the person may 'escape' into space and detach from connection in the present.

As a dominant, you are not a therapist. If you encounter this experience, stop the scene immediately and wait until the person comes out of the altered state. Do not try to comfort them unless they ask for comfort. Do not try to tell them what makes you feel better. Simply wait, listen and when they are functional again, seek joint therapy with a KAP member to find out what is the best course of action if both of you wish to continue exploring kink together.

Moving Within Space

It is my suggestion that you practice space techniques first without deploying other sensory stimulation or distractions. This will allow you to get a feel for what is happening within you and your submissive's minds in the simplest form or without the complexities of physical stimulation to complicate responses.

Use the same techniques to make your submissive feel as comfortable and safe as possible. Your submissive should know what you are both doing and can and should be fully informed as to what both of you might expect or feel during the exercise. This will reduce fear and anxiety and narrow your submissive's attention to directly focusing on the exercise or experience itself.

Don't create performance anxiety. While practice will assist everyone in recognition and control over their own mental states, no two people have the same abilities. Some people have trouble sleeping without pills, others fall asleep in any position and with loud noises and lots of distractions. Altered states exist across a spectrum and every person has different abilities and issues that can impact how they experience any state.

Once your submissive is comfortable you may discover that they may launch into space rather quickly. Often, especially if an experience is relatively pleasant *(space is often very pleasant)*, the individual will learn the location and characteristics of space in their mind. The more frequently a person is in that space, the easier and faster it will be for them to find that space. Once within space a person can drift along quite comfortably for hours. Some people focus on some slight sound, perhaps your heartbeat or the whir of a fan. They are waiting for either an increase in intensity, a direction or some change.

A change of state is movement. A change within state is also a movement. A change of state means that a person who is in a state different from their norm, will note changes. I've described some of the effects that are commonly noticeable early in the process. You may have other sensations. There isn't any right or wrong to how you experience an altered state. Often the objective of entering an altered mental state in connection with kink is to allow the body to assist the person receiving direction (the submissive) in pain management and in tissue recovery.

A change within state is how a person can act to influence their state while they are in that state. If you go back to my earlier discussion about the firefighter and training, you will recall how I noted that he trains himself to continue to function along specific protocols while in this state. The firefighter is still hyper-aware of the fire, the danger, the possibility of needing to act quickly to locate and save people and animals. This doesn't mean that the firefighter isn't in an altered state, it means he is moving and guiding himself while in that state.

The difference between staying mentally alert within an altered state and releasing your intellectual acuity in favor of a pure experience of the space is significant. In general, most kinky scenes do not require a submissive to retain acute mental processes.

Some people can develop their mental controls sufficiently to shift into altered states at will and to assist their mind in shifting into deeper states more easily.

It's also important to talk about how most people tend to identify spiritual states. Space experienced at the same time as the flood of chemicals and energy released during the event often produces experiences of euphoria. Some people will feel these experiences in deeply spiritual ways and they may regard their partner as a vehicle or conduit of divine potentials. Some feel all of the attributes associated with spiritual rapture. In this regard the dominant or partner is essentially 'god' in human form much along the lines of ancient ideas of how a priest receives divinity and passes it to others. A dominant should be aware of this potential and be open to discussing the experiences with their submissive or partner in the days after such an experience.

This also indicates how vulnerable the submissive may become to the intensity of the experience and how they have interpreted what they felt at the time.

Questions & Answers

Can I be hypnotized to make me 'more' submissive?

No. Space is not hypnosis. Anyone who tries to hypnotize someone into behaviors against their consent is unethical and likely to receive the just rewards of being manipulative, a failed relationship. However, some people in kink are experts at hypnosis and routinely incorporate hypnosis and NLP in their interactions.

Discuss and negotiate such interests prior to scening.

Can I be forced to do things I don't want to do when I am in space?

Yes. You can be coerced to agree to 'change' your limits while you are dis-inhibited during a scene. When you recover from the experience it is common to feel grossly violated and disgusted with the other person. You can also feel pressure to conform to the requests or needs of other people. If you believe you do this too often seek therapy for basic self esteem issues. If you select a partner who frequently violates your negotiations take a step back and examine your criteria for partner selection.

Can I hurt my submissive by taking them into space?

Not usually. Space is a natural place inside of the mind. Humans normally enter space. As noted earlier it is possible to inadvertently scene with a person who uses altered states to detach or escape from abuse. Any scening with a person with these issues is dangerous for the mental health of the individual. Stop scening and seek professional help to sort out the best way to proceed with the least danger to either of you.

Are their negative side effects of space?

No. However, many people discover that they have a lot of issues from their childhood that they haven't fully processed. Accessing altered mental states coupled with faux-trauma or intense stimulation can cause these issues to surface vividly and unexpectedly. If this occurs the scene should stop and the partners should discuss the old event or what is happening. It may be necessary to go to a therapist to work through particularly difficult issues. Only discuss what the person having the experience feels comfortable sharing. This isn't about the power exchange in your relationship. Don't impose rules that may negatively effect the mental health of your partner.

OTHER ISSUES

Venturing into the realms of altered mental states should be done carefully. The human mind is vulnerable to suggestions. People often have an enormous desire to be part of something greater or more important than themselves. Many people want for their life to have visible meaning, to be worthwhile and of significance. This desire makes them vulnerable to other humans who have no scruples on using their needs against them.

Within kink there is a strong underlying belief encouraging voluntary focused enthrallment. This predisposition towards 'thralled' positive responses can influence the mind and leave a person open to simple hypnotic triggers. This sometimes allows people with questionable motives a means of manipulating another human's mind.

People often seek help from qualified and licensed hypnotists to help them with minor lifestyle problems such as overeating or smoking. These real life hypnotists are generally quite good, and almost never attempt any type of mental manipulation, as such non-voluntary manipulation is unethical and fundamentally wrong.

With the opening of the online community many more vulnerable kinky people have become accessible to huge numbers of unknown individuals. Within this group have been a small but growing number of predators. Not all human predators like to physically molest, rape or kill other humans, some like to toy with other people's minds. Many new or emergent submissives are vulnerable to the lines or lures offered by these predators. Exposure to kink often opens up huge windows inside a person and it can make them unsafe. These changes, much like all types of changes in life, leave the individual groping their way along on a pathway of information seeking education and exploration. Their formally well known and understood rules suddenly shift or change and quite often they do not have sufficient information to correctly identify one of these masked predators when they have met them. In many ways their defenses have not gained a level of understanding to insure their integrity or personal safety.

Many people feel an instinctive desire to trust. Especially if that person offers themselves in the role of dominant and speaks to them with interest or kindness. Often the predator is quite charming and innocuous in online appearance and demeanor. They will seek out and tell you the things you may wish to hear. It is relatively easy to be swayed into believing them when in all likelihood they have offered nothing of substance for you to base that trust upon. Your desire is your vulnerability. Your submissive interests are a clue and key to further opportunities for them.

If you are a new or emergent submissive and any online dominant tells you that they can take you into space or hypnotize you for any reason online or on the phone, know and understand that such suggestion is a demonstration of a lack of care for your personal safety. Hypnosis is only safe when done in person. A submissive entering space is vulnerable to significant detachment from physical reality. That detachment can make them unable to rationally discern true danger. A real dominant will never willingly risk the life and mental health of any submissive.

I have also noted a growing trend of online trainers. It is my considered opinion that such training especially online is almost always flawed, often significantly. A large percentage of these trainers are simply individuals who want access to submissives without taking on the responsibilities inherent in a relationship. No one needs professional 'training'.

Most people start off engaging in one-time casual scenes with people they feel are friends. There aren't any rules to how you behave. You don't have to kneel on command or wear a collar or look down or any of the hundreds of other 'rules' you will hear about online.

You do need to ask questions and figure out what you like to do and how you like to feel. This is about you liking yourself and feeling good. The fewer pre-conceptions you have about your role and what you must do in order to fit in with an imaginary community, the better. Show up. Be yourself.

You might want a mentor. No, they don't need to be dominant. Yes, they do need a little more experience in real life than you have at this moment. Most importantly, you need to like and respect them. They may live up to your approval over time or they may turn into an un-friend. You may have several mentors, advisors and particularly good friends over time. Check out your local groups and in particular try to attend a few play parties, workshops or other events where people are busy scening. Pay attention. In this way you will hear lots of gossip about local people, you will see lots of behaviors both good and bad and you will hear lots of advice. All of this is the type of information you just can't gain online or from books. You will discover that there are innumerable points of view about everything. As I said, there aren't any rules beyond common courtesy. None.

If you are fascinated by altered mental states you will find you aren't alone. Look in the piercing and suspension groups for people who really, really want to experience mind-blowing vision quests and epiphanies through space. Attend conferences that offer spirit circles and other spiritual practices. Explore. It's your head.

High End Submissive

Early submissive conditioning is common for many females and some males. This conditioning doesn't act upon all individuals in the same way. Some individuals respond to conditioning by adapting to its confines without a great deal of emotional struggle. These individuals have what are called mutable characteristics. Mutability is often identified as being particularly adjustable, with an understanding nature, one who is good at analyzing and who is also extroverted.

From the outside a mutable personality can be expressed as self-assurance, yet, if you look closely you will often find that the mutable personality is aligning and acting upon persons in their life that are more forcibly aggressive or ego-centered.

Sometimes this will show up as peacemaking, a good listener or a person whose advice is well-trusted. They will generally be quite bright, articulate, charming, loving, giving, career oriented and willful. None of these characteristics will identify or reveal this individual's truth. Often this person will learn very early to mask their truth. They will recognize in terror the potentials of their conditioning and their struggle to overcome their responses and they will often take serious measures to obscure any hint of their mutability.

Some will spend enormous amounts of time watching

television and movies to align their behavior with what they see based on how they believe others expect to see them. This is a form of self-training or self-shielding. They will often be extremely well read for the same reason. They instinctively know that survival requires for them to blend seamlessly into society as much as possible.

These masks can be enormously effective allowing this submissive to manage themselves without attracting the true attention of others. It is common for some people to create alternate personae to deal with the outer world. They will usually have a defender personality that will appear to be quite dominant. Often this defender will be loud spoken, assertive and almost pathologically defensive. Many submissives will actually name this defender. They will generally have a normal persona as well. They will usually take on their given name and will incorporate enough of the defender personality to maintain a wall or safety zone for the inner self. The core being or true self, will hide.

I am not talking about a split-personality here or some kind of mental disorder. This is just the way the features of the personality are set up. The individual is fully aware of what they have done and why. Their life is an ongoing challenge to negotiate the constant temptations of offering service towards others. It isn't that offering service is wrong but our culture is set up to value independence and celebritized or monetized creative results. Wanting to do something merely because another person mentions a desire for something, isn't valued.

When a mutable person finds kink and discovers a world full of people giving direction to others it is something of a dilemma.

In the last chapter I talked about 'focused listening'. In general, the mutable conditioned individual has been using tightly focused listening their entire life. They hear *into* the emotional combinations of other people, they literally *feel* their needs. This *feeling* can be as intense as if the feeling emerged from their own desires or experiences. It can even seem *stronger* than their own feelings.

I have chosen to call the individual with these potentials who discovers kink a high-end submissive. This doesn't relegate them to being submissive (this may seem confusing) but they will often choose to role-play submission to mask their conditioned and mutable responses.

The high-end submissive is not a volunteer. When in the presence of any person emoting using elevated energy and an assertive tone, this submissive will feel compelled to respond. This is not a thought. The response feels more primal and the individual may move towards action before they think about it.

Often they develop strategies to avoid following through with their first inclinations. Using a motto famous in Clint Eastwood's movie Heartbreak Ridge, this individual will "improvise, adapt and overcome" the obstacles or issues they are faced with.

Most people have rather poor emotional management skills. Many people act out when they become angry and they yell, gesture and project violent intentions towards others. Earlier I discussed some of these features around what happens during trauma. These aren't new behaviors. I also talked about the two choices that every person faces during trauma.

Some people with a more mutable personality seem to manage to survive such situations where others don't do so well. Why? It seems plausible to me that there is a mutation or adaptation present that acts upon the aggressor and increases the survivability factor.

All humans appear to me to have both dominant and submissive sides. At any given time they may feel more comfort in expressing one side over another. Any individual may become involved in a situation which brings out their dominant side such as during parenting or as a teacher.

As a child, a person with a more mutable personality may find themselves literally throwing themselves physically between two fighting persons or otherwise trying to intervene in the midst of very excited and dangerous energies where they are likely to receive injury.

This would seem counter-intuitive. The reaction is spontaneous and terrified. The individual *needs* the aggressor to stop, to control their energized emotional emissions. The mutable child doesn't know this – exactly, they only know that the situation *must* stop.

They will often placate both of the people fighting and it may not be clear why. Their behaviors towards the aggressors will be non-aggressive and designed to reduce the altercation. They may go so far as to plead with one or both of the aggressors in order to end the situation. They will sometimes offer themselves instead of the other person.

What is going on?

Remember what I mentioned about focused emotional listening? In an altercation one of the two aggressors is likely to desire not to be involved. They may be broadcasting this emotional plea even when they are fighting. Remember my comment about the two choices and how escape strategies are negotiated.

The mutable person is not trying to hurt themselves but they are more 'able' to deal with the aggressor directly than they feel able to deal with the emotional pleas they are receiving.

By projecting acceptance toward the aggressor the mutable person acts upon the source of aggression. Since it is unlikely that the aggressor has elevated emotion towards the mutable person this behavior 'shifts' the dynamics. In addition, the mutable person 'receives' the energy of the aggressor.

Energy circulation is something I discuss in more detail in Extreme Space II: Kink Secrets (available in February 2013) and if you are interested in more of this process I encourage you to purchase a copy of that book for the details. For this text, it is only important to understand that some people can draw off the energy of others and reduce the intensity of that energy.

The interface of this process will often shut down the explosive or violent encounter. Sometimes the submissive will redirect the energy of the aggressor and they may find themselves within the whirlpool of uncontrolled violence of a person out of control.

This reaction or response is irrational to many outside viewers. After the event ends the individual may find themselves verbally chastised by friends and family for the stupidity of what they have done. This second companion experience often serves to isolate the person from these same friends or family as they cannot readily explain what has happened to them or why. This type of event is how most people with mutable personalities get their first taste of this aspect of their personality.

What actually happens? A mutable person can often go into an altered mental state just by listening too closely to two emoting people. They can experience proximity energy that is elevating, they 'feel' or 'hear' or otherwise receive or analyze body language and other subtle information that conveys a message that includes the elevated chemical signature of impending violence. When they receive this signature it is as if they are inside the event, their system corresponds in kind.

Early on they become experts at management. They learn how to cope with sudden space events. They learn how to make jokes about speech gaps, slurring and detachment. Often they may allude to being out of it. They learn how to recognize and exit the presence of a person verging on a strong emotional display without openly expressing their true nature. They manage. Their greatest fear and desire is for their attributes and responses to be recognized and taken advantage of by others.

The advent of the Internet created new opportunities for a person with a mutable personality and new problems. Their patterning and masks are primarily constructed through physical actions and responses. The limitations of the Internet to written communication may tend to strip away some of their hard won strategies.

Couple this with their 'interest' in kink and you can see why it is a problem. The sudden ability to be open or free to express this aspect of their inner self often leads to a false sense of security based on the illusionary anonymity of the Internet. The submissive may throw themselves happily into the safety of the Internet experience, not truly realizing that their mutable characteristics will continue to make them vulnerable, perhaps even more so in this subtle venue.

Any person with greater sensitivity in any area will have associated problems. Being sensitive and reactive to elevated energy, command structures, emoting voice, directive inflection and other things are coupled to their adaptability and childhood submissive conditioning. Some people discover that they 'read' more closely than other people in a continuation of the acute listening behavior they are familiar with.

Analyzing writing can also trigger some of the same responses if the individual 'speaks' what they read in their head. Their brain doesn't clearly distinguish differences between self-spoken direction and read direction, particularly if the individual is trying to reach out and understand the other person for a potential relationship.

Reading a book in the safety of your home and knowing that the characters are fiction is vastly different from an online conversation via email or IM.

The safety of 'fictional' fantasy relationships, often an escape for people with these characteristics is now transformed into a new problem because the nonfiction reality of an online conversation has potentially real consequences.

The submissive having learned and patterned through extensive reading is now vulnerable to something that was never interactive before. What was part of their defenses now reveals itself to be a gate for the unwary.

I want to restate at this point that while some of

these traits are familiar and common to most people, a person who is very reactive in this way is quite rare.

Most people 'feel' anxious and emotional when confronting a strongly emoting person. This is normal. Few people are truly auto-responsive and subject to non-consensual access and manipulation by a others.

You may feel like this article describes you. It is likely it describes how you feel at least some of the time and to some degree. But, most people have sufficient personal shielding to resist access and the capacity to rationally consider decisions in addition to the decisive ability to say simply, no.

If you work as a psychic or psychologist or in any of the fields that rely on intuitive, empathetic or similar types of 'subtle sensory' information reliance, then you may have some of the issues described here.

Submissive Manifestations

Manifestations: one of the forms in which an individual is actualized.

Self-actualization is a term used to describe the process that a person takes as they try to move towards their full potential. In kink this idea can be somewhat applied to how a person tries to reach their full potential within the role of submissive.

Each person responds to stressors differently. In a perfect world there wouldn't be any stressors and a person could perform with their behavior of choice. But, we don't live in a perfect world and stressors are common. No only is our behavior shaped by our internal processes and experiences, it is also shaped by our external environment and ecology.

This means that distresses that affect us are not all internal. If you live in circumstances where it is difficult to pay your bills and feed your family due to circumstances outside your control such as no available jobs or jobs you aren't qualified for because of a lack of education due to poverty, then your behavior will be affected by the elevation of your energy and the release of stress hormones into your body.

How a person behaves under stress is often a more accurate reflection of their personality than when a person is performing for personal gain such as at the beginning of a relationship.

The aspects of the personality that are more influential under stress can be sharply different. What does the individual do with these differences if they are attempting to establish and live inside an intentionally created relationship dynamic such as D/s or M/s?

Most people like to visualize or fantasize about a D/s relationship primarily in terms of when everything is perfect. They imagine no real problems, no internal challenges, no great difficulties. Somehow the stressors of the world will be magically swept aside and the D/s will cure their problems.

Unfortunately, even in the best situations all of the same ills of life will show up and your habitual responses will also show up. What can this look like?

What do you normally do when stuff hits the fan?

What do you do when your partner does or says something that you not only disagree with, you actually think it is rather stupid?

In a D/s framed relationship the fantasy is that this wouldn't happen because the submissive is supposed to always show respect for the dominant and the dominant is supposed to never do stupid stuff.

Let's look at another scenario for a moment. Often a newcomer shows up on a fetish website and joins a newbie forum. Soon after they confess that they are married or in a committed relationship and they want to submit to someone.

Often a veteran will ask them, why aren't you submitting to your current relationship partner?

It is common to hear that their partner isn't into kink or isn't dominant enough or they tried it and it didn't work, but the most common response is that the submissive doesn't want to submit to their current relationship partner. They don't *want* to.

Does this sound off to you? It doesn't mean that this person doesn't truly want to be a submissive in a kink interaction. But it does show that submission isn't the everyday behavior of the person. The explanation commonly offered is that it's because the other person isn't dominating. This suggests that their submission hinges upon the presence of domination. Why?

As I noted earlier each person is composed of many sides. Who shows up for any particular event or situation is a composite of the majority of characteristics that pertain to that situation. So, in the effort a person puts forth to maximize their individual submissive actualization, keep in mind that it is likely that only a slight majority of the person's personality is contributing to this process. The rest isn't, won't, doesn't like it or is ambivalent one way or the other until something goes wrong and then they will internally smack down the parts that are trying to reach this goal.

People who are focused on submissive actualization are likely to present the following behaviors when they firmly believe that everything is excellent, in those times when the stressors of life are more remote.

Posturing: Posturing is when the submissive naturally assumes a submissive posture. This is without training or request by any individual. Such a posturing pose can include the lacing of fingers behind the back, the lowering of eyes, the crossing of fingers in the lap if the submissive is seated. When lying down the hands seem to find themselves above the head *(some submissives have difficulty growing aroused with their hands down)*. This type of submissive posturing is so commonplace that it is often overlooked.

Posturing can be habitual, conditioned or a natural feature of the persons personality. Often the position of the body is unconscious and merely experienced as comfortable. More often it is learned or self-taught, sometimes when the person first discovers kink and when they get very interested in becoming kinky and fulfilling the ideal of the perfect submissive.

Some body positions reflect self esteem. Some don't. Some posturing can occur when a person is performing. It doesn't mean they are particularly submissive, but it can reflect an enthusiasm for participation in kink from a submissive perspective.

Sheening: Sheening can best be described as an exuding of chemicals through the membrane of the skin. These chemistries are oils as well as pheromones which when smelled by a potential sexual partner are designed to attract their attention. This sheening often occurs in moments of heightened energy and proximity and may be accompanied by feelings of detachment, wobbliness, trembling, slurred speech, heightened hearing and near panic.

It is also common for one human to look for signs of arousal on the skin of the other person. The cones inside the eyes that allow humans to see color were developed specifically so that one human can notice color differences in the skin display of another human. These color cues register as sexual arousal.

Riveting: Riveting is when the one person becomes totally focused upon their partner. The surroundings seem to fade out or become insubstantial, eyes may dilate, hearing will sharpen, often the individual will note a distinct alteration in their heart rate and breathing. They can become so focused that they experience difficulty standing still. They may fumble, stumble or otherwise indicate symptoms similar to intoxication.

Command Structures: People approaching a kink interaction often become tightly focused on giving and receiving direction. From the submissive perspective they will reach towards their partner trying to hear every word, nuance and tone, interpreting all at the same time. These words are sometimes called commands and the submissive will hear them differently from common speech. At times they can confuse the two, particularly if their partner is having a conversation on the phone at the same time they are interacting with their submissive. The submissive will often listen to both trying to sort out what is a command and what isn't. Keep in mind that this is happening in the context of the submissive already entering some degree of altered state where reality is slightly distorted.

Heightened Senses: When in the presence of a dominant the submissive will often note a heightening of their senses; sound become very acute. *(In scene sound often becomes critical, tiny sounds can seem as loud as cymbals)* Vision alters. Many submissives will note an increased ability to see in darkness. Bright light can become physically painful and very hard to tolerate. Many notice an increased sense of smell. Sometimes things which have smelled unattractive to them before will smell enticing in scene. They can usually clearly smell the natural odor of the dominant near them and can sometimes read that smell or interpret the scent to identify or help identify the mood of that person. A submissive will also note the ability to endure certain tastes that they cannot tolerate when they are not in the right head-space.

Then of course we come to touch. Submissives become highly sensitive to the slightest touch. Many submissive females can arouse and orgasm from something as light as a touch to their hand. They can feel that their whole body is waiting to be plucked like a violin string. How they feel or experience touch alters and evolves depending on the circumstances, the depth of their connection to the dominant, the strength of the dominant's presence or energy and other factors.

Bonding: Bonding or attachment between partners is driven by two major influences. Human beings are born with a propensity to align with authority. In childhood the typical authority figures are parents. The second influence is the faux-trauma effect described earlier.

These two elements work together along with physical attraction, desire to form a relationship and sexual interest to trigger relational hormones in the body.

The Voice: When a person is giving direction they will tend to speak differently from when they are engaging in conversation. As an example, when a parent is teaching their child they will use a tone of voice that indicates that they are conveying something important. The same is true for the speech attributes exchanged between a dominant and a submissive. This familiar speech type is easily recognizable by a submissive and identified as 'authority speech'.

Slurred Speech: Some submissives will notice that their speech slurs, their ability to be witty diminishes, they may get tongue tied, embarrassed or flushed, tingly, light headed or they may say things that seem very stupid and unlike them when they are in altered mental states. This is temporary and can be corrected using the practices mentioned earlier. It can still recur during intense scenes when the attention of the submissive is not focused on producing legible speech.

Other Manifestations: There are a variety of other characteristics that some submissives may discover, feel and experience. The most common and obvious one is the ability to arouse very quickly. Some female submissives may experience vaginal leaking where they become so aroused, quickly and for longer periods of time that their vaginal juices can soak their underwear or run down their leg.

Heightened arousal appears common to both male and female submissives. Orgasm as a response to arousal, particularly when no direct stimulation is present or in greater frequency for the age of the person becomes more common. Sexual fixation, frequent sexual or kink thoughts and a strong urge to interact with other kinky people is also common. Some submissives seem to be built to absorb higher levels of stimulation both physically and mentally. This may go so far as a hooded clitoris and a thickly-padded labia on a female to high pain thresholds for both sexes.

THE WALL

The Wall: The wall is one way to describe the limit that the mind and body are physically, mentally and emotionally capable of processing. Not all people have robust mental health when they enter kink. Many people have minor to serious mental illnesses or disabilities that affect their mental health. This doesn't preclude them from enjoying kink interactions. However, kink can pose serious challenges for many people.

Toleration of stimulation varies wildly not only between people but within a specific person. What stressors an individual can tolerate when they are at a moment in life that is relatively stress free will be very different from a time when they are under more stress.

Stressors are cumulative. Stimulation, such as through focused interactions and scening, are also a form of stressor. The body, mind and emotional state of the individual are challenged to meet certain goals that are often difficult.

As stressors accumulate and are experienced as a

burden upon the mental state of the individual the responses that the person will give may seem to be stable but internally the person may find it increasingly difficult to maintain the appearance of stability.

Every relationship includes expectations placed upon each person to perform based on the dialogue and agreements each person gives to create the type of relationship that is desirable. These expectations form silent stressors in that they become fixed rather than flexible and if a person fails to measure up to the fixed state they have agreed to share then there are often strong negative consequences in the relationship.

This means that the existence of the relationship is also a stressor and can contain other performance stressors simply to continue to exist. Now you add in external stressors such as jobs, illnesses, family problems, broken cars, financial pressures and you begin to see how each person carries a 'load' simply by being alive and walking around.

When you couple a lowered resistance to stress with a constant daily load of stressors you can end up with scening and relationship issues due to conditions that include physical fatigue, psychological duress or resignation culminating in in-scene fatigue.

During a scene the submissive burns energy at a fairly high rate that is often notable in nutritional requirements of proteins, carbs and electrolytes as well as symptoms of rapid dehydration. They are also using up their reservoir of mental and emotional tolerance. As noted earlier, this reservoir is dependent on many factors both internal and external and it can vary from day to day and from moment to moment.

In general, we like to think of scening at peak health moments where both partners are alert, well rested, nutritionally supported and fully hydrated. Under these conditions a 1-3 hour scene is probably doable. However, it depends on the intensity of the scene as well as the orientation of the submissive to the scene stressors.

Because most people scene within the fetish interests of both partners it is likely that these fetishes will elevate the energetic responses further than normal and that they will venture into areas of past experiences that may be challenging or very difficult for the submissive to process.

If the stressor threshold is running low (such as when a person isn't in their peak shape and when they have many additional external stressors weighing on them) then it is logical to realize that it becomes easier to exceed the threshold of the individual.

You might think that this condition would immediately trigger the activation of a safeword but this just isn't true. Most vanilla people only encounter this type of physical and emotional threshold under extreme conditions and with great rarity over the course of their lives. This means they have minimal experience in recognizing the symptoms of psychological fatigue where they simply cannot cope with the requirements being presented to

> *While having an intense scene may sound like exactly what you want, you can't know your own outer limits and neither can your partner unless you know each other very well, and even then you may exceed the limits of the mind.*

them in a functional way.

It doesn't matter if the person is in a altered mental state, that state doesn't prevent this problem. The altered mental state we have talked about most in this book is part of the body's stressor management system. It has limits.

Kink scening can shift from consensual interaction to orchestrated abuse if the submissives mindset at the time moves from the grasp of the submissive-positive internal personality aspects into a more holistic involvement by the entire being. Some people don't know they are in trouble until they are in trouble. The entirety of their being may try to rally or escape the conditions causing the excessive experience of stressors. If they are unable to physically or mentally withdraw then extreme measures of escape may happen.

An extreme measure can be a mental break. The person may resign themselves to circumstances they cannot change. They may become numb. They may display rapid jerky pointless movements that have no direction or focus. They may become rigid and lose control of their limbs. They may find it impossible to comprehend the situation around them.

All of these potentials exist for every human being regardless of their background, mental health status, physical health, age or intellect. If you are human, your body and brain have these potentials.

From a scene perspective, the longer that a scene takes the more the submissive becomes energy depleted and the more psychological load is created.

It is essential to provide recuperation time and to know and advocate for yourself if you are not in the 'mood' for scening.

While engaging in space can produce some euphoric experiences, it is not a remedy for acute stressors and mental threshold breeches.

As you may have noticed I described how a scene can slip from consensual into nonconsensual in a heart beat. All of your intentions going into the scene are meaningless. Don't try to 'break' the mind or mental health of other human beings.

Develop good strategies to openly communicate your current mental health status in terms of interacting with your partners in safe ways.

If any dominant tells you that they can identify the symptoms of a pending mental break and that you are safe in their care because they will protect you from this potential – leave!

While it is possible to tell when a person is stressed, submissives and masochists in scene are always under and experiencing some level of stress, that is part of kink.

With any signs of mental and emotional distress, seek immediate help from a professional therapist or psychiatrist.

If you scene with a partner with known mental health conditions it means they are more and differently vulnerable to having and experiencing problems during scenes. Many people move in and out of consent during scenes particularly when they are strongly triggered by the contents of the interaction.

Create a safe and open space for frequent and in-depth dialogue about mental health safety and about issues that are happening when you experiment with different triggers.

With an establishment of trust between a dominant and a submissive the submissive will generally begin to lower their mental walls or shields and allow their dominant greater and greater access into their private realms. Trust is coupled to the ability to process information. The stronger the trust, the further the submissive will allow themselves to go.

Achieving space for a new submissive is generally not intentional, it simply happens. There is a desire and a willingness to try, and at some point that first barrier or mental threshold will be crossed and the submissive will find themselves in space. Often this is a frightening and exciting experience. A dominant should not press that first experience of space but allow it to be full of pleasure and positive chemistries. This will encourage the submissive to actively go to that place in their minds during a scene.

To deepen an experience of space, the dominant needs to proceed slowly and cautiously. It is essential to remember that trust is the key, if the dominant says one thing and does another they are providing an unstable surface and the submissive will not trust them as deeply. This will tend to prevent the submissive from releasing their vulnerability further. From a dominant's standpoint the deeper you can take your submissive, the higher they can fly and the more stimulation they can sustain. Again it is important to note that there are sincere limits.

Submissives vary from day to day and moment to moment. On Monday they can space and be at maximum from having nipple clamps while on Tuesday they may need or want zippers, full CBT or waxing to achieve the same euphoric state. It becomes essential for the dominant to become so attuned to their submissive's current state that they know where their submissive is at on any given day. There is no right or wrong here. It is merely the current threshold of the individual.

There is some stress relief involved in scening as the submissive becomes more free to express and release pent up feelings and frustrations. But, doing more doesn't mean you will gain further relief.

Relief or satiation is a threshold well below psychological fatigue, it is a point where the submissive can let go and release. Once release occurs, it is like crossing the finish line of a long race, the submissive cannot run again until they have had recuperation time. Again, there is no right or wrong, simply variations. Learning such intimacies between partners is crucial. Making an error can propel a submissive into a horrendous event or a scene that they later feel to have been in violation of their needs, wants and desires or it can cause a break such as I've described. This leaves the dominant in a somewhat precarious position if they only play with that submissive occasionally. They simply cannot know what is going on.

For deeper or edge play, I sincerely recommend that the people involved spend a great deal of time together learning each other prior to attempting to play along the threshold. This is not an area where you want to make any mistakes in evaluation or judgment.

The deeper a submissive goes into subspace, the worse their communication skills can become *(verbal)*. The dominant should assume that not only can their submissive not evaluate what is dangerous to them, but that the chemicals flowing in their blood stream will essentially mask their body signals which would normally tell them there are problems. When a submissive is in subspace, all the responsibility for that submissive's safety and welfare rest squarely on the dominant.

A submissive deep in space can endure broken bones, severe lacerations and many other forms of severe damage without knowing it. Since this type of damage is not what BDSM is about it becomes very important for a dominant to know not only their submissive's skin, tissue, bone and muscular responses to various implements or toys, but also the full potentials of each implement or toy. Many submissives in deep space will appear or tend to encourage a dominant into extending the play beyond the limits that a toy or implement has been used on them in the past. Essentially the submissive is intoxicated, the sensations increase their feelings of being high and the submissive enjoys that continuation. However, this is also how serious damage occurs. Once the chemistries retreat from the bloodstream and brain the submissive will feel everything. The aftermath can be absolutely horrendous in part because the dominant will not have known the damage they have delivered until sometimes several days after the scene.

When a couple have played together a fairly long time, they tend to relax into an understanding of each other. At this point many submissives will be able to enter subspace quite easily. *(The dominant is sometimes the net or the safety string that returns the submissive to 'normal space'.)* Often both the dominant and submissive will jointly decide to try something new or go somewhat further.

Safety in edge play is tenuous at best. The very best safety is simply the deeper the understanding that can only be achieved by long term, frequent interaction. People that play on the fly or casually, essentially cannot know their casual partner as well. The risks of doing damage increases. To some degree people who desire heavy scening or edge play with basically unknown strangers are suggesting potential mental problems. BDSM is not about a desire to be damaged. A sincere desire to be damaged or injured reflects a mental problem which reflects impaired judgment. This, by definition, challenges the individual's ability to make sound, reasoned, safe, sane and consensual choices.

THE VOICE

Although I've already spoken briefly about how voice impacts a D/s relationship, the topic is worthy of a bit more exploration. Voice, choice of language, command structures and delivery are perhaps the least understood, most illusive and hardest to convey concepts in text form.

Human beings are somewhat hard-wired to attempt to bond with others particularly in conditions where interpersonal relationships are the objective or are essential to the activity. Bonding is a process of attachment. This attachment is not based on love in the classical sense. Preparing to interact activates energy in the body. Elevated energy is associated by the brain with either flight or sex. In modern culture we often exercise and people become somewhat addicted to how they experience the energy and chemicals that are released simply from activating or challenging their body.

At the beginning of a kink interaction the two people usually spend some time talking to each other. Some of this will be normal conversation and some of it will be role establishment types of communication. Both normal and role establishment will elevate the energy of both people and boost up some of the brain chemicals and some hormones. These are all features of courtship and in many ways early kink interactions fall into that category.

As I mentioned earlier, it is common for both people to focus more intently on not only what their potential partner says, but on the physical cues that are also present in the conversation. Many people use a softer tone when they are trying to seem pleasant or sexy to a potential partner. They may make attempts to create humor and they will couple all of this stuff with gestures, physical excretions, body odor, mirroring, touch and other subtle cues like swelling of the lips, changes in skin color etc.

If the two people decide they are interested in continuing then often the way they will use language will also shift. Each person is likely to interpret their potential role and begin to exercise that role in the interaction.

Some of these cues continue to happen in phone conversations and today many people are exploring text only communication or some mixture of text, webcam, phone and more prior to ever meeting in person.

The problem with establishing a relationship without physical cues is that some information is lost that most people use to inform their choices. In a D/s context the preset for the relationship adds additional challenges when each individual layers their need and expectation within the D/s context on top of the stresses and excitements of any new relationship. This means that it is more likely for a person to make a judgment error in a potential kink relationship than in a vanilla relationship.

Early kink infatuation is driven primarily by each individuals personal needs, not by the relative quality of their potential partner. In a sense, each person is infatuated with themselves and their own needs and the potential posed by the other person to be used to meet those needs.

Initial bonding is often followed by frequent contact to reinforce the connection. This is similar in many ways to brainwashing techniques, or even the techniques used by religious or political groups to orient the individual into alignment with the program. It can be considered a form of enthrallment, capture, and non-consensual bondage in the sense that intellect or reasoning is often in a deficit compared to need. Consent requires clear thought.

Bonding and attachment occur to both the dominant and the submissive, though the intensity appears to be stronger on the part of the submissive in many cases. Each person develops mental and emotional shielding that they use to create some distance from others. At the beginning of a relationship, particularly in kink, it is common for the submissive to open their protective shields very early in the relationship process. This is usually done because the person believes it is the 'way' things should work and they want the dominant to take control of them.

This relinquishing of barriers on the part of the submissive is not without risks. When people want something they are often willing to accept any version that seems sort of close to their ideal.

Every person is somewhat subject to 'hearing' and attaching interest when a speaker is charismatic. This is fundamental to evangelism where a good speaker will rise in popularity and control very quickly. This doesn't mean a person with a authoritative manner is worthy of this type of adulation. In fact, the opposite is just as likely to be true. A person attempting to gain control over others may have serious ego issues that they aren't dealing with. When a person *wants* to believe, they are *likely* to believe.

The more invested a person is in kink or the idea of D/s, the more likely that person is to attach quickly and without a lot of critical thinking taking place.

Some people go through life listening for authoritative voices that they can follow. They want to follow. It feels comfortable to have a direction and someone else in charge. They like the sensation of diminished responsibility and the increase in motivation and support that the direction of others provides for them.

This potentially makes this type of person vulnerable to being 'taken' by any aware dominant whom that submissive may 'hear'. In addition, an unattached submissive can and may enter space in public when in the close proximity of an emoting aggressor. But, you will also find a person with these characteristics captured by musical performances and singers. The sound of the voice or music is just as powerful as an aggressive emoter.

People in these conditions listen and wait for command. Many hear deep, personal messages in the musical content. Some allow the music to provide personal guidance. If the dominant person remains unaware of the submissive they will at some point move out of range of the submissive and the submissive will resurface. In the case of music, it is likely the individual will carry the music with them constantly to reattach and comfort them while they are living their lives. Fandom is the meta label for this process. Any reinforcible vocal content can maintain the enthrallment of the individual. Eventually there is some decay of the attachment and the individual is likely to seek out the next attachment person, song or dominant.

The voice is not entirely about words. From the dominant's perspective there is a sense of sending information at the submissive beyond just the words they use. This can be both verbal and mental. There is directed intent. In a kink setting the dominant is acutely aware of the submissive and the delivery of command tends to feel more like packaged groups or clusters of information. Often the dominant will learn to groom their physical voice and discover and use particular inflections of sound which appear to penetrate the resistance of the subject submissive. Feelings, emotions and desires are projected along this same connective frequency, sometimes without the companion word structures.

It is the dominant's desire to intercede with and override what you might consider to be the software programming inside of the submissive's brain. Alignment in some ways appears to open a conduit into the interior programming of the submissive. The dominant may wish to control certain ideology, thought and responses inside the very core of the submissive's command center. In some ways they may appear to attack the independent programming and overwrite that programming with directives or alignments directly to their command and design.

> *Sound is a powerful tool. Do you know how specific sounds and favored music affect your responses?*

This is usually done through the creation and application of rules in the relationship and with constant repetition and the inclusion of rituals. Dominants often desire for the submissive to conform to their personal rules. This indoctrination period is literally the taking of the submissive. The simplest way for the dominant to accomplish this is through frequent repetitious sounds, directives and commands. The simpler the form, the more successful it will be. From the submissive's perspective all applicable decision making processes will include an awareness of and responsibility to the rules and requirements of the dominant prior to execution.

For a submissive to detach from a strong dominant is quite difficult even when both submissive and dominant willfully agree to separate. They must be able to blockade the voice so that they don't automatically respond when they hear commands. This is generally difficult if the submissive remains in physical proximity to the dominant. Severance of contact, physical or phone, may be necessary for a considerable timeframe for the programming to dissipate and the shielding or buffers of the submissive to be reinstated.

An individual will continue to be susceptible to a

former partner as those access corridors may continue to exist for many years. However, when the submissive attaches to a new dominant it becomes easier to shield from old temptations.

The submissive will continue to be aware of or recognize other dominants by their emoting presence, but will in most cases not be vulnerable to being affected by them.

However, it is possible for a submissive who is bonded and attached to be taken by a dominant who is stronger (or in some way more attractive) than their dominant. It is considered extremely bad form for a dominant to trespass upon another dominant's submissive. It's called poaching. It happens more often when poacher is somehow celebritized. In general, in social settings and online, a dominant will actively 'not emote or project energy' at or toward any submissive not their own.

How well you listen or hear depends in part on your personal history. If you have had the need to listen for risk around people in authority in your life, such as with alcoholic or abusive parents, then you are more likely to have developed and practiced hearing techniques.

The same goes for projecting your voice or energy. A predisposition to project instead of receive signals can be triggered initially by a life event. Often this behavior emerges from a person strongly desiring a particular outcome in a situation. In the situation they accidentally combine their speech with their need and boost it with the energy of their need and they experience a positive result.

This positive reinforcement encourages them to

practice this behavior on others. Practice is a requirement of mastery. Not all people who role play dominance can project energy and many don't have a good control over their voice. This doesn't mean they are good or bad at being dominant with a submissive, it simply means they don't have these specific tools to use. As I noted earlier, many people predispose themselves to enter into a relationship merely from the amount of need they feel to seek out and engage in kink interactions. You don't need a skill set or even any real experience to be granted this type of eager participation.

A more intuitive dominant can also hear the submissive. Some feel or co-experience a scene from both sides. Many don't have this experience. Some dominants will find that they hear most submissives, particularly after they have worked with a number of submissives over many years. Again, practice changes things. This can create problems when the dominant 'knows' that a submissive *(not their own)* is in trouble in say a public scene. In the vanilla world this dominant may find themselves caught in situations where their senses indicate or trigger the protective aspects of their inner self into action, sometimes on behalf of total strangers. This is considered bad form. In a public venue, if you believe a submissive or masochist or bottom is in trouble, contact the DM (dungeon master) and ask them if there is a problem. They can check it out and evaluate the circumstances for themselves.

The Alpha Dominant

I'm sure you've heard a lot about alpha dominants, or alpha males. This has become a popular label or designation eagerly sought by many people who believe that they are superior and that their superiority should be recognized by everyone around them.

The alpha animal is an animal within a social group who demonstrates some characteristic that gives them social status. In many animal groups the alpha male fights other males, sometimes to the death, in order to acquire the position of top dog. In other animal groups the alpha male is selected by the alpha females from among the group of males. In such groups status moves through the female lines not the male lines. A male can also acquire status through the status of his mother.

An alpha frequently gains privilege and preferential treatment including: access to better foods, access to mates and other 'goodies'. In modern American culture the primary privilege metric is financial success. A person can gain status from inherited money, received money, accidental acquisition of money or through the ability to wield the money of persons of greater wealth. Other metrics for improved status include: physical appearance, mastery of specific skills, crafts or abilities that are valued or celebritized by others. The other metric for status is through belonging to the right social group or through alliances with persons who wield social or financial power.

You can see from this list that the quality of the individual in terms of character, ethics and substance are generally not part of any of these metrics. The decline in valuing qualities of character can be seen in the rampant and wholesale savaging of the planet in favor of monetary profit. It isn't as if the super-wealthy are at risk of not having enough money to purchase any thing or person they desire, from their perspective it appears that there is never enough money or perhaps there is a sadistic delight in destroying in order to support the ego.

However, most people in kink are not super-wealthy regardless of what you might read in erotica novels or see on film. Still, most people within the culture 'believe' that this money-grabbing behavior is correct and right because they follow the same process and behaviors in their personal spheres of influence. I note this here because you are going to either believe you are an alpha or you are going to meet one or more dominants who claim to be alphas.

To evaluate such a claim you need to identify their community of reference. Whom gives them preferential treatment and based on what criteria? Who is your specific individual competing against and in what way are they demonstrably superior to others? Who exactly are the others and do the others know of or specifically offer privilege to the person claiming alpha status?

Generally, most people will claim alpha characteristics based on how they feel about themselves. This self-analysis usually doesn't emerge from any visible real life circumstances that have anything to do with social relationships or intimate personal relationships. Often the peak experiences of a person's life are related to some distant event that has long since passed into obscurity or was only of note to people who are no longer germane to the 'alpha' persons life. Perhaps they won a high school trophy, or got a substantial raise at work or they were in some event that made it onto the nightly news or maybe they won a lottery.

What does any of this mean in terms of dominance? Nothing. The idea of the money metric as a measure for qualities of character simply doesn't work. And, if the act of caring for the life and wellbeing of another person for any duration of time do not require qualities of character then what does?

This means that you need to go outside the current human (American) metric values to determine the qualities of character that will be beneficial for you in terms of kink.

Unfortunately I cannot tell you that a person with good social status inside kink social networking is any better a guide than the money metric. In fact, the social organizations derived from the mainstream culture will mirror the features and values so prevalent in the mainstream culture. So, having good kink social status merely means that the individual has chosen to create status within kink through this mechanism. Kink social status is a type of internal celebrity that brings with it a certain amount of power and all instances of power can be wielded for good or ill. A person in relative power also has to protect their power base and this makes them less able to go against the values of the peer group that supports their apparent status. This disables their ability to challenge the same 'errors' that are prevalent in the mainstream culture. In addition, persons reverenced in kink are given more leeway to transgress within kink. What happens is that people of lower status in the same social network are invested in supporting the network to support their own status and some of their own status is derived from association with or 'knowing' people that others venerate.

This means that the very people you think you should be trusting because they have big names and travel the country doing workshops and interacting with other big names are often hypocrites. This is the same process you might see with a religious minister who is 'given' power by those who celebritize them, and this is the same minister who violates the very rules or ideas that is being demanded of others.

Are any of these people really alphas?

An alpha is any person 'given' that status by others for some perceived merit in any sphere where the merit has value.

You will find a lot of people with great skills, plenty of money, great looks and a life that looks fabulous from the outside. Should you value these metrics in your explorations for a partner? It doesn't matter what I say because you will invest in these metrics to some degree because you are a product of this culture.

But, what really matters is not what a person says about themselves or what their friends and social network say about them. The only thing that matters is how you feel and what you experience when you are in a close interaction with that person. If they make you feel cruddy then it is obvious they aren't very alpha when it comes to relationships. If they think alpha means they are a tough guy who wears black leather and doesn't take shit off of anyone, well, that is the exact description of an ego-centered person who is too rigid to admit their weaknesses and you can't work on stuff if you refuse to admit you have stuff that needs work. Alpha isn't belligerence or toughness or intelligence or driving a nice car.

Alpha is a person completely committed to improving themselves and their world in each and every moment. No one ever *'achieves'* alpha status, they are always chasing it and encouraging the same improvements in others.

Edge Play

For the purposes of this section I will assume that your submissive is new to kink and that you have participated in discussions and negotiations that have included base limits that you are using as boundaries in all interactions.

Edge play is any interaction that explores the body, mind, emotional or psychological state in areas that are identified in advance as being challenging, risky or dangerous.

There is edge play that is physically difficult or dangerous and it is easy to identify that this type of play is near or over the edge of where the dominant or the submissive have ventured before. But mental, emotional and psychological edge play is a lot more tricky. The areas of strongest attraction in terms of fetishes or fantasies are likely to also represent the exact areas where the individual has had prior nonconsensual experiences. This means that there is 'stuff' inside every fetish and fantasy and this stuff is a can of worms.

When you engage in edgy play you are putting these states of mind on the table. While a person may feel a deep and passionate *need* for specific types of experiences, this doesn't mean they are magically able to participate in such experiences without having problems.

This is why edge play is edge play. It is unpredictable. In a best case scenario the scene will result in a cathartic experience where the submissive can process out some of the 'stuff' with some degree of safety provided by a careful top or dominant.

In a worst case scenario the scene won't result in a cathartic experience and the submissive may experience new damage including emotional and psychological problems.

It is important to realize that a dominant, top or sadist is likely to go to their limit rather than to the submissive's limit and call what they are doing edge play or pushing limits. Is it edge play? Yes. Is it disingenuous? Yes.

A submissive produces distinct types of energy during a scene. You might consider these types as *flavors*. Often the objective of the dominant is not any particular goal such as an amount of time on some apparatus or device, the real objective is the *emotive state* of the submissive. The dominant wants that *flavor*. Many dominants will push their partner until they receive that flavor from the submissive. Often that flavor comes out of dark places. Think of it a little like crossing the line from wanting to elicit pleasure when you really want to elicit the pain, fear, anxiety and pleas just beyond that threshold – that 'real' stuff beyond where the submissive finds it *easy*.

Many submissives want to toy with this edge too. Deep in their mind they may carry around a belief that they have unpunished sins that no one ever caught and that they want to feel purged from inside of them. People have all kinds of self talk informing their choices. I'm mentioning just one here so that you get the idea of how edge play sets up for both partners. Some submissives want to 'give' this experience to their dominants and this suggests they know it's there long before they ever get into kink.

It's important to remember here that both people have things they want to 'get' from the experience and that these 'things' are likely to be different.

When a submissive first meets a potential partner they are likely to discuss areas they share in common. What a submissive cannot know is how that area actually sets up for the other person. Each person has a different script for a scene. Some submissives will go so far as to write out a story about their fantasy so that every element is known. This still doesn't mean that what they experience will follow that storyline.

Recently I listened to a discussion where a female submissive was questioning her physical encounters with one particular dominant. They met 6 or 7 times over a period of two months. This followed a month or two of online and phone contact and a neutral meet-and-greet. This means she followed all of the normal advice about meeting someone. She also knew a little about the man's reputation locally. Several people knew him and although she didn't question these people directly about his conduct, they seemed socially friendly to each other.

On their first meeting after the meet-and-greet they were in a semi-public kink-friendly establishment that had horseshoe shaped booths and some availability of food and alcohol.

After making themselves comfortable in a booth a waitress approached and the man ordered alcohol for himself and for her as well as finger foods. She declined the alcohol. He placed a knife at her throat and proceeded to run his hand up her skirt (she wasn't wearing panties based on his request).

This 'scene' partially fit the fantasy scenario she thought she was getting into, except for the knife and the alcohol. She became troubled and confused because her fantasy now felt like a non-consensual violation yet it wasn't straying too far from what she had imagined in the safety of her home.

He drank some, continued his behavior and she didn't say "No." because she felt like she had 'agreed' to the basic scenario and he was simply embellishing it with features she didn't like. This general scenario happened upon each of their subsequent meetings where what she imagined wasn't what she felt was happening during the encounters. She felt something was wrong but she didn't trust her version of reality in the unknown spectrum of kink enough to validate her reality. After each 'meeting' or scene she confronted him with her issues and his behavior and he talked it off as completely normal and exactly what she wanted, after all she was wet the whole time. She couldn't argue that the interactions excited her physically and was that the measure of her pleasure or compliance?

After the last interaction she had enough and she refused to meet with him again. By then she had met other submissives in the local group and one had become a friend. In the aftermath she eventually confided in her new friend about how confused she was by the experiences and how she felt violated and a lot like she had been raped in some instances.

At that point the other submissive told her that there were other rumors about similar problems. The submissive who had experienced these interactions and who had been 'around' other kink people when some of the knife play was happening questioned why no one had told her about the rumors or problems.

As you can see this is a complicated situation. It is obvious there are several possible valid viewpoints to use in considering how this situation played out. There are many layers to social networks, to self advocacy and to validating reality through an unreliable partner.

I've described this scenario here so that it becomes more clear how a shared fetish interest can be quite different based on how each person expects it to feel like as it plays out. While the apparent scening incorporated the shared 'range' of both partners it's obvious that the needs of the edge play dominant trumped the needs of the submissive. The dominant in this instance was interested in what they wanted for themselves and it was obvious that what they wanted was to get past the fantasy of the submissive into 'edgy' territory where consent was questionable. Further there was active manipulation in validating her reality which is a form of psychological abuse that wasn't negotiated. And, the social network of this fairly well known person didn't inform her that his reputation included rumors of non-consensual violations by other newbie submissives.

This should illustrate the complications of edge play and the continual differences between the wants and needs of each person in any kink interaction.

The best case scenario for positive kink interactions centers on getting to know your partners over some time and trusting your gut when it tells you that things are wrong. The illusion of authority projected by a dominant is not real and it shouldn't act to silence the submissive.

The Threshold of Flight

There is a moment when the individual moves from normal space to altered space. This shift occurs in all realms of the human being. As the person moves along this altered space corridor, they will at some point cross over a threshold. This is the point that I call *flight* because on the inside there is a sensation of physical, spiritual and emotional freedom. Everything feels lighter and the sense of touch is distorted enough that it is easy to lose grasp of down and gravity. Sometimes your limbs can feel weightless and you can feel certain that with one tiny umph of energy you would surely rise up off the floor and drift in air, weightless.

Manifestations of flight vary from individual to individual, but many aspects appear to be uniform. There is a moment when the intellect portion of the mind withdraws in favor of the experiential and sensory channels. With some people this will appear to the movement from considering something in a negative or resistive way, to considering that exact same thing in an excited, aroused or positive way. The resistance is in part the social or conscious part of the brain constantly informing the individual as to what is acceptable, appropriate and sometimes even allowable as an action or thought within society. By breaching the range of this conscious voice the mind is freed to consider the action, idea or thing from other angles or perspectives. This freedom sets aside the societal consequences for possession of these non-conforming thoughts and through that release allows the individual to explore this forbidden area.

Many people are unable to explore this area alone and it is only through the interaction and external actions of their partner that they can relinquish responsibility as the awareness of consequences for entry into forbidden space. The submissive, in this instance, will deliver the responsibility for their actions and feelings onto their dominant. This removal of societal viewpoint allows the submissive to experience the event with fewer inhibitions. Some people struggle or have trouble letting go and to some extent the dominant consensually 'forces' them to get out of their head and out of their thoughts about everything. This shuts down some of the brain chatter.

Space itself is progressive and moves through identifiable stages until it reaches a depth where flight becomes possible. This depth is where the brain detaches completely from reality structures and allows itself to process information without using its standard criteria as a guide.

This process is accelerated by the application of sensory stimulation. With the removal of normal thought patterns the brain shifts its focus to absorbing the data streaming into it from a single source, the dominant. The dominant, through the application of mental and physical challenges, forces the brain into a more involved or focused state. In a sense the dominant is tricking the brain into believing that a new set of problems is occurring, requiring coping techniques that standard or normal processing will not properly address.

As the dominant slowly increases this process, the submissive will pour more and more focused energy into solving the faux-problem.

Pain and pleasure share the same nerve endings in the human body. The interpretation of whether a sensation is painful or pleasurable is a decision that the brain makes when judging the incoming information. By alternating pain and pleasure along both the nerve endings and the thought processes, the mind becomes filled up with making constant evaluations of this incoming data stream. The mind must decide whether to respond to the conflicting information as positive or negative.

To complicate this process further, every time that the brain decides pain it responds by releasing a complex combination of chemicals into the blood stream of the individual to help that person cope with the ensuing pain. These chemicals include adrenaline and endorphins which are potent drugs to deflect or dull the sensations and allow the body to survive the situation. By alternating the sensations, the dominant begins to drive the release of these chemistries and of the brain's decision making apparatus.

There is a point where the mind and body reach a threshold. This is an overload of information and sensation. The brain recognizes that it is unable to process the conflicting information successfully and further decides to process all further information as positive and pleasurable until it can catch up a bit or discover a solution for the situation. At that point the submissive begins to fly.

The body continues to pump chemicals into the blood stream while the brain finds itself free of all normal constraints to work on just this one problem. This combination opens doors within the mind that are profound, mystical, explosive, euphoric and transcendent. The freed mind explores a universe that is unavailable to them in their normal space. Thought becomes clear while problems, issues and troubles diminish or vanish altogether as minor considerations.

Processing information through this space tends to cleanse the information or how the mind may view that information. The experience is humbling and ecstatic at the same time.

Blended Space

There has been considerable focus placed on subspace within kink because for a long time many people believed the dominant was not experiencing the same types of issues because he wasn't *receiving* obvious physical stimulation.

But, of course the dominant is receiving obvious physical stimulation from their partner. There is an idea that touch is required for stimulation to be *real* even when people know perfectly well that all kinds of non-touch stimulation effects them.

There is a logical disconnect around anything acting *on* a dominant and their behavior. While I'm positioning the dominant in some of this text as male this is simply because some of the content is hetero-focused. Gender is not germane to how the body responds. Men and women have very similar physiology and while there are cultural and some small gender differences, none of these rise to the level of any significance in terms of what I'm talking about. Space doesn't differentiate by gender or sexual orientation or your beliefs, values, ideas about god or what you had for breakfast on Sunday.

No dominant is spanking anyone's butt unless they are *receiving* stimulation from the action. The physical act of spanking is exactly like exercise. You have to use your muscles and target specific spots and swing over and over and trust me, muscles tire, the back gets sore, you sweat like a pig and this is just the beginning of what you are receiving. So, you are exercising. Well, not exactly. This is like saying sex is exercise. It includes muscles and movement but if sex is like exercise you are really doing it wrong.

Dominants and submissives have split viewpoints. Often they will find both sides of the imagery of a scene exciting. A submissive may get excited by what they imagine their dominant will think, say, feel and especially see as a scene begins. The awareness of their partner is complete and a big part of the turn on. This is a joint venture only it's deeper than imagination.

One of the intriguing aspects of kink is the desire to co-experience. Many people take photos of their scenes or even home movies and long after a scene is finished both people will watch or look at the images, revisiting not only their own experiences but exploring the cues on the face and body of their partner. They are being voyeurs physically to aspects of the scene that were not visible to them at the time of the actual scene. In fact, often they like looking at their partner in the images more than looking at themselves. The dominant tends to do exactly the same thing.

It is common for each person to feel like part of their experience is held captive inside the other person. During a scene many people are so tightly focused on each other that they experience sharing. It may sound odd to think that a dominant can co-experience the sensations of the submissive indirectly, but, it is this movement and sharing that is so powerfully attractive to both people. This is a type of intimacy that many people don't experience except during sex.

See, what you are exchanging, while connected to sex and sexual potentials, isn't really about sex. What you exchange is more fundamental, more primal and often more rich than the quick squirt of bodily fluids. It isn't love, or admiration, or adulation or even excitement, it's like a shared vision quest with some physical, some emotional and a whole lot of spiritual elements all swirling around together and between both people. It is raw potential and the stuff of magic or dreams, all that indefinable stuff that is so drummed out of everyday life.

As the scene progresses this blending deepens causing the scene to intensify. Some people will report that they experience a movement between both viewpoints in a circular fashion, as if they are in both bodies at the same time. The energy streams move faster and faster as the essence of each person flies into the other. This becomes an experience of duality.

When a couple has been together for several years, it is common for them to state unequivocally that they hear each other mentally. *(This is called being clairsentient.)* They express that this hearing is not necessarily in verbal words, but often in packages of information or feeling *(this is described somewhat in the section titled the voice)*. It appears that shared or blended space opens up new areas of communication in nonverbal or mental ranges. These abilities are not limited to just your partner but appear when developed to work with any person who is in a space condition or within close proximity. It is fairly common within kink to find people who have developed empathic techniques or abilities.

It does appear that some people have a natural aptitude or ability to develop this skill beyond what would be considered normal even in kink. However, it is fairly clear that the majority of kinky people develop or already possess this ability when they first encounter kink and with practice their abilities expand and grow stronger.

Lost In Space

Most submissives who experience subspace will also get lost in space. This is when reality becomes slippery. This is actually quite common for submissives and may occur virtually every time they enter space. The submissive solves this problem by a sort of tethered attachment to the feedback of the other person. They rely on their partner to walk them through the features of the shared reality. This may be as simple as guiding them into undoing a buckle or moving in a specific direction or noticing something. All this means is that they are not tracking the overall scene. They may be aware of a pinched bit of skin and be completely unaware of a dripping candle.

This state of mind goes further than tracking items in physical space, they will also have difficulty tracking non-material items such as information they should know. When asked questions they may not be able to recall their location at that moment or whether there is a bathroom in the building. Logic fails.

Some people in altered states also gravitate towards spiritual experiences. They may see, feel, and interact with dead people. They may speak in tongues. They may engage in religious commentary that may seem to have nothing to do with the scene itself. All of these are possible and indicate how far out the submissive may be. You can think of this type of manifestation similarly to being high on drugs. Some people hallucinate or expose psychotic behaviors.

No matter what comes up or out of the submissive, they are relying on the dominant to guide them down for a safe landing. Often it is a good idea to speak with them in calming tones and to remove stimulation so that there is less for their brain to process.

Once they are completely free of stimulation you should keep them warm and comfortable in as relaxed a position as possible until they connect with you in ways that make sense.

There are times when a submissive will detach from the dominant. They may occur if the dominant has flattened mental stream, if their focus or attention is not upon their submissive or if they have a weak dominant presence. This is rather more common in new dominants and submissives especially if they are unfamiliar with the existence of subspace or have never before encountered it.

A dominant may also push off a submissive attachment if they are not cognizant of what that attachment is or if they just don't want to be intimate.

Some new dominants are uncertain how to maintain a continuous strong presence and if they are also new to the toys and tools they are using they may shift focus toward the techniques instead of maintaining attention on the submissive. This would be something like what you may have experienced when learning how to drive a car. At first the details of what you are supposed to be doing totally overshadow the focus on driving itself. If you are thinking about when you are supposed to shift you may not be thinking about what that car in the other lane may be getting ready to do or even where you are going.

With practice these details diminish until at some point you are no longer consciously aware of them at all. You learn to drive and 'driving' becomes one single thought rather than dozens of individual thoughts. It becomes a habit.

Submissive Frenzies

Submissive frenzies are a state or condition that many if not all submissive will experience at one time or another. Many aspects of BDSM produce the same characteristics of other chemical related addictions. From this perspective the frenzies can be considered to be the withdrawal stage of the kink addiction cycle.

The peculiar thing about this state is that a submissive (or kink newcomer) need never have engaged in real life BDSM to actually experience this state of need. Although I've called this condition *submissive frenzies*, this doesn't mean it only happens to someone if they self-identify as submissive. Frequently a submissive will begin to experience symptoms of frenzy shortly after they encounter a kink environment such as an Internet website, group, forum or other similar venue.

It is common for most people who eventually explore kink to have some history of fantasies that included kink elements long before they officially discovered kink. The fantasies and desire to experience specific types of sensations is usually kept as a secret from friends, family and romantic partners in fear of receiving censure or a negative response. It is also kept as a secret because it is like having a special gift that you don't have to share and it never seems to get old when your imagination plays with this gift. In some instances the submissive can't clearly identify the source of their interests or even the time when they first experienced their first fantasy. Many have a vague idea about circumstances that might relate to the interest. As much as they enjoy the fantasy it is often coupled to feelings of guilt, shame and anxiety. If they have been raised with religious sexual constraints they are likely to view their fantasies as some kind of sinful weakness. But, the images, thoughts or desires don't go away. Often they have worked out tricky ways to implement aspects of their fantasies while alone. Generally these self application measures never feel complete but they seem to reduce some of the agitated energy.

Frequently people notice that their fantasies or desires are not constant but rise and fall like waves inside their body and mind. Usually the individual is unable to note events in their life that seem to trigger a rising up of their sensations of need. Seldom do people try to match up interactions in their life with the close onset of these feelings and driving impulses.

Eventually most people notice that the intensity of their interests and feelings is increasing. Eventually the sensations are so strong that the person toggles on some S/m porn or website and discovers that other people share similar perverse interests.

That moment alone can thrust a person into a frenzied state. What was once a lone exploration of a personal fantasy now becomes a possibility to play out their needs in a more real way with another person, someone they can feel safe sharing some of their secrets with. This trigger they recognize.

With the discovery that kink is real and not merely

stuff made up for books and television, many people feel a corresponding surge of excitement. They can immediately recognize the potentials that kink might offer for them to realize their deepest personal secrets. The realization or identification of this can be both positive and negative.

For many there is a period of denial, anger, repugnance, fear, hesitation, temerity and hope. All of these emotions seem to occur simultaneously, leaving behind wave after wave of confusion and anxiety. Some try to limit their visits to online sites as an effort to demonstrate to themselves that they have control over this 'thing' that is happening to them.

When they find it difficult to resist the sites they can feel new worries. What's wrong with them? They often feel they can't risk getting involved in the perversions that kink represents. Many people have deep involvements in church, community, religious families, friends, and work environments that they logically understand would view such interests as repugnant. The risks are too high.

Sometimes they will view their own attractions towards their secrets and kink as repellant and they will punish themselves physically, mentally and even speak out against such perversions in an effort to purge their own 'unclean' state by becoming an advocate against such things. This makes their secret even more profane because it doesn't go away, it isn't fixed by their efforts of denial and refusal. They aren't magically cured of their desires. If anything, all of their efforts to resist seem to intensify their needs. They sometimes hate the power their hidden needs now have over their mind, thoughts and feelings.

At some point they experience a type of break. This is a moment where their resistance reaches a point of fatigue and they give up on trying to maintain the lie of all of their efforts. Once again they find themselves online at some website or forum, creating another new fake name, desperate to find some way to release all of the build up they feel over their internal struggles.

Their first need is to feel accepted by others who know at least part of their secret life. After all, the perversions of their thoughts and fantasies are obviously, at this point, a part of who they are as a person and everyone in the media and beyond urge each person to acknowledge their personal truth.

This first step of self-acceptance may not include actually talking to anyone or trying to meet anyone. It can simply be showing up and watching other people talk and in their talk seeing and hearing echoes from inside yourself that parallel their state. Now you know you aren't alone and at least it's a shared *fallen state*. It doesn't mean you aren't possessed by demons (one of the beliefs that equates sexual sins with demon possession), but it does mean that lots of other people are experiencing the same sorts of things.

As they read or listen or watch they will hear other people discussing these issues in ways that don't line up with whatever story the individual has heard about sexual exploration. Two things often happen at this point. There is a desire to accept the self and the knowledge that these perversions don't necessarily equate to moral bankruptcy. And, the accompanying realization that it's possible you might not know yourself as well as you thought. These realizations push the individual towards sorting the events and motivations that have occurred over their entire lives, seeing the patterns, the hints, the presence of their desires in so many different ways.

Many people have no intention of actually doing anything kinky with other people. They have an express promise with themselves to restrain their interests to reading and chatting online. They are seeking a way to *fix* the problem that their errant fantasies and needs have now become. Self analysis coupled to online reading and listening begins to offer clues to their previously unexplainable actions and feelings and many begin to consider the world from a changing viewpoint that incorporates this growing self knowledge. As this process unfolds they become fully aware that addressing their suppressed needs and desires is possible.

This presents a new conflict. Feeding their fantasy with information isn't quelling their needs, it is growing their inner hunger. Some pull back and force themselves away from the Internet sites and what they view as a diabolical temptation that will certainly ruin their life. Others struggle with the terrors of what will happen if they actually meet with someone. Could they have just one experience and would that end their fantasy?

Others leap for the ring. At some point the risks are outweighed by the intensified needs. What this *means* is set aside for after, later, in the distant future of days or hours when the need isn't so loud.

What occurs next is a mad dash or race toward finding that special person who can attend to those so long unattended needs, coupled to a desperate desire to gather more and more information. This plunges the person into a frenzy. They give themselves *permission* to set aside their fears, judgments and confusing beliefs and simply reach for the tantalizing promise that kink seems to dangle before them.

There is an increasing and progressive growth of need. This need is often felt inside the body like a groin ache coupled to a heady mixture of emotional, psychological and mental deprivation. You can imagine what it might feel like to be deprived of water for a couple days while it is hot outside. At some point your entire mind and body are utterly captivated by the single thought.

The awareness of deprivation and denial are usually restrained behind deep internal walls of habit, fear of loss of family, fear of loss of reputation and community status and other similar fears. The depth of these sensations are frequently masked by food addiction, alcohol, drugs, and other addictive behaviors such as excessive exercise, gambling, texting, collecting items, shopping or any number of the hundreds of similar behaviors. These tools no longer work and once the individual discovers they can't rely on such tools to mask their feelings the effects of these tools drops off suddenly leaving the deprivation and denial fully exposed in one complete bundle.

The magnitude of the repressed needs far exceeds anything the individual had any reason to expect. In their mind their fantasies were small little things hidden off in some dusty corner to be played with when no one else was looking. Now they discover that their repression masked a huge part of their feelings. It's too late to call these feelings back into hiding.

Fairly quickly the desire to get their fix becomes supremely important. Some people become irrational, willing to make poor decisions. They become rash, impulsive and generally stupid regarding risks and protections. The need is freed and it races around inside their bodies like a *mad* thing. A submissive in a frenzied state is at their most vulnerable to succumbing to the ploys of those less than admirable. They may become easily enthralled, believe themselves in love, willing to give over anything *(sometimes literally)* in order to fill the newly realized enormous void swallowing their senses.

Contact with a dominant of almost any kind will rivet their attention. The very thing the submissive gives away here is their common sense. They invest everything, believe everything and leap at the first opportunity that comes along. They gush at the perfection of the stranger they meet, investing in that stranger all of the unearned adulation of their imaginary fantasy ideal. Too often they discover they have grabbed at a tin ring instead of a brass one. But this doesn't happen until after a wild jump into some interaction, when the experience isn't so great but bits and pieces offered new hints and teases that more was possible, but maybe not with this first sort of inadequate excuse for a dominant. They get a taste coupled with a virtual slap in the face. The kinky fruit dangles, still tempting, but now they are just clear enough to pay slightly more attention to the hand offering the fruit.

What happens is that the first experience or first several experiences reduce the initial degree of need to a point where some common sense peeks up over the edge and thinks, for a moment, that while you like the *action* there is something wrong with the other person.

Some people flee kink five minutes after their first

scening interaction. It's like when you have sex with someone who really isn't your type. Once the orgasm has squirted or oozed its inevitable path out of your body, then you look over and notice that big, hairy mole on the side of the other person's nose. Meh! You have orgasmic regret and you hurry into your clothing with an excuse and out the door.

This is the same satiation coupled to regret that is common in kink. People run off, they feel better, the need is depleted and obviously it was a one time thing and now they can go back to their normal life and it's done. They almost can't imagine how they were so foolish in the first place. The frenzy is a distant foggy memory they would rather forget. It was scary. Now it's done.

Here we go, back into our safe world of sexual deprivation and denial. What do you think happens next? How long it takes for the need to build back up depends on two factors. Each person has a different history. Need is partially associated with negative personal events. If a person has a tragic background then it is likely that they have a lot of stuff to process. This stuff is the fuel of need. The second factor is how much stress does the person experience in their daily life. There are normal stresses such as dealing with traffic during a commute. Then there are stresses on the psyche where the individual is *performing* to the expectations of others and where this performance is at odds with aspects of the individuals actual personality. This performance stress is like a tug-of-war within the self. Where rush hour traffic abates after a short duration of time, internal conflicts do not abate but are a constant stress that require consistent energy. As energy goes down, wounded fuel rises and is drawn into the body to support the internal conflict except that this wounded fuel is tainted with need. This means it will be drawn towards the need side of the internal conflict while the daily energy reserves are on the other side, supporting the expected performance behavior.

Over time the need side will increase as the performing side decreases. Often the person will overeat, drink alcohol or otherwise use their familiar addictions to combat the rising need. In the midst of this they will have memories of the positive bits and pieces of their last kink interactions. The dangling fruit frenzy of increasing need starts again.

> *Buyer's regret, kink version, is common to many early interactions. What do you do if your scening partner has suddenly vanished? What do you do if you are the one who checks out?*

Kink interactions often include the most potent chemicals in the body coupled with excited energy states. These features are addictive. The state of natural euphoria that a submissive may experience during a scene can set off a hunger to experience that again. This addictive package is coupled with the individuals sexual fantasies and augmented by the sexual hormones and hormonal cycles experienced by both men and women.

A submissive in a pre-frenzy need state will often become very alluring, flattering, flexible. They will mirror the apparent needs of a prospective dominant they are talking to in order to appear to be the perfect candidate for a future alliance. The are predators on the hunt. Many people viewing D/s from the outside like to imagine that the dominant is the hunter and the submissive is the prey. In fact, both are hunting each other. Both are primarily concerned with meeting their own personal needs but they try to convince the other person that they are interested in meeting the other person's needs. Otherwise, they would be rude, right? Though the submissives, in general, do not tend to lie here, many only present partial truths. One said to me, "you have to ask me the right question." This is a lie by omission statement.

A person's judgment depends on where they are in their personal need cycle. If they wait till the last desperate moment to seek out a potential partner, then it is highly likely they will end up with a less than stellar partner and experience. They will shop on impulse and make rash decisions.

Frenzy is ongoing in a person's life. It may appear to go away when a person is in a stable relationship that addresses some of their needs. But, it isn't gone unless the person does the work to reduce some of the factors feeding the need. In most cases a person will be with one or two partners that meet the bulk of their needs.

Frequently a person will start to complain about not receiving the level of kink they signed up for early in the relationship. It is very common for both persons to have selected their partner when they were both at peak moments of personal need. But, because each person has a different rates of recovery one may often be ready for interaction on a very different time frame from the other.

In early explorations of kink it is common to invest

deeply in the *myth* of the D/s relationship that sets up a lot like the knight in shining armor – there is only one perfect dominant idea. In the fantasy the libidinal drives match perfectly and everyone is horny at exactly the same time and each knows exactly what the other needs without any words being spoken, etc.

The reality is often quite a bit different from this myth. If two people have different libidinal needs you end up with dissatisfaction and interpersonal conflict. This doesn't sound romantic because it isn't romantic. Some partners choose to add access to additional play partners to 'cover' the gap for the more active partner. Other partners break up and move on looking for a better match.

When you are early to kink the idea that one submissive may scene with several dominants in an ongoing basis can seem rather shocking. This isn't the fantasy. Many people resist this idea and they create a lot of 'firm' rules about not wanting anything to do with this type of arrangement. Typically they develop these rules with minimal knowledge of their own libido around kink. This is an intellectual decision not based in what their body is doing. This is a disconnect that can cause a person a lot of hardship when what they impose on their relationships turns out to be deal breakers in the long run.

Unlearning conventional concepts on dyad relationship models is quite difficult. Our culture doesn't include conversations about compersion (the opposite of jealousy) and about honoring your actual needs versus making choices based on what you think you *should* do, say or think.

A more experienced, yet unattached person, or a person in a long-distance relationship, will recognize that they have a need to have their edges taken off, and they know exactly how that can be done through their own experience. The difference is that the older submissive can then evaluate what part of their need is pressing upon them. Many then learn to go to a dominant they are not bonded to and ask this person they trust *(often as a good friend)* to relieve their physical need *(play)*. Many dominants *(experienced ones)* will be open to assisting or aiding their friend, knowing that keeping the submissive's edges down will allow that submissive to retain the majority of their rational functions while they are seeking their next mate or until they can meet with their person of preference. This action reduces the submissive's vulnerability to experiencing frenzy.

From a dominant's standpoint it is preferable to discourse with a submissive who is in their best condition. It is very important for the dominant to learn to recognize the symptoms of frenzy and allow for the premise that the submissive's judgment may be impaired when speaking with them, This allowance should propel detailed questions. Also the dominant should give few hints as to what they may be looking for. The submissive is more likely to reveal themselves as they do not have a guide to go on. By this I mean that the dominant should take control and ask what the submissive is looking for instead of offering or directing the submissive's attention as to what the dominant is seeking.

In this way the dominant can generally get a clearer picture of where that submissive is in their need process. It's also important for a dominant to prevent a potential submissive from thrusting their submissiveness at them. What I mean is that some submissives wield their readiness and submissive presentation intentionally to trigger the dominant and increase the dominant's interest. You have to remember here that both people are experiencing some degree of frenzy or fluctuating needs. Either person can attempt to manipulate the other in order to push the situation towards the conclusion they desire. Back off.

Instead of going into role play immediately, tell the other person to respond in neutral role. Some people will chastise a person for this request. Move on. A submissive can be told they aren't a *real* submissive for making such a request. A dominant can be told they are weak or a fake and that they don't know how to handle a strong submissive.

This kind of petulant rhetoric clearly shows the degree to which the individual is impaired and under pressure from the state of their own needs. Request that no honorific titles be used by either person and that no 'role' activity and interaction will occur until both persons have an opportunity to get to know each other.

If either person is on edge from need, have a friend work with you to reduce the need safely. Meet a few local people and become friends. The idea that you can only scene with someone you are in a deep and passionate relationship with is just not accurate. Take the time to select your more important partners slowly and with care.

You want to be in a competent, comfortable head space at any time you are making important decisions. This is equally true for negotiating limits.

Dominant Drop

There is a persistent myth that the dominant, top, or sadist (by any name) doesn't enter space in the same way that a submissive or masochist does during scening.

This is true. But, it isn't completely true. Applied stimulation certainly activates physical responses that are not activated by the person giving the stimulation. However, there are other factors that contribute to altered mental states that can significantly change the experience of the dominant.

One of the most important factors in scening is physical touch. Many dominants opt to use lots of tools and implements on their submissives. These look cool and are more effective than the hand. But, tools, objects, devices, mechanical toys and all manner of artificial restraints create a distance between the dominant and the submissive.

Touch conveys information. Direct touch flows that information faster and in a more alive state than what a person receives standing even a few inches away. Think about it this way, you have an energetic body that is radiating energy through the membranes of your tissues and skin. When you get excited this energy moves more quickly. The closer you get to your physical body the higher quantity of energy is present. This diminishes rapidly with distance.

This means if you are standing a few feet away from your submissive and swinging a crop or whip, your submissive will be radiating massive amounts of energy and you will pick up only a trickle.

If, on the other hand, you rest your left hand on your submissive while engaging in something else with your right hand then you will greatly enhance the amount of energy you experience from your partner.

If you were having sex in missionary position, your bodies would be touching at several spots and your plexus points (chakras) would be as close to touching as possible. This close contact jacks your energy and your partners energy and their contact with you does the same. Sexual excitement is a result of both people passing energy quickly back and forth. This is why some positions tend to feel much more intense than others. This is also why when a person is closed down, why they will not be passing energy during sex. Some people hoard their energy behind closed systems.

By resting your left hand close or near a main trunk or primary plexus point the chakra or confluence of nerves in the palm of your hand will receive the high energy flow more directly and this will pass through your hand, up your arm and into your trunk near your heart. The energy will split and run up and down your spine enervating and accelerating your energy system at a much higher rate than if you were not touching. Information passes inside energy.

Some dominants don't like to physically touch their submissives because they struggle with moral questions about causing pain or they experience difficulty going further when their partner cries out. This is more common with newcomers than with people with some experience. Unfortunately, distance often becomes a habit and it will limit and seriously change your experiences.

When a dominant spanks or restrains using their

hands and their own body weight they become more involved. When you spank with your hand it will sting your palm at the same time it stings the butt of your submissive. This stinking sensation done long enough will be painful. The same factors that trigger and elevate a submissive in this way can do much the same for the dominant. Using your hands and body weight as restraints means that if the submissive struggles (and a lot of them love to struggle) that the dominant will be hard pressed to be successful. This struggle is very physically challenging just like any hard work out. Again, this physical interaction will ramp up your system much faster than the distance of toys and tools.

If you are a person who doesn't want that contact, it doesn't mean you won't get excited. If you didn't get excited why would you do this? You will get excited anyway and your energy and body chemicals will ramp up – anyway.

When a scene ends and both partners are finished, the dominant is just as likely to experience drop as the submissive. Usually, the dominant will think that this drop or lack of control is un-domly or something and they will attempt to act as if nothing is happening to them. This is unfortunate because their body doesn't give a damn what image they want to project towards others. Their body will experience the ramping down of their energy and just like after an intense sexual experience, particularly if the scene concludes with ejaculation, (presuming the dominant in this instance is male) then the male will want to go to sleep.

I don't mean to suggest that this only happens to male dominants. It is just as strong for a female dominant. She may or may not engage in intercourse but it is very likely she will experience a strong energy drop after the scene is complete.

Many dominants engage in a relationship which begins with the establishment of rules, boundaries, and instructions for the submissive to follow including immediate directions of conduct, behavior, attitude, etc. An example of this is to immediate require that the submissive call the dominant an honorific title such as Master, Mistress, Sir, Lord, Lady, Ma'am etc. The submissive is told that they must be deferential, humble, obedient, respectful, etc. at all times. The submissive is then given a list of objectives, requirements, and things which that dominant feels are important for the establishment of boundaries between the two of them. On the surface this all sounds wonderful.

However, in a real life or a functioning full time relationship, this type of construction causes problems. If you set up the relationship to only exist within these parameters, then what you are creating is a cage. You are forcing the existence of role or scene to occur at any time you are sharing the presence of each other. Initially this may seem to be exactly what you desire. You believe you require this totality of apparent commitment by the submissive.

> *Do you prefer to use toys and tools on your submissive rather than try to make intimate connections with them using your hands or body?*

However, as you move forward with the relationship you begin to feel stressed. Identifying the source or cause of this stress may be difficult. You may find your language becoming constrained when you speak with your submissive. You may feel tight. You may look at the relationship and to all extents and purposes it is perfect, exactly as you have created it to be. So, why are you feeling so trapped? You may find yourself exploring new submissives, you may feel guilty, shamed, embarrassed and unhappy. You really like or love your submissive, what is happening?

One of the least visible aspects of a dominant/submissive relationship is also something widely talked about but poorly understood. Exchange; many people equate this to an exchange of power by the enforcement of roles *(especially in scene)*. This exchange can be better understood as not an exchange of power but an exchange of energy. By creating an artificial arena or environment, the forced introduction of requirements, rules and boundaries, you are also constructing the identical requirement, rules and boundaries for yourself. You become trapped within a performance role whenever you are with your submissive. Far from addressing your needs as a dominant, the relationship now becomes an exercise in assumption of role regardless of where you are at the moment.

By requiring your submissive to be submissive at all times when around you, you are also requiring yourself to be dominant at all times. This inevitably becomes a burden, causing stress both mentally and physically. It can go to the extreme of driving the dominant to avoid their submissive, because that submissive has obeyed them to the letter. The flaw was within their perception of what a viable D/s relationship should be like, not in the submissive's execution of the dominant's desire. How does a dominant undo such a thing without losing the respect of their submissive?

This phenomenon, similar to the depletion of energy immediately after a scene, is sometimes called dominant drop. The requirement to sustain role at all times, drains the dominant's energy reserves, when they exit the immediate proximity of their submissive they feel depleted and sometimes even physically ill.

There is another aspect which I also need to talk about. Many people feed on the energy of their partners in and out of scene. A great submissive/dominant relationship passes or exchanges energy so that no person is actively depleted. However, especially in new dominants and submissives there tends to be a more focused need emanating from the submissive. The submissive wants to experience everything they have imagined inside of them. To bring this into fruition they launch themselves at the dominant in full submissive regalia. They are only too eager to trigger that dominant response that feeds their needs. They are only too happy to call the dominant an honorific title and follow directions. They cling to the rules like leeches. To a large extent their submissive response forces or attempts to force the dominant into dominating them. For those in casual relationships, occasional meetings, phone or cyber this type of incessant role-playing may be viable. For those seeking real life or a more full time interaction this kind of relationship seldom works.

I sometimes explain it this way. I am me all the time, I give direction intentionally and by choice. It is essential that all aspects and parts of my personality are fed and well tended. That means my vulnerability, my need to cuddle, my desire to laugh, to dance with my man, to do dishes and vacuum, whatever it is that pleases me and brings me fulfillment and joy in my life needs to have the space and freedom to exist. All aspects are part of me, integral and necessary for me to feel whole and healthy. There are no rules which say you as a dominant must do one thing or the other. You are unique.

To address dominant drop in my own life, it became necessary to view my primary relationship in other terms. It is my desire to control when and where I turn on *(or give direction to others)*. To accomplish this the most simply, I don't impose D/s on myself. When I am with a partner, we are both in neutral space. This allows open flowing conversation, debate, humor, the sharing of ideas, doing things together etc. When I feel a desire to engage or take control, I do so. I may do this physically by touch or verbally by shifting from neutral language, where I use his proper name to scene language, where I use my chosen private name for him. This simple construction is quite effective, It blockades the submissive's potential desire to force me into role, it negates the building of stresses by offering open exchanges of conversation and at the same time allows me total control over when and where I exercise my role of choice to its fullest. I do not experience an energy rape. I found over the years that this arrangement works best for me.

A submissive experiencing a dominant in dominant drop may notice a sudden withdrawal coupled to an unsubstantive reason for the detachment and/or removal of presence. The submissive may go into a panic or frenzy bombarding that dominant with gifts, cards, flowers, phone calls, etc. Each of these will compound the problem and make it worse, adding stress to the dominant. These are demands for attention that the dominant is simply unable to give at that time. That inability can be driven to the point of a complete severance of the relationship in order for the dominant to recuperate. If the dominant has avoided the submissive they may also feel too embarrassed to continue the relationship.

    A new submissive should consider the act of alleviating the stresses of the dominant as a priority in their life. Learn to be patient and await the natural waves of energy (and need) that all of us produce. This learned behavior is something that makes more experienced submissives such a joy to be around. A submissive should seek to blend seamlessly into their dominant's life, sharing in that excess of dominant energy when it is available and feeding their dominant with ease of spirit when that dominant is low on energy.

Coping with Release

    Relationships end. In general, D/s or kink components add an additional layer to a relationship and you can equate this to new and challenging stressors. This means that a new D/s relationship is under more challenges than a similar non D/s relationship. In either case the ending of a relationship is painful. I receive frequent letters asking about coping in the aftermath, both from dominants and from submissives. What kind of aftercare should exist? What obligations continue even after the relationship has ended?

Many people seem to believe that the dominant side of a relationship experiences fewer emotions than the submissive side. This belief seems to stem from the posturing some dominants like to use to 'show' dominance. This posturing often includes a stiff or closed demeanor and language distancing themselves from their partner. In addition, many dominants who try to include several submissives in their home or family will seem to treat the submissive as a disposable object rather than a person they are in a deep relationship with.

In some cases this posturing is correct and the dominant individual may not be as deeply invested in the relationship as the submissive. But, in most cases this is just posturing to hide the emotions.

When a relationship fails part of what breaks are the expectations and promised future (future constructs) that both partners to the relationship have created about the relationship. Frequently a promise of 'love' or any equally committed state also includes nest building, friendship associations and networking and goal setting.

> *D/s style relationships tend to last from 2 months to 2 years, usually on the lower end of this metric – are you prepared for a D/s relationship failure?*

If a relationship has lasted more than two years the tangle of the interwoven lives can include adopted children, shared property, shared investments and other financial and legal issues. Even with short relationships these mingled issues can become prominent.

Any relationship failure can cause people to act out. Kink failure is no exception. The behaviors people demonstrate while in a relationship can be markedly different from their exiting behaviors. When you are exploring a potential new relationship it is critical to talk to friends or former partners of your potential new partner and ask questions about how they behaved during the break-up of their former relationships.

You won't want to ask those questions because you will want to believe that *you* and *your new relationship* are special or extra special and asking about break-ups is going to some how ruin your blissful new relationship. Wrong. Most relationships begin with a detachment of the critical thinking and skepticism parts of the brain (read my new book Extreme Space II: Kink Secrets for more detail on why this happens). This contributes to a state called *New Relationship Energy (NRE)*. Within NRE everything is wonderful and those bits that aren't perfect seem minor and unimportant compared to how wonderful you feel.

However, how a person behaves during any large disappointment is likely to be the pattern for future large disappointments.

Has your partner ever been the subject of a restraining order or been accused of domestic violence? Did they move out of state during their last break up? Did they continue to support children created or adopted in prior relationships? Do they describe their former relationship partners in hostile and unpleasant terms? Is the responsibility for former break-ups always positioned on the former partner? Do you frequently hear stories about why the former partner was so bad, wrong, evil, sick, mentally ill, damaged, mean, deceitful, hurtful, detached, sexually barren, too assertive, argumentative, unpleasant or similar?

Imagine your new partner describing you using all of the *same* words they describe their current former partners. Look up their divorce papers. These are public records. Read about the divorce and the claims made during the divorce by both partners.

Does your current potential partner maintain friendships that existed during their former relationships? Why or why not? Have you met these friends? Have you spoken with your potential partner's family? What do they say about the former relationships?

It is likely that you won't do anything that I suggest here. You will trust your feelings for the person.

Now, look at your behavior during your former relationships. Do you like to argue and fight? Do you scream and scratch? Do you try to hurt the person? Did you do things to be mean? Did you make up stories to explain everything to your friends and family? Did anyone put a restraining order on you? Did you stalk your former partner? Did you try to ruin your former partners job situation or relationships with others? Did you harass them on the phone? Did you try to find out who they were dating and cause that person embarrassment or harm? What is your pattern and strategy for exiting?

Many people believe that because a relationship starts out full of excitement that it needs to end the same way. Their former relationship partners must be enemies that are denigrated in all future comments, forever. One of the reasons this behavior is so common is that the person doesn't want other people to talk to their former relationship partner. They want to cast themselves in the role of the victim, the person to be valued and sympathized with in new relationships. Few people want to admit to their part in why their relationships failed.

Every person has both good and bad behavior habits. Every person has things that they do, issues that they possess that contribute to problems within relationships. The two top areas of relationship failures are problems with perceived cheating (the idea someone is cheating is often enough to create domestic violence) and problems with money.

These issues don't magically vanish because you like a person. Unless a person does work to correct bad habits these habits will persist. If a person couldn't manage money in their last relationship it is likely they can't manage money right now. If a person was accused of cheating (and they were actually still technically married while dating you) then they will continue to cheat on you with others in the future.

Your new relationship isn't the solution to former bad behavior habits. Your new partner simply hasn't met your well-screened less favorable habits yet. In all likelihood you entered your new relationships on your best behavior. It isn't your best behavior that fails. You cannot maintain the artificiality of 'best' behavior for very long. It is your normal or typical behavior that is the measure upon which your relationship will actually function.

While you may be determined to *change* so that you don't repeat the past. Determination isn't change. Determination is an intellectual exercise while relating is an interpersonal practice that involves all aspects of the being including the emotional, psychological, physical and spiritual states.

Now you've added kink to that package. In your kink mode the pressure of the *changed perfect performance* is significantly added pressure to the already difficult requirements of relating.

So, your relationship fails. How are you managing that failure? What skills have you developed to assist you in dealing with rejection, sorrow, grief, anger, pain and disappointment? How does kink make coping with relationship failures different?

At the first sign of trouble in the relationship seek relationship counseling as a couple. Most people won't do this. There is a hidden taboo in kink regarding mental health issues. Although most kink people engage in the idea of the consent process, beneath their participation they still hold some belief that what they are doing is perverse, sick and sinful. Going to a relationship counselor sounds like it is likely to expose their flaws. If they are trying to live the 24/7 D/s prototype relationship style, they have a role to maintain and exposing the stuff they haven't shared with their new partner is likely to impact their roles.

Some people have very weak self esteem and yet they select a role where they are *supposed* to have great self esteem. When problems show up they feel guilty for not being able to magically know everything about solving relationship problems. Maybe they project themselves as a slave master and they have created a belief that of course they know how to manage a slave. Except, now the relationship is heading on a fast train to Suckville and they can't seem to force their slave into whatever might work for the slave to be fixed.

Face your fear, get help! You will discover that both of you are doing, saying, thinking things that are contributing to the problems in the relationship. You will also discover that you weren't magically *changed* by wanting to change after your last sucky relationship. You will discover that you have to actually work hard at changing and that confronting the real issues is ugly, painful work and that no one but you can do that work.

If you can't afford to get help or no matter what I say you ain't going to go to any therapist and have them delve out your secrets then you must follow the guidelines of any deep personal loss.

- Don't ignore your pain.
- Feel your feelings.
- Cry.
- Allow anger to pass through you. Don't interact with anyone while you are angry.
- Don't deny that the relationship is over.
- Don't place blame on the failure on the other person or on yourself.
- Don't try to create bargains to salvage or save the relationship. Don't promise change.
- Expect to feel sad and depressed.
- Fight depression by good nutrition, daily exercise, plenty of sunlight and good sleep. See a doctor to assist you.
- Grieve. Loss is loss.
- Don't punish yourself with regret or delusions about how it could have been saved or avoided.
- Don't wallow in negative self feelings such

as guilt, humiliation, and embarrassment.
- Seek support from friends and family or by seeing a therapist if necessary. Support groups for loss can also be helpful.
- Avoid alcohol and drug use to manage your feelings of pain and loss.
- Let go of your 'old' goals for your 'old' relationship.
- Don't create stories about why the relationship failed. Don't tell these stories to others in order to feel justified in what happened.
- Don't stalk your former partner. Don't threaten your former partner.

Many relationship break ups feel like a death. You may not have the symptoms or responses I've noted here. You may have a few or all of these reactions and more. Often responses to a loss come in waves. In addition to these standard relationship loss reactions it is likely that you may also experience a rising need for kink interactions. At this point you *should* know a few other people in your local community who are kinky. You can request scening from friends that isn't particularly sexual but it can relieve some of your need or frenzy symptoms. This often sounds wrong or odd to newcomers because many people associate kink with being in love or in a personal committed relationship. These two are actually separate issues.

There are other common issues that occur during a relationship loss or failure.
- Create a reasonable financial exit strategy.
- Know where your legal papers are located

and make copies to be kept in a safe and distant location that only you have access to.
- Keep a phone book of all of your friends and contacts and keep it in a secure and distant location from your residence.
- Seek legal advice if you have given your assets to your partner and are now facing financial ruin.
- Leave any shared residence if you are threatened with physical harm.
- Move children away from threatening conditions before they become dangerous.
- Tell friends and family what you are doing and why so that they can document and support your process.
- Don't bad-mouth your ex even if you feel very hurt and angry. Words are weapons that are easy to cast and hard to retrieve.
- Set reasonable goals for the dispersal of joint properties and let a lawyer help you handle negotiations, particularly if you are emotional.
- Don't try to turn mutual friends against your ex. Don't try to shame or humiliate your ex in public, in their family, private life, job or among friends.
- Recognize that anger is part of grief and it is temporary and covers other 'real' emotions. Try to feel the emotions that anger covers up. Work on processing your grief.

- Don't try to punish your former partner financially.

If you are homosexual and your relationship is not officially recognized seek immediate legal help. If your partner has died you may have no legal right to assets you have contributed to creating. Prepare in advance by legally negotiating a trust in each partner's will.

Anything you do to or towards your former relationship partner will have internal consequences inside of you. While revenge may feel good in the moment you commit any negative act, in the long term your revenge will eat at your spirit. It will become a cancer inside of you. What you do to others you are also doing to yourself even if you can't see it, feel it or experience it in the moment of your actions.

When you construct your new relationship you may be tempted to remove all independence from your submissive partner such as by controlling credit, checking accounts, income, access to friends, family, support groups and more.

While this sounds romantic to some newcomer submissives, it is a very bad choice. While you may choose to functionally live with the illusion of these roles you need to maintain control over your separate income. You need singular access to your assets. You need to control and maintain health coverage and insurance. You need to retain control over your property and assets that existed prior to the relationship and those assets created during the relationship.

Everyone dies. If you are in a long-term D/s relationship it is highly likely that the (male dominant) will die first. This is based on life expectancy statistics for men and women in America. Any relationship should include this understanding and calmly prepare for the eventuality of death.

Most relationships fail. This eventuality should also be calmly planned for at the beginning of a relationship so that both parties to the relationship are adequately protected by this likely result. By approaching the relationship pragmatically both persons can shape the way future loss can happen. Such a business-like approach doesn't raise the specter of imminent failure, it recognizes the inherent value of each person and expresses a loving desire to promote the wellbeing of that person should such an event happen.

Planning for your future makes each person a reasonable custodian of their own life. No person should become homeless and destitute when a relationship ends. If you don't know how to plan for such things there are classes online, financial and legal planners and life coaches who can offer a physical and emotional plan for how to create the necessary documents and strategies. Don't think that you can avoid these things because you only have a few dollars in the bank. Few people are taught by their parents how to manage their own finances and legal business. Even fewer have good relationship role models coming out of childhood. How are you going to learn these things without seeking out the educational opportunities that are readily available on all of these subjects?

Coping takes different forms for each person. The added element of kink in a relationship sometimes creates lifelong sensations of shared intimacy that simply don't vanish because the relationship has failed and both people are off in different directions.

What you have shared with a kink partner has many of the aspects of shared trauma, such as you might see with war buddies. Dealing with these additional connections, sensations and feelings can be very difficult. To some extent an old kink partner will know things about you that no other person will ever know. The same goes for your knowledge of them.

One way to help lessen the power of your old connection is by journaling. The process of writing a journal allows you to document every tiny detail of a scene or relationship that you remember. Try to remember smells, sensations, tastes and every thing in as vivid detail as possible and ask your brain to help you process these into quiet memory versus a charged memory full of energy. Use energy discharge techniques to release energy associated with this type of bonded attachment. (Extreme Space II has a good energy discharge technique near the back of the book).

Form an intention to move toward health, wellness and personal happiness. Recognize that while a relationship may fail and your old goals may no longer be viable, you can set new goals that will be equally rich and important for your happiness and continue to move towards those goals. You don't end because a relationship fails.

PAIN

In kink there is a continuing and growing focus on masochism, so much so that a person's submissive interests are often evaluated by their willingness to endure pain, humiliation, degradation, mental and emotional damage and other 'so called' submissive acts.

Masochism isn't submission. Ever. It's masochism.

Receiving direction need not ever include acts of punishment, discipline, humiliation, degradation or any types of mental and emotional damage. Receiving direction doesn't require the repudiation or rejection of spiritual concepts, beliefs, understanding and veneration of ideals and the sacred. Being submissive or seeking out kink interactions doesn't mean that your motives should not be pure, that your spiritual life must cease to be recognized or valued or that you should somehow reject the necessary analysis of your feelings and behaviors. You will encounter kink practices that are counter to your personal viewpoint and ideals. It is likely you will feel conflicted and challenged as if your possession of restraints upon your behavior and choices are some type of 'brat-like' behavior that needs to be removed. It is likely that your religious mores will stand in opposition to acts you are requested to participate in and that you may feel pressured to convert to a non-spiritual identity, as if this is a worthy and necessary goal of kink.

Submission isn't directly about any of these things. At its core the desire to submit from one person towards another is simply to receive direction. The quality and content of the direction that is given depends on the mental, emotional and psychological state of the person giving direction. Simply because any person is choosing to give direction doesn't mean the content of their direction is not damaging, irresponsible, flawed, riddled with thinking errors, based on lack of education and insight, or otherwise not worthy of being followed. A dominant doesn't have some special inside channel of good guidance towards others.

Today, most people on kink or fetish websites conflate submission with some masochism. Most dominants expect to spank their submissives. Most expect to give pain and have that pain eagerly received.

If you like aspects of submission but have no interest in receiving pain don't be bullied into believing it is necessary and part of your role. It isn't.

D/s, on many levels, is a permission process. The dominant (by any name) is seeking permission to engage in acts that are unavailable in a normal relationship. A submissive (by any name) is also seeking a partner willing to participate in acts that are unavailable in a normal relationship and for that access the potential submissive is willing to give permission for a list of potential shared acts.

Few persons interested in submission would include on their list things like: the desire to be emotionally damaged, the desire to shorten their life by practices that cause long-term health problems, the desire to lose relationships with friends and family, the desire to acquire sexually transmitted diseases or to experience damage to their tissues and organs, to experience nerve damage from pretty-looking but poorly applied ropes, etc.

Few persons interested in domination would include things on their list like: the desire to mentally, emotionally and spiritually damage other people, the desire to cause physical injury that reduces the life expectancy of others, the desire to separate other people from their jobs, support systems, family, friends and important relationships, the desire to pass sexually transmitted diseases and to cause nerve damage or death all for the fun of it.

These things sound like fun, right? Of course not. But pain, damage and destruction are not limited to physical evidence. No dominant is playing just with the body of their submissive.

Every kink interaction encompasses the entirety of the person. This means that anything you do will affect the entire person. Just because you intend only positive outcomes doesn't mean this is what you will do or how your partner will feel. Intent is an empty excuse. It is necessary for both persons to take ownership of the whole potential of what is possible when they interact.

Let's talk specifically about pain.

Most people have a good understanding of what pain is but often they don't think about it very deeply until they are involved in something around kink and suddenly they have to take a deeper look.

No one likes pain. Pain is a warning system in your body used to indicate when something is not working correctly or when something is wrong. When you accidentally stub your toe on something hard and sharp it is highly unlikely that you immediately retraced your steps so you could do it again and again because it was so good. No. It is likely you jerked away and expressed some verbal curse words while checking your toe for any lasting injury. There, your warning system worked properly.

A true application of pain is the presence of a warning interpreted as a warning and processed as a warning.

When someone spanks your ass it may feel painful but there are multiple differences in the experience versus the raw pain of the stubbed toe.

First in these differences is consent and the intentional choice of both participants to engage in spanking. You may wonder why this makes any difference at all in terms of how you receive pain.

We've already talked about the response processes but it should be made clear here that those same response processes fired at the time you stubbed your toe. If the spanking is sudden, hard and unexpected the individual is quite likely to have the exact same response to pain that they would have with the stubbed toe.

While they may have a blanket consent offered to their partner, a sudden and unexpected physical contact is no different from a non-consent accident. After their first 'non-thinking' reaction the information will reach their cerebral cortex and it will process *with* their thinking, ideas and agreements around their relationship.

This means that your preparation and thinking influence your experience. No surprise there. However these processes can radically alter how you process the nerve-sending information after first *sudden* contact or from the onset of a scene.

Our culture likes to promote the idea that all pain is very similar. But, many kinds of pain are much more difficult to 'manage' than other types. Example: if you have an abscessing tooth it is extremely unlikely you will find it sexually pleasurable and that you will intentionally try to maintain infected and abscessing teeth for your sexual pleasure. I'm not saying impossible because I too have seen "Little Shop of Horrors" with their dental scene, but, serious infections in the head are generally met with the shortest trip possible to the dentist for pain relief.

Deep body aches, points where bones crush against each other and many more painful symptoms of disease and injury are extremely unpleasant and very difficult to deal with.

This doesn't mean how you think about the pain shouldn't be applied to these pain challenges. Many people use meditation, bio-feedback and altered mental state processes to assist in pain management with significant success. Your brain is both the implementer of the degree of pain that you experience and the potential moderator of that pain. How you think, how well you train and use your brain, and how you interact with your own nervous system all play key roles in how you experience pain.

Pain tolerance develops differently for each person. In general, women tolerate pain better than men. Each person has different pain thresholds that shift depending on the time of month, the time of day, the hour and even the minute. Many external factors alter how pain is identified and processed. If an injury happens in conjunction with some separate event that is a priority to the individual, the person may not even realize they are injured or their experience of the injury may be only a momentary glance to evaluate risk or response levels before the person moves on. They don't actually 'feel' the injury. Does this mean the body isn't sending the signal or is the signal dampened by the intense focus of the person coupled to a *mental evaluation* that the other event is more important?

How you tolerate pain is going to be unique to you and it shouldn't be compared with other people as a measure of anything. Many people use kink as a means to overcome persistent and chronic pain because a kink scene that includes stimulation will elevate their system and for a time it will reduce their experience of chronic pain. Some people cannot physically scene because they are too sensitive to pain and any stimulation feels overwhelming and is difficult for them to deal with. I mention both here because we tend to have multiple thresholds of what we can tolerate. I don't mean with pain specifically.

The factors that you manage in your daily life affect how you process information. Pain is information. Interacting in a relationship is information. The more stress that you experience daily the lower your threshold is for additional information. At some point your brain essentially throws up its hands and gives up on trying to process more stuff. This impacts how you receive further stimulation.

Some thresholds are aligned with inhibitions and when a threshold is crossed the individual is likely to feel released from their inhibition. We don't tend to think of inhibitions as thought barriers but to some extent we tend to maintain a persona that includes the features we like to present to society and to our partners as our outer face. This persona maintenance takes a conscious application of energy and attention.

Scening and the elevation of sensory information tends to break down the amount of energy that can be diverted into maintaining persona. When the threshold is reached, the persona fails and the individual is exposed on a more primal, less formally structured, basis.

You can expose earlier and alter personas. An earlier persona is a persona a person used at an earlier point in their development. Usually this is how they perceived themselves at that time period. An alter persona may be a particular persona that the individual likes to use deep in their imagination about themselves. They might experience an animalistic, primal state or a regressed state from what they feel is a former lifetime. How these persona set up inside the person is less important than how they emerge and how they feel when they emerge.

In some cultures these states are considered part of vision questing where the individual looks for clues about their life and experiences. If they experience primal animal states they may feel these experiences are affiliated with their inner totem. As you can see, many of these inhibitory releases require spiritual explanation from the individual's unique perspective. I've only mentioned a few possibilities of a dis-inhibited state, there are many other aspects or sensations that can emerge at different times through this process.

Some people believe that their shift of experience is directly correlated with how much they trust the person they are interacting with. However, this may simply be wishful thinking. I have known people who have had similar experiences with virtual strangers. The only truly common factor appears to be sensory stimulation and potentially how much work the individual has done to overcome internal obstacles. Inhibitions are not the only obstacles to how people experience their worlds. Incomplete past experiences that have remain 'alive' and unprocessed are also obstacles that inform space. In some cases the uninhibited state may be a flashback to a very traumatic experience. As you might imagine this type of unexpected exposure of an old trauma can be incredibly painful in a way that has nothing directly to do with the ongoing scene.

During each day each person has a certain amount of internal room for 'new stuff'. Mentally a person can want to scene while physically they are tired or they've simply exceeded the amount of decisions they can handle for the day. It is not possible to predict today what you will feel like tomorrow.

We are also effected by the rhythms and systems of our bodies. Our moods and feelings are subject to changes in our bodies such as the rise and fall of hormones. We have cycles and these cycles change our responses. New participants of kink are well served to take a month or two and track their feelings each day and also track their daily activities to see how different experiences, events and behaviors impact their pain levels.

Going to the gym will effect how you feel and how your body reacts. What you do at the gym also makes a difference. What you eat, how long you sleep, how stressful your job is, and many other typical daily routines all impact how you react.

Do you do any mental training? This is a choice such as NLP training, hypnosis, meditation, some kinds of yoga, martial arts and other practices that require sustained mental effort and interaction. I don't mean education or school although these are helpful in other ways, I am speaking directly with working on noticing how your brain works. Much of pain management is associated with awareness and interaction in intentional ways with your brain.

If you are masochistic you should be dancing, stretching, and doing muscular exercises for flexibility and strength as well as regular aerobic exercises. Swimming is good. I mentioned dance because it requires mental as well as physical coordination. You don't need to be good at it, but it helps to work at it trying to improve your skills.

Music can also play a key role in pain management. Many cultures use drumming and chanting to enter trance-like states. These types of music are readily available online. Try out different music from what you typically listen to during your regular musical enjoyment times. Notice how music effects you and what works quickly versus what works more deeply.

> *Is shared pain play your primary attraction to kink versus traditional sex? Or are you trying to gain regular access to sex and believe that kink provides more opportunities for sex connections?*

Much of kink is a lot like a sport. You train for it. You work on becoming more fit. You value your fitness as part of your ability to interact and move yourself towards personal and relationship goals. I am not speaking to weight or physical size as much as I'm speaking to an orientation towards better fitness overall. It's very simple, the better your health, the easier it is for you to explore physical, emotional, mental, psychological and spiritual mysteries.

I've focused a lot here on the physical aspects of pain. But, mental health, emotional health and psychological wellbeing are easily as important or even more so than physical pain. It is extraordinarily easy to inflict hurt on others through words, attitudes, gestures and behaviors.

In kink it is common to intentionally use derogatory language as part of making a scene hot. Unfortunately, the individual doesn't always stay in the mental state of consent during a scene and this means that words that sometimes make a scene hot can within a split second cause hurt and damage. How any person receives charged language and behaviors is tricky. Your assumptions that consent is the only essential ingredient guiding what you say and do with your partner is foolish.

If you like to belittle, humiliate, denigrate and diminish your partner thinking it is how you elevate yourself in the relationship, or how you indicate status, or how D/s must set up to be real, then you are likely to verge comfortably into abusive behaviors and end up with a partner with damaged self esteem, self loathing and ideas that they have minimal value. At some point this denigrated person will cease finding you interesting or tolerable and they will leave.

While scening these fetishes can be exciting, it is also quite dangerous. It should not become rote. You shouldn't fall into the idea that fetishes are some license to disrespect your partner. At some point the fetish aspect will wear off and you will be left with a person you have been abusing for your pleasure. That isn't kink.

DESENSITIZATION

There is a lot of emphasis placed on how much pain a

submissive can take from a dominant.. Many equate the ability to take significant amounts of pain as being superior to a submissive who can only endure a small amount and sometimes no pain at all. There tends to be an elitist attitude where photos of extreme results that are posted to fetish websites as 'evidence' of a submissives masochistic value are rewarded with streams of complimentary messages from both other submissives and other dominants. Deep bruising, tissue destruction and other evidence of serious physical trauma is valued as a trophy and accomplishment. This creates an atmosphere of trophy hunting and performance as a goal of scening. This type of trophy hunting concerns me deeply, as do the self-abuse aspects, which I often consider mentally unhealthy.

In order to look at desensitization, you need to look at the underlying desires on the part of the submissive and the dominant very carefully. Why do they want to extend the pain threshold? And, is it possible?

Part of the experience of s/m is pain; the infliction of and the receipt of pain. However, for most people the desired experience is not merely to feel or give pain. Pain is generally a tool used to create sensations and experiences that may be only accessed through the pain. I will focus this section on those people who use pain to achieve a desired effect.

When a submissive first enters the lifestyle everything is new. While they may have been exposed to relationships which included violence, the non-consensual infliction of pain is often a completely different experience from how pain is received from within a consent process. So, a consensual process of pain is new.

Intellectually it is popular to view one or more eras from the past as idyllic in terms of how the people appear to have related and behaved themselves with others. In particular, many women are attracted to gracious clothing and the gentlemanly behavior of the men that they see in period movies or read in romance novels set in a specific period.

What they frequently don't realize is that the lives that are documented or written about are not only fictions, but they are fictions of people living in wealthy circumstances. You don't see many films or books in romantic settings of tenements, poor houses, families crowded into one bedroom walk-up apartments or living in shacks on the estates of some wealthy person.

In the fantasy past, everyone seems to be elegant and wealthy. This creates a belief that in the time before the women's suffragette movement, relationships between men and women (in undisturbed patriarchy) were better than mainstream modern relationships.

It is true that divorce was quite rare in such past times mostly because it was almost illegal except in extraordinary circumstances. It was also very expensive and because women were not allowed to own or manage property or their own wealth, they frequently could not bring suit to escape abusive and loveless marriages. There was also the 'rule of thumb' a quasi-legal term that indicated the size of rod (thickness) that could be used to beat a woman if she disobeyed her husband.

Most people who long for the past believe that their modern rights would exist in a past setting. What images of the past look like and how hard such lives were in reality are two different things. Still, the imaginary past is a popular fetish in kink. In many cases the submissive desires to return to a simpler time, a time and place where the rules were straightforward, not fluid and shifting from day to day. In addition there are underlying desires to be captured, taken and used. Often the mind views these fantasies as the escape from the limitations of modern society. This fantasy world is a place where the individual, in being bound, is set free from responsibility of self care and reputation and in this inability to maintain their formal presentation in the world, they feel more able to be fully themselves. This suggests that what they consider to be their true self is at odds with the dictates of normal society.

The other attractive part about the past is the appearance of romance. Women tend to believe that romance is all of the stuff around relating and sharing time with a man without sexuality. They would like for a man to focus intensely upon them in appreciation and admiration across more time in the relationship instead of just when a man is attempting to overcome some disagreement or when a man wants sexual release. This desire for sentiment, intimacy and the features of romance are invariably sewn into the attraction towards kink.

As they begin to explore this new world, they frequently come to believe that engaging in S/m is essential to fitting in and being 'popular' or appropriate as a potential kink partner. Some genuinely enter kink wanting to experience pain, control and to abandon the good girl aspect that they feel they are forced to fulfill in most of their daily life. All of these things are forms of mental release. However, every individual is unique. In the heightened focus on this aspect of D/s there is pressure for a submissive to be able to take a lot of pain.

What is the advantage for a submissive to become more masochistic? From the perspective of the submissive they might tell themselves that being able to take more pain from their partner is a part of giving to that dominant or showing the level of their devotion. This sounds nice but it is really what is happening? This positions pain as a necessary ingredient of devotion. That said, what pain does the dominant give as a necessary ingredient of devotion to their submissive? They don't. This makes this idea just that, an idea that isn't supportable in fact. Pain is not a component of submission in any part. How much pain a person can or is willing to experience has nothing really to do with their partner unless they wish to justify their behavior using this argument.

> *What is good pain?*

Why would a dominant want to have a strongly masochistic submissive? If a dominant is sadistic they will want to exercise their sadism on their partner. This exercise of sadism is not an act of love or caring, it is to pleasure the sadist and only the sadist. In a sadistic view the pleasure of the masochist is incidental and helpful. To retain sadism within kink the sadist must acknowledge and prefer the consent of the masochist. This doesn't mean the sadist desires for the masochist to experience pleasure, some don't.

Sadism and masochism are common and both are closely related to mental illnesses. A masochist can be self destructive and seek to find and use a sadist to intentionally damage their body, mind, emotional state and spiritual state. Often this emerges from low self esteem and many former experiences of devaluation. The individual may consider themselves to be damaged and worthless goods. They may also consider all forms of their own sexual desires and needs to be inherently wrong or sinful. Receiving pain can allow a person to feel useful and correctly treated. As you can see all of these potentials indicate some potential mental health concerns.

This doesn't mean that all masochists are mentally ill. Kink is a mechanism that allows people to more safely release pent up beliefs and feelings from their body and mind. But, it is a tender threshold. The practice of encouraging physical damage can push individuals who are on the edge mentally or emotionally into exceeding that edge in order to receive the praise and reward offered by others. In this way the receipt of pain can be equated to increased value. But, the price is heavy. If the individual goes down this path without good mental health support also in place, then they may become more damaged and less mentally well. Remember, good mental health is necessary in order to provide consent. If a person is consenting to damage their body they are not a good custodian of their own body and it means they are incompetent to offer reasoned consent.

There are some positive reasons for desensitizing a person. If you are a newcomer submissive with little or no experience of any masochism then it is difficult to find a dominant who isn't a little bit sadistic. Many dominants are fairly light in terms of their level of sadism. Most want great sex with less argument and more compliance in other areas of the relationship.

Most people have a history of light discipline from their parents during their childhood. This means that they associate 'spanking' with 'how someone who loves me treats me'. Often, in childhood, discipline was structured, discussed and then applied. I'm not talking about a child being hit randomly when a parent lost its temper. Measured discipline, in this way, is sometimes viewed as an essential marker of shared love.

Modern American society is steadily moving away from the concept of disciplining children by striking them as it is becoming clear, through psychological studies, that this type of discipline has serious long-term consequences on the child. Consequences that are viewed as unfavorable. (I suggest you look up these studies to better understand them.)

However, if you are an adult reading this book you are likely in an age group where spanking discipline was still common and you will have integrated that concept into your world view already.

There is no correct level or even desired level of masochism. While I have spoken to the submissive perspective here, let's take a look at the dominant side. We would like to think that all persons entering kink are in good mental health. But, this isn't true.

Each person is a product of their life experience. Not only does the potential dominant have the same probable life experience of spanking that their potential submissive shares, the dominant is also likely to have adult romantic relationships that have failed. In those relationships if the dominant is male, the dominant is likely to have experienced masculine role confusion. As our culture moves towards the center where men are experiencing reduced power and privilege, women and culture are demanding that men adjust their behaviors and expectations to recognize the increasing power of women in relationships. Unfortunately, most men have been raised in cultures and at a time when these changes were not prominent or to the degree that they exist today. This means that many men were conditioned to present their masculinity by dominating and then when they grew into adulthood and adult relationships the formula no longer worked and their relationships began to fail.

Rather than adjust their behaviors, some of them found kink where they can impose their conditioning upon women who are supposedly compliant with the old paradigm. In addition, some dominants emerging from modern romantic relationships have unprocessed anger towards their former spouse or significant other. This anger is often centered in how the woman in their last relationship censured them for trying to domineer the woman in the relationship.

In their kink relationships if a man has these issues they can project their anger against a former relationship partner on their new kink partner as a form of venting. By treating a kink partner as a person of reduced status and as a dependent, they move the status of the submissive into a position where the submissive can never have equal voice. In this way the dominant hopes to escape future censure for his bad behaviors.

Although I'm speaking about a male dominant, a female dominant exiting argumentative or abusive former relationships can victimize submissive partners in exactly the same way.

D/s isn't about silencing your partner, projecting your anger instead of doing your psychological work or somehow rolling back time to a rigid patriarchal framework in order to evade facing modern issues.

It is likely you bring some or all of these issues with you into kink. But, this doesn't mean you need to exercise or practice kink from this viewpoint.

The aspect that triggers me internally is creating and directing action which elicits the response I desire. I do not derive personal pleasure from the infliction of sensation for the infliction itself. I derive pleasure from the reactions or responses of the submissive. When the relationship is new, the response I might be looking for may take only a minimal amount of action or sensation to achieve. Often, since everything is so new, the submissive will reach that place quickly. Over time as both partners grow accustomed to each other and as the submissive becomes used to certain types of sensation occurring frequently, they learn to process that information differently. Then, in order for the dominant to achieve their desired reaction they must alter the action or intensify it.

This is not consistently true however. It is important for the dominant to actively seek out what the underlying mental trigger is inside of the submissive. If a submissive is triggered by a desire to serve not by application of pain then their ability to process pain information is not necessary. A dominant pressing such a submissive may mentally injure that submissive by implying that they are not good enough in some ways for not processing pain in a manner the dominant believes is required. For a serving submissive they can generally process a certain amount of stimulation comfortably and will attempt to please their dominant by allowing this application to themselves. They will not ever need or desire serious or heavy scening in the pain infliction arena. A dominant should not try to convert or force such a submissive. A submissive's limits can and should be pressed in the area of their trigger. This will increase their sensations of pleasure or responsiveness. In my opinion the enrichment of each others lives is of considerable importance here. For the submissive who triggers on sensations of pain can and will become somewhat desensitized to light forms of play. Again the same principles are at work. Their mind learns to process the information and requires different stimulation to respond or react.

    The dominant should always remain aware that the submissive is not a constant force. The ability to process information will vary. The level or range of pain or stimulation that the submissive can endure will never remain constant. It is quite common for the submissive to have an intense scene which takes them further then they have gone before, to be immediately followed by a withdrawal or inability to process the level of sensory input that was standard before the limit breaking scene took place.

    This reaction often surprises both the dominant and submissive. It is a recuperation period. This period is sometimes quite reactive and a submissive may find themselves lashing out at their dominant at this point or resisting direction. Returning to the level that was normal to the intense scene may take several weeks or it may never occur a second time.

I find that frequent scening, even daily scenings do tend to extend the initial limits or range of the submissive. However, it is my opinion that a significant part of this effect is a result of increasing trust as much as of desensitization on the part of the submissive. Often a submissive desires to go further. As they develop trust, they relax more and more into the direction of their dominant.

The critical factor is to listen carefully to the submissive and resist the urge to push. If you, as a dominant, are not getting your needs met by the level of masochism of your submissive, start asking some serious questions about what is fueling your needs.

As a submissive, do your work. If you have low self esteem and low self worth get help. There are kink-aware professionals in every area of the country who can assist you in assessing where you are in these areas of your life and how you can improve your mental health.

All humans age. As we age it becomes more likely that experiencing pain will be problematic. If you invest in the idea that your value is based on masochism, age will defeat you. Your value is not based in how much or how little pain you can tolerate for others. As a dominant if you only seek out masochists it means you are probably not working on your stuff. While your moments of sadism will temporarily reduce your unwanted feelings and emotions, they will continue to exist and they will eat you out from the inside. Do your work. If you learn other management skills it doesn't mean you will stop being sadistic or dominant, but it does mean that you won't push others just to ease your unprocessed pain.

Cutting

Many people who seek out kink have been triggered by years or sometimes a lifetime of physical molestation, violation of trust, faith, belief, love and hope. Abuse may be their norm.

One response to chronic abuse is cutting or other types of physical mutilation.

Cutting, in particular, is when a person uses a sharp object to cut their skin so that the blood will flow out quickly. Often cutting occurs immediately after a distressing or stressful experience. Usually cutting occurs in private. Some cutters will use anything sharp that they can find. Others are quite particular and use only specific items and they may view cutting as a ritual that is almost spiritual in nature.

Penetrating the skin kicks off a slightly different response from touching the skin. The skin is a barrier that can be viewed as parallel to personal privacy. If a person is experiencing chronic abuse, their personal privacy is being intentionally violated by others.

To relieve this stress, the person, in turn, violates their own privacy barrier.

The person may feel that the stress or distress is physically captured in their skin and that by cutting or opening their skin, they can allow the stress to escape.

As blood flows out of the cut wound the individual

often feels sensations of deep relief.

It is now common to see needles and cut play in kink. It is also common to see people scene until blood is flowing from the butt or tissues of the masochist.

For obvious reasons this is unhealthy and dangerous.

If you feel that this is the best mechanism to relieve the pressures inside of you, it is likely you need to seek out other forms of stress management so that your reliance on cutting and physical damage are reduced.

The objective is to feel less distress and to reduce physical damage at the same time. It is possible. Stress processing is a learned skill. You aren't born knowing how to deal with confusing, hurtful or damaging experiences. What you discover first, is often what you use and what you think works for you. It does work for you. But, it is costly and dangerous and there are many other processing skills that you can learn to help you deal with abuses.

Scening kink may provide some necessary relief for a cutter's distress. But it isn't a solution either. Take the time when you are not in immediate distress and seek out other processing techniques. All you need is the desire to learn and to value yourself enough to give that learning to yourself.

If you scene a cutter, seek solutions with them as an ally and partner. Don't judge, you haven't lived their life.

Shifting Roles

Online you might come to believe that roles like dominant and submissive are fixed features of a persons personality. But, they are really roles. You can view a role as a collection of personality attributes. When you gather one group together you can present yourself as a dominant. When you gather another group together you can present yourself as a submissive.

This may sound confusing. Good. You are confusing, complicated, chaotic, diverse, changing, growing, transforming and always in the midst of reshaping yourself.

While roles help newcomers to grasp a specific viewpoint, they are roles.

Some people barely grasp any role for any length of time. Often their personality is a mixture of all kinds of roles smushed together. To present as either a dominant or a submissive means they must restrain other aspects for a duration of time. Usually this restraint fails under pressure and the conglomeration of their natural personality will manifest.

I'm not talking about a switch.

A switch is a person who likes to select different roles to meet their person needs at any particular moment.

When a person *shifts* roles it can often happen in the midst of already being in a role.

If a person is presenting themselves as a submissive and they shift, it is called 'topping out'. If a person is presenting themselves as a dominant and they shift, it is called 'bottoming out'. Many people move in and out of both roles as often as they inhale.

Usually they will want to primarily be in one role. Example, it is common for a person to dominate a scene until it comes to the sex part. Then they will shift over into submission for the sex.

The reason for this is that the submissive gets the good sex. In order to have really good sex, you have to be relaxed mentally so that your mind can let go of earthly concerns and run around in an altered erotic state.

Most people in kink don't really talk about this very much. Submissives want to trap their dominants into being dominant all the way through the sex part. Why not, they want the good sex.

In truth, the best sex is when both persons are submissive during the sexual act. No one really wants to be on top.

Pride and Punishment

Pride: A reasonable or justifiable self-respect.

During a recent all dominant gathering, a comment was offered regarding the stripping of pride as part of punishment for a submissive. The comment disturbed me and has lingered in my mind. There are many aspects to pride, some good and some bad. However, I have a continuing belief that pride is important. Or, to be more clear, self-respect is important. A healthy person takes pride in appearance, action, accomplishments, their home, their children, their country etc. Part of respect of these things includes a respect of self.

Self-respect is crucial for everyone. So often I am confronted by broken people who believe that all that is left is the submissive. This analysis always stuns me. To me the submissive is not the residue of life's battering, but a choice that occurs in the heart and soul to explore this aspect of self for a moment, a day or a lifetime. Submission is a learned and inherent aspect of human beings. The very first state of all humans is as a submissive infant in the care of others. When a person is at their peak, strong, healthy, happy, content, assured, and stable, they can then reach within themselves summon forth the aspect of their presentation that they wish to explore.

A lack of self respect suggests a lack of respect for others too. If you cannot value yourself enough to make positive healthy choices in your life, then you are demonstrating poor mental health. This is usually visible through slothful habits, (untreated) depression, drugs, alcohol, poor self care, bankruptcy, violence and abusive situations in the home, or out of control children, among others.

Kink is not a management system to rescue the victimized or those who have abandoned their own self care. At its core it requires hard and continuing work, particularly if you are preferring a D/s or M/s relationship. If your faculties are impaired then your consent may be invalid. For those exiting traumatic relationships or situations I suggest taking the years necessary to gather the controls in your life prior to venturing as a newcomer submissive into kink. Most of the practices in kink require strength, both physical and mental. It requires commitment, on levels and to issues more difficult than those confronted in the larger world.

The objective of anyone entering kink should be to enhance and improve their life. Destruction is not positive.

Pride isn't the same as vanity or excessive ego. To some extent pride is how we create value for behaviors. If you are working on a project you are likely in the position to choose whether to do that project well or marginally. Many people opt to do work only sufficiently enough to be paid. Some like to create the illusion of working hard while they really cut corners. They are putting in time. The work itself has no real value for them. The work is seen as a necessary hurdle to achieve what they actually value.

In a job what is usually valued is the money received for the work. Our culture is steadily moving the only metric of value towards monetary compensation. People are informed that money is the arbiter of status. Without money, the person or item is without value.

This is an unfortunate metric for any culture or individual to adopt. This type of metric devalues life and it devalues most of the joys and wonders of life. Money reduces value to a disposable currency.

Pride can be directly associated with the money metric. Most people buy new objects to demonstrate their level of value in a money metric society. By wearing new clothing, driving a new car and using a new cell phone they silently inform others of conformity and agreement with the money metric and they demonstrate their worth. This means they have a finite cash value. They are told they are worth X dollar amount. Often they express great pride at this applied number.

The number doesn't have anything to do with whether they are a good parent, whether they treat their elderly parents with love and kindness, whether they assist their community in supporting incompetent or dependent people such as those who are mentally ill, indigent, homeless, or without food or shelter. It doesn't mean they care about the quality of their water supply, the toxins in their food, the destruction of wildlife habitat, and the growing inequity between the poor and the wealthy. Your value number only recognizes how much cash it takes to buy your time, your life.

Pride in your work or working hard and well because it has its own value is often a metric that is talked about but not practiced. Most companies want their employees to work hard but they also want to devalue that work by paying very little for that hard work. It isn't any surprise that many people don't work hard and they don't find any satisfaction or take pride in their actual work.

In this way you can see how pride operates both in positive and negative terms. The same is true in pride of self, or self respect. No two people in kink have the same goals but in general, most people want increased satisfaction. That satisfaction may set up as a relationship or a singular kink sexual encounter. How they get to that point is often considered work.

However, this is a mistake. Self respect is the view each person has of their own actions and behaviors. It's possible to respect yourself if you achieve a goal you set for yourself. But, once you achieve any specific goal it moves into the past. You cannot hold it as a constant in the present no matter how much you want to do so.

Some goals you never actually achieve, you are always in the process of achieving them. Eventually you notice that the process of achieving has its own values. They may not be based on the money metric. In fact they are seldom related to money in any direct way. Taking pride in all of the tiny choices and behaviors that you do each day produces good feelings.

While your results may be temporary, quickly swept away by time, there is value in self investment. Fulfilling any role in kink is about continuing choices over time. You never actually become submissive or dominant but you make choices, hundreds of minor choices that show your interest and commitment to your path for yourself. Your choices are not actually for your potential partner. The relationship you are building and supporting is your relationship with yourself. You learn self value by practicing self value.

Where you practice is in all of the minutea of your daily life, it isn't centered in a scene or kink interaction. You are visible at all times to your own mind. It is your mind that assigns personal value, not persons outside of you. You may listen and believe what other people tell you about yourself, but, beneath the viewpoint of other people is your viewpoint of yourself.

By refining and taking value in your own capabilities you support your inner truth. Today I'm writing this book. I am working very hard to create the best possible material for you to read and think about. I have some pride in this effort in the sense that I believe my strong interest and tight focus is producing the level of content I believe you deserve to read. You deserve my best.

I could write something simple and easy. I could repeat what other people say and call it a book. If I did, I would be doing you a disservice, in my viewpoint. The value of my writing is not based on how many people might buy my book, but by how many people might find comfort and support in my work, in my words. By how many people will be inspired to challenge their own obstacles and seek out new ways to remove those obstacles. These values are intangible.

In this process I try hard to guard myself against delusion and ego. I make every effort to remain humble and simple. My writing is my conversation with you. Without you, my conversation is only with myself. I need you for my conversation to thrive and flourish. It can never be otherwise.

The dominant and submissive are roles in conversation with each other. One cannot exist without the other. One person cannot silence the other. When they try, they speak only to themselves and they are alone.

You probably didn't approach kink to be alone.

PUNISHMENT: Punishment is the imposition or removal of something for the express purpose of retribution or the intentional modification of thinking or behavior.

If you enjoy the idea of including punishment in your D/s or M/s relationship you are essentially establishing a dependency based relationship. This is a relationship similar to a parent/child dynamic. Keep in mind that the outcome of most dependency relationships is for the dependent to exit the relationship dynamic.

To some extent there is an existing time limitation to acceptance of a dependency relationship. Frequently, since we are speaking about adults who are intentionally re-instituting the framework of a formerly failed dependency, it is common for independence and dependency to be the actual issues that both partners are working on.

Just because you are strongly attracted to a dependency relationship doesn't mean your attraction will prevent potential relationship failures. The actual practices of dependency may fatigue quickly.

That said, how do you formulate the punishment structure between adults? You cannot assume that childhood punishments will translate. Some people increase this dependency by incorporating age play where the submissive partner is also perceived as much younger. In this way the punishments are actually part of the scening and fetishes.

This means they are not punishments. Actual punishment in this instance would be the removal of scening with the fetishes. In this example you would cease age play and discuss the issue as peer adults. Scened punishments that are fetishes are fake punishments. They are actually scening rewards. In other words you cannot use a scene punishment to correct behavior or express disapproval towards your partner. If you do so, you are actually rewarding the behavior in question.

What does your partner truly dislike? I guarantee that after a fairly short time interacting with your partner you will know enough about them to understand their triggers both positive and negative. Punishments should be based on activities the submissive dislikes, in general this is usually a level of attention removal. A dominant can show displeasure and direct the submissive's attention toward what needs changed most effectively by using variations on this technique. A healthy submissive wants to please the dominant, and most often will self-punish when he or she feels they have failed them.

Some submissives desire and need to feel and be humiliated. The action of humiliation and degradation employed during scene between a dominant and submissive is not punishment. For those most often participating in this aspect of BDSM it is a very real part of their need and pleasure. It is the action of the dominant focusing time, energy and attention on that submissive in the manner agreed to as part of the range of play.

Punishment is the removal of that which summons pleasure and joy. A submissive being punished should not be in scene in any form. Play or the giving and sharing of attention is the reward for accomplishment.

- Avoid corporal punishment. If your submissive is masochistic this is a reward. If your submissive is not masochist it can be abusive. You can 'scene' corporal punishment with a like-minded masochist.
- Avoid verbal battery. Calling your partner names in anger will torpedo your relationship and your partners self esteem. Leave or find a separate space to calm down. Exit D/s relationship roles and talk

together as peer-adults.
- Don't make threats. If you can't communicate without threats, go see a relationship counselor who offers communication classes. Practice.
- Any punishment you create should be positive. Your creative punishment should relate to the infraction in some way while not being destructive.
- Use rewards to motivate behavior changes. You know what your partner likes, use your knowledge to encourage them.

SERVICE is one of the most overlooked aspects of a long-term D/s full-time relationship. Service is the orientation of both partners within the relationship towards each other. We often hear of service submissives but very seldom does anyone talk about service dominants.

The ideas are not mutually exclusive. D/s relationships tend to be very intimately involved and often present unique and complex issues. The majority of a couple's relationship exists outside of the play arena or scening. Living within the structure of D/s outside of the scene is quite often much more difficult than anything else in BDSM.

It is relatively easy to be dominant or submissive in short spells where the focus tends to be toward pleasure, scening and brief weekends of role-playing the relationship. It is much harder to extend those roles into every aspect of your daily life. Rules of conduct which seem so necessary in short term affairs can quickly become non-functional when the necessity of altering or shifting roles occurs within a full time relationship.

The simply fact is that rules limit behaviors and can stymie growth. You may see some real apparent benefits to having these limitations at least in the beginning. It looks and feels like a D/s relationship. Everything is nicely compartmentalized; one person is on top who is responsible for all the decisions and one person is on the bottom who is responsible for accepting all the decisions. Only, unless you are with someone 24 hours out of every day and unless your submissive has no opinions about their life, wants and needs at all then this simply doesn't work. Relationships do not exist in a vacuum. Life is in constant change, it can and often does require spontaneous decisions and demands a level of flexibility in order to move through the chaos with some level of dignity and hopefully happiness.

Rules created to foster rituals of respect or limit the mental freedom of another person usually end up constraining the creator of them. What is less obvious is that each of those rules takes maintenance. Should a rule exist that is temporarily suspended for some ongoing real life issue or problem then that rule is demonstrating a failure or rigidity. If life changes *(as it always does)* requiring partners to share their responsibilities differently, then enforcing these rules can become not only impossible but totally impractical.

Rules that are present but not enforced are meaningless. Sporadic enforcement will elicit feelings of contempt, frustration and disrespect. In general, the fewer number of rules the better. Utilizing the full potential of your partner's abilities without feeling challenged or personally threatened by their personal power is essential. If you control out of fear of strength then at some point you will choke off a majority of the good things which exist between you.

We talk a lot about trust relating to scening, however, trusting the choices of your partner is even more critical. Respect moves both ways within a D/s relationship. Fear of allowing your partner to make choices can cause your partner to lose respect for you, or they may become ego damaged with heightened sensitivity to failure. In either case your partner will not perform to their capacity, a part of their energy will be eaten up in maintaining the knowledge that you fundamentally distrust them, which is another form of disrespect.

With a healthy relationship each partner will have an awareness of each other, they will essentially be oriented toward aiding, assisting, lifting, propelling, or otherwise making life better for their partner. There is a fundamental truth that by making your partner stronger, you make the relationship stronger. You are actively demonstrating both trust and respect which builds that strength. The delegation of power is a demonstration of strength. Expressing respect through trust is enormously important.

Many people appear to believe that strength encourages conflict and through that belief develop a concept that strength should be broken. The reverse is actually true. If both people believe that they are working with and for each other, then the need to be visible by argument, challenge or otherwise confronting their partner will diminish. Conflict generally occurs when one person feels devalued, not adequately trusted or respected, or simply ignored. If you are in the habit of silencing your partner you are in the business of creating conflict and hurt feelings.

Control through intimidation or fear leads to misery, abuse, feelings of extreme negativity and eventually brings devastation to whatever relationship continues to exist. We can be afraid of many things: we can be afraid our partner will cheat on us, afraid they will make bad decisions, afraid they will hurt us, and afraid they will leave us. All of these types of fear can create great personal insecurity that can be expressed outward by manifestations of lack of trust. Often issues, events or problems are created through expressions of fear. People literally create the very thing they are afraid of.

You have to set aside fear.

Control is the voluntary cooperation of two people within a relationship. Increasing or enhancing the desire to voluntarily cooperate is at the heart of building a long term 24/7 relationship. We encourage this cooperation by honoring, respecting, trusting, desiring and caring for our partners. By expressing positives, encouragement, approval and general agreement our energy is directed toward building or creating.

If either partner is focused on their personal needs or is overly attentive to the play or scening aspects of BDSM, then working through the often mundane challenges of daily live will be done with a strong lack of enthusiasm, which their partner will inevitably sense. This lack of commitment towards the core of the relationship *(which is serving the needs of someone else)* almost always results in fractured relationships. Many such people will create situations of conflict in order to escape the work of building a life together. Sometimes they try to use D/s or their role to force their partner into inappropriate scening rather than listening to criticism or sharing their part in making the relationship work.

Rituals
Presentation
Ritual: Formal or customarily repeated act or series of actions.

Rituals are most often associated with religious faiths or beliefs, but in actuality they exist throughout our daily lives under other names. Some are habits. Some are routines or duties. All of them are patterns that we follow in the performance of daily tasks. By doing actions in certain patterns we feel better or tend to believe that something has been done properly. In extension this can be a form of direct homage or an offering of respect.

The removal of or altering of patterns within our lives causes stress on the individual. We tend to feel secure within our known habits and the expected behaviors of others around us. This is shared culture. Things outside of these norms are always different and may make us feel out of control or unsafe. Most people try to do things the proper way. This can be all the way down to such things as deciding whether the toilet paper should fall over the top or pull down from under the bottom. Such detail may seem idiotic when looked at externally, but within the individual things out of proper order lead to feelings of insecurity and disconnection.

We create rituals, habits and patterns to help us manage or cope with our lives. Within these rituals we are in control and existence or even reality can appear measured and understandable.

For many people within kink there is a desire for new rituals that are kink specific. The most common rituals are titles and wearing certain clothing or lack of clothing, and creating a series of behaviors to indicate the entering of a kink scene.

Presentation Rituals

There are numerous presentation rituals. Essentially a presentation ritual is a customary pattern of actions that the dominant within the relationship creates for the submissive to learn and use when that submissive presents themselves in submissive role before that dominant. The individual ritual is designed around the circumstances particular to the submissive and their role or roles within the relationship. Some general or broad rituals will be described below.

Public Greetings

Within most kink greetings in public spaces there is generally a desire to maintain relationship privacy while at the same time demonstrating cues regarding relationship status if the meeting is with other kink related persons.

At a first time meet and greet, the dominant within the relationship should instruct the submissive prior to meeting in the exact manner or language they find acceptable for a socially open meeting. Many dominants do not allow a submissive to address them using their proper name which forces the submissive into addressing the dominant as Sir or Ma'am in public. In general most dominants do not wish to be openly associated with the kink community in public. The dominant should offer an alternative title or name that is acceptable for the public venue.

By addressing your dominant as Sir or Ma'am you immediately fall into normal or vanilla formal protocol or detached proper social behavior. This type of protocol will serve a submissive quite well in virtually all situations. Formal etiquette creates a distance between the two people and demand responses that are less familiar than say those demonstrated between lovers or close friends. If Sir and Ma'am sound too formal for the known intimacy of your relationship *(as in if your friends, family and co-workers understand your relationship to be boyfriend/girlfriend or engaged or even married)* then you should create appropriate specific 'names' which can be used to indicate intimacy-these might include 'pet' names or nicknames which are acceptable in any company.

In addition many dominants do not allow a submissive to touch them without permission. A submissive should wait for the dominant to indicate through body language *(such as an extended hand <to shake> or open arms <to hug>)* when such touching is permissible. If a dominant does not indicate this, then the submissive should not attempt to promote it or force it by extending their own hand or arms.

It is common for many submissives to follow a protocol of lowered eyes. This gesture is supposed show deference to and before their dominant until, unless or when that dominant should give them formal permission to lift eyes.

Personally, I prefer to talk to people and look them in the eye except during some scenes. In public I am not looking to perform for others as it is just not my kink.

Private Presentation

This type of presentation can vary in literally hundreds of ways so I shall simply describe a few options to show what types of rituals can be easily created.

In general when a dominant and submissive are alone there is a mutual desire for a full expression or demonstration of role between them. This ritual is an offering and the submissive should consider that every time they present themselves. The quality of the presentation should be a full reflection of their feelings for that dominant, the respect and admiration they have for them, the desire they have to serve and give of themselves fully into the care and concern of that dominant.

The object is not to simply kneel quickly, but to kneel beautifully, joyously and fully. If that's not possible, don't make a hash of it. Dominants like to look at their partners because it is fun. On the other hand, if your knees are crap, don't kneel and damage your knees. Say something. Sit sideways or in a way that is pleasing to your partner and not hurtful to your body. A presentation can be luscious, sensual, erotic and completely unique to the individual couple. It can also be interactive.

As you age a lot of so-called submissive rituals become painful or impossible. It's okay. You are only capable of what you are capable of. Be serious if your interaction is serious, be playful if that is appropriate, be naughty too or resistant.

A ritual should work but it shouldn't squash relating. It is like shaking hands. Maybe it is more. Maybe your rituals are deeply important. Structure them to fully meet the needs of your relationship.

In new relationships rituals help both people establish role and demeanor in scene. After a time these rituals may lapse into disuse. This doesn't mean you aren't kinky but it may mean your needs have changed as the performance around new relationship shifts into regular behavior.

Most kink rituals are so infrequent that they don't become habitual unless a person is engaging in them with great frequency.

Creating rituals reinforces many things between the dominant and submissive. It is important for the dominant to clearly teach or show the submissive what they personally desire and expect from the submissive. A dominant should not assume that a submissive will just know things. A large majority of common kink rituals are based on military positions and formal or court etiquette.

A submissive may have been inside the lifestyle for 20 years, yet they cannot possibly know your individual needs and requirements. Design rituals around simple forms which are pleasing that your individual submissive can easily *(physically)* accomplish. These rituals are often called homage rituals. Since a large percentage of those initially created are used to directly reinforce the roles of master/mistress and slave, the submissive is giving homage to their dominant.

A dominant who likes rituals should create a small number of rituals which they should train their submissive to follow. They should repeat or use these simple rituals as often as possible to enhance and reinforce the connections between themselves and their submissive. Repetition creates a habit, eventually a habit becomes so internalized that it is simply part of the response and it will not require thought. This is essentially how you train specific response behaviors. It is usually the desire for the submissive to behave as you wish for them without stress or conflict. With a perfectly trained submissive the responses become so fluid as to become automatic. Eventually the submissive will fully claim the response as part of their normal or natural responses. It will become integrated and simply how they present themselves during role and often in general. It simply becomes as common as shaking hands or saying hello.

Management

Many things go on during the evolution of a relationship between a dominant and submissive. In the beginning both people are filled with somewhat nebulous hopes, dreams and ideas. For the submissive, they mentally decide that they can submit fully even though this is for the a completely untried state and a long time frame.

It is fairly easy for the mind to accept a role in the short term, as in small clusters of time with their dominant. External to those short periods of time that submissive returns to their normal state or condition which is likely not the least bit submissive. Their mind creates a window of time where it permits the submissive to present their submission but that isn't how it feels to the person. Many feel that this is their natural state and what they do the rest of the time is the unnatural state. This, in many ways, is a delusion.

This is what the person wants to be true. This is the story of how they want to be a full-time submissive. This submissive practice period can extend for a long time, sometimes years. The submissive can become quite comfortable with this version of being in submission and usually they consider themselves to be a full submissive. Eventually, many arrange to join their dominant so that they can live together on a full-time basis.

While this shift doesn't seem like a big difference, it is. When you live separately from your partner you invariably dominate your life choices including the time and how you will submit. When you move in with the other person, all of this is disrupted. It is likely that you have been unaware of your recovery time between being or performing actively submissive.

Once you move your submission has no escape. No matter how well intentioned or trained or committed the submissive is to making the new relationship work, they will encounter the same frailties of their previous romantic relationships.

The discovery that their dominant is imperfect is often expected yet unpleasant all the same. What does a submissive do when they are confronted with behaviors they never really noticed in their partner prior to moving in with them?

The romanticized version of D/s doesn't really offer great suggestions for how to communicate when stupid little things bug you. Yes, you've read here and everywhere about communication being the key but this is D/s and you have agreed to comply with direction and possibly you've agreed not to question what your dominant does, says, thinks, or otherwise expresses.

I'm potentially talking about bad habits. Annoying bad habits. What does the submissive do to tell the dominant that they have issues or problems or bad habits? In the mind prior to all of this no contingency was created to deal with bad behaviors on the part of the dominant. Not big bad behaviors, but the small stuff.

What if your dominant is lazy? What if he doesn't like to put his dirty clothes in the hamper or he leaves the refrigerator open and food spoils? Trust me, every dominant has bad habits of some kind or the other. If you set up a relationship with only one-way directional balance, then one person will push and the other will be pushed over.

This is D/s but it is B/s too (bullshit). D/s as an excuse for being suddenly lazy and unwilling to do your fair share of help in the relationship or the shared home is not D/s.

The mind of a submissive is determined to reshape their world into D/s perfection but functionally the human being is able to perform a role for only a limited period of time before the other aspects of the personality increase pressure until they can release. And, they will release and usually it isn't soft and cuddly. Often the submissive is somewhat unaware that any of this is occurring and may find from the inside that they feel restless, angry, resentful, combative and destructive but often the source of these feelings will be unfocused. It couldn't be the way their new relationship is set up it must be something else. Maybe they aren't submissive enough or their new partner isn't dominant enough. Maybe they are too strong for their new dominant to control. (That is a favorite.)

To turn their whole world around they have convinced themselves that they are perfectly submissive. Often, especially for new dominants and submissives, there are elaborate creations or expectations on what a full D/s relationship is going to be like in the real world. People build up fantasy worlds of submission and dominance. Moving from a somewhat infrequent or occasional meetings to a relationship where two people live together instantly puts the submissive and dominant in a state of performance pressure.

There is usually a genuine desire to maintain the roles they have created and often a complete inability to do so in the created form. Adjusting from the illusion to reality is perhaps one of the most difficult things a submissive ever does.

Typically the two people need to take a break from the initial form of the relationship and talk about it again. In fact, they may find that they have to do this adjustment process many times before they can work out a structure that is workable for both people. Will it be 24/7 D/s. Probably not. It is likely that D/s will continue to be important to both of them but it is unlikely that everything that happens inside the home or when the couple are private will be kinky.

It is important that during this process that neither person should worry that their partner is looking elsewhere. If either person is shopping for a replacement partner it will destabilize the potential relationship further.

Sometimes the non-submissive parts of the submissive will want to destroy the relationship because it requires constant submission and no person is constantly submissive. Inside there are parts of them that will not wish to surrender the last vestiges of control.

If a dominant is pushing for additional submissives they can pretty much guarantee that their current relationship will decay and probably end quickly. Poly is not a solution for relationship problems.

Both partners need to discuss what is happening and why. Both need to come to terms with the challenges of constant performance and they need to find ways to recuperate in safety and in assurance that these periods of non-D/s are necessary and important for both people.

You can't punish away these kinds of issues or problems. You can't use discipline.

Be sure to set up your relationship so that it is manageable. In this I mean that a submissive is not submissive all the time, nor is a dominant, dominant all of the time. Create space where both can relax and be vanilla, talk openly without reprisal and engage in exchanges where both are equal. These spaces do not challenge the roles, actually they release the needs of the psyche to express all sides of itself.

Neither person should believe that they should be in the business of micro-management of every detail of life. Discover what each person is good at and give that person authority in that area. Create ways to come together and express their D/s interests in loving and enjoyable ways. If D/s is used as the means of control then it will quickly be something that is unpleasant and that defeats the purpose. Be in control of when and where you require the submissive to be submissive to you. Successful relationships require hard work and consistent focus and attention from both persons.

Passive Discipline

Discipline. The word is part of BDSM but its definition is a bit elusive. In general, in kink, it tends to mean any type of sensory stimulation applied to the body of another person. Is this stimulation done to actually discipline the person? Not usually. Mostly it is done for fun and because people want the experience.

The discipline as a frame is quite popular. You will see lots of fetishes that incorporate someone being naughty and someone *disciplining* them.

These are scenes and most scenes incorporate some kind of discipline. Again, it isn't intended to actually correct behavior, offer training or anything else.

A scene is one person giving another person their attention.

Many people want to experiment with real punishment and real discipline. If you are one of these people then one possibility is through passive or non-responsive discipline. This is the opposite of giving attention or giving direction. From a dominant's perspective it is often the most effective discipline that can be implemented to correct inappropriate behavior actions used by a submissive if your preference is not simple communication. It is important to remember that most submissives take action to gain attention or test the focus and strength of their dominant. These behaviors are most common in less experienced submissives, and in submissives who are in the first 2 years of a potentially long-term relationship.

Sometimes discipline works, sometimes not. The reason it might work is because the recipient wants it to work. The reason it doesn't work is because it is applied towards the wrong issue.

If a person is not receiving adequate attention to begin with and you withdraw more attention, it is likely not going to turn out particularly well and in reality it may mean that your libido for kink or your rate of renewals are too far apart for the relationship to work.

Still, lots of people want to try this because in their past relationships they tried the communication thing and it didn't end well. Usually they were made to feel wrong about one or many things and they don't want to feel like anything might actually be their personal problem.

Discipline can allow the dominant to shift responsibility and blame onto the submissive. If a submissive is acting out the objective isn't to stop them from acting out. The objective is to find out why they are acting out so that it won't be necessary for them to use this tactic in the future. Applying discipline can be effective at silencing the submissive and temporarily changing the offending behavior.

Generally a submissive will behave to perfection in the first 3 to 6 months of the relationship. This is quite similar to a vanilla honeymoon phase. Their dominant/master/mistress is perfect. They are so lucky. The world smells like roses and honey. Life is so fabulous. They are so happy. Then small things begin to be noticed. Their master/mistress has flaws.

The submissive doesn't really want to focus on these flaws but they can see them very well. And, shouldn't they help their dominant by pointing these minor things out, especially if their dominant is rather inexperienced? And, there is this edge of restlessness, the collar they have accepted so eagerly is getting a bit tighter now that plans are underway to possibly merge households. As the time grows closer their restlessness and sense of impending real confinement grows more real. A part of them isn't really sure that they are ready to relinquish control.

Sometimes a submissive just has needs. They may have an almost insatiable appetite for attention. To attain this attention they will utilize almost any type of emotional outburst or ploy. Some of the favorites are "I am not worthy of you…" This is a demand for the dominant to reassure them again, that they are so special. Then there is the guilt "…You promised to call me…I waited for hours…" or something dramatic happens. A personal crisis; they are devastated, crying, overwrought, clinging like a noose.

Often a submissive will do something they know is forbidden, plunging the relationship into serious waters, creating a potentially relationship breaking crisis. In the midst of this they will often plea for forgiveness, saying that they are a terrible submissive and that their dominant should get rid of them. All of these are fairly common submissive voluntary actions.

With a new dominant such actions can be baffling and very hard to cope with. Talking with their submissive can feel like they are in a small boat being buffeted by huge waves of energy or perhaps on the movie set of some overly dramatic story. Fairly quickly the dominant will realize that the submissive is creating scenes; emotional, distraught, conflicting scenes. Nothing positive is gained during one of these scenes except that the submissive gets fed energy. Sometimes hard words are said. In the end the dominant often feels totally drained, frustrated, irritated, empty and alone. It becomes essential to consider how to direct a submissive out of what is essentially old familiar vanilla habits so that these scenes do not destroy the complete relationship, the feelings of trust and respect.

One choice is to be non-responsive to any submissive who is improperly acting out or offering direct challenges to the direction or word of the dominant.

A better choice is to step out of D/s. Indicate to the other person that the role play will cease until the source of the issue is identified and until the submissive creates a plan to address the source.

By making behavior correction the responsibility of the person with the behavior the dominant (in this case) is not 'topped' into scening.

If your partner has physical needs you can't address don't tell yourself that they can 'stuff' their needs until you are good and ready. What happened in their last relationship? Each person is primarily interested in their own needs first. No matter what they say and how desperately they try to convince you otherwise, each person is living with their own need state. They are visiting your need state.

Work together to resolve imbalances in the relationship. Discover if one person prefers to be pushed. Some dominants actually feed off the bratty behavior of a submissive in order to propel them into a 'spontaneous' scene. Pay attention and learn about how you behave and what works for you.

Don't blame others if this is a process that you are actually reliant upon. Talk about it.

How to engage in productive communication:

You are going to have communication problems with your partner. It is likely that your upbringing did not make you an expert at productive communication. Most people 'wage' communicate. This means they allow their discontent to build up to the tipping point and then they throw words and accusations at each other like they are waging a verbal war.

The result of wage communication is that no one listens. While one person is yelling the other is planning out what they are going to yell when the first person takes a breath. Both will yell and escalate until one person leaves or until someone gets hurt.

That isn't productive.

Try the egg timer method:
- Use a 30 minute timer.
- Set the timer. While the timer is running only one person talks.
- When the buzzer sounds ask the person who is listening what they heard.

Often it is a good idea to use a tape recorder for your first few experiments or require the listening person to take notes.

- Have the listening person state what they heard, not answer what they heard.

This will be difficult for most people. Most people have never practiced active listening or good note taking. The listener should be able to reflect exactly what the other person said, not what they think the other person meant. This may take 15 minutes or longer. While they are reflecting back the content of the first person the first person should not argue. If they feel they haven't been heard accurately, have them play back the tape recording of the section that hasn't been heard, asking the second person to listen again.

The first few times you do this it will be frustrating

because people are invested in being right and winning an argument. They are less invested in being heard or listening carefully.

Once both people believe the first persons content has been properly heard it is time for the egg timer again.

- Use a 30 minute timer.
- Set the timer. While the timer is running only the second person talks.
- When the buzzer sounds ask the person who is listening what they heard.

Both people will quickly learn that this is a very challenging exercise. Because neither person is given privilege and both are tasked with careful listening it becomes much more difficult to power 'over' the content of the other person. By listening carefully each person must actually 'hear' the content of the other person.

This will be uncomfortable. You will hear things you want to deny are true. Instead of rushing to defend yourself, listen. Each person's viewpoint is valid. There isn't a right or wrong. Instead there are two views of the same situation.

The workable solutions are usually between the two perspectives.

Usually a couple can only manage one of these complete sessions at a time. They are emotional and difficult. Once both sides have been correctly heard, don't do an answer or explanation session. Agree before you start (at the very beginning) that each of you will take your notes and go to another room separately and think about what your partner said.

Refrain from talking about it for 24 hours.

- The next day. Sit down with your partner again.
- Apologize to your partner for causing them distress. Each person should do this.
- Tell your partner that you 'listened' to them and their viewpoint was important for you to hear. Each person should do this.
- Ask your partner if they have any requests or suggestions for resolving the issues that have come up.
- Allow your partner to speak while you take notes and remain silent.
- The second person then asks the first person if they have any requests or suggestions for resolving the issues that have come up.

At this point both people are likely to have reasonable control over their emotions. By indicating that they value the perspective of their partner and by both people equally offering suggestions they can begin to see their relationship as teamwork.

Some people find this process helpful weekly. At some point it is likely to become less formal and each person learns to listen instead of yell.

Cooling down periods allow both people to think about what has been said. A cooling down period should never feel threatening or scary. It prevents a furthering of the commentary when heads are hot. At the end of sensitive communications each person needs time to absorb and reflect on what they have learned.

You can apply similar techniques for online relationships. Tell your submissive that if they become argumentative, manipulative, disagreeable, whiny, overly dramatic, overly emotional or excessively needy online or on the phone that you will restrict them from contacting you for incrementally increasing periods of time.

Move your contact from email to snail mail. Have them write out (by hand) a list of their biggest concern. The act of writing by hand slows down communication and forces a person to think about what is important.

When you receive the letter in the mail, read it and then allow at least 24 hours before you reply by letter, in the same way. This forces the communication to a week or two from beginning to end and it challenges the motivation by either person to receive instant attention. Much will happen over the weeks that it takes to communicate by mail.

The most common excuse used to *avoid* this method is concern over releasing your home address if the other person doesn't have it already. This is an excuse.

Purchase a P.O. Box and fund a similar P.O. Box for your potential partner if they claim inadequate funds.

The process of making this arrangement indicates the sincerity of the issue.

If one person has significantly more money than the other, that person can send a book of stamps, envelopes and notepaper to the other.

Some people will argue that they can't go to the post office or mail receipt center easily. If they continue to protest this 'method' then express your regret for their choice. Give them your P.O. Box and tell them not to contact you except through that box until the underlying issues are resolved.

People will bail. But, if a person is sincere in working through issues they will use regular mail and they will be forced by the process into some thinking time instead of impulse time.

Be sincere.

Hints for long distance cyber or phone training

Many people prefer the anonymity of cyber relationships. They want the interaction with another person but they want to avoid messing up their real life.

I will assume here that your relationships are at this point exclusively cyber/phone. I will further assume that this is by your willful choice and desire *(to keep a distance)*. When your submissive is at a distance from your physical reach you immediately become confronted with problems. When you or your submissive is new to kink the first thing to do is engage in mutual education about kink. Locate articles online and have each person read them and then you talk about what you have read. This allows you to engage in a conversation together while learning about kink and each other.

The objective of domination is to give clear directions. The objective of submission is to receive directions and comply or act upon those directions. You achieve both of these objectives with practice.

Most people like to set up web cams so that when they communicate online they can each see their potential partner. This can cause problems if one or both persons are married or in primary relationships and if they are hiding their activities from others.

However, you *should* set up web cams. Identify times where both parties are safe to use their cameras in privacy. The first obvious benefit for web cams is to provide real life footage of the other person. Online, many people pretend to be someone they aren't. Sometimes they pretend to be female when they are males or they hide their appearance behind fake photos.

Don't listen to excuses for why they don't have a web cam. No web cam, no online relationship.

Once web cams are up and running you can see and interact more directly. You should be able to quickly become expert at positioning the cameras to the direction where you can see what you want to see.

Avoid any interaction that places the submissive in danger. No candles. No electrical scening etc.

Typically people want to see genitals and breasts and a lot of fondling happens. Usually both people try to masturbate for satisfaction. The D/s comes in with one person giving direction to the other and both people enjoying the D/s aspect.

Humble

Humble: *not proud or haughty, not arrogant or assertive, reflecting, expressing or offered in a spirit of deference, respect or submission, unpretentious, lacking all signs of pride, aggressiveness or assertiveness.*

Humble behavior is perhaps one of the most difficult things to do. Our culture doesn't tend to value humility very much anymore. When a person responds humbly they may be subjected to teasing or derogative comments by others. We are taught that the idea of humility is great but this teaching usually doesn't translate into how we experience the world when we are actually humble. Often humility is considered to be faked in order to present a certain goody-two-shoes type of projection. By considering the behavior to be fake, people viewing humility can distance themselves from their own actions which are encouraged to be grandiose and self centered.

If you are humble other people will want to believe you are lying in order to gain positive admiration for your achievements without looking pompous. This is all a twisting of character values and self esteem. Many people think that self esteem is reflected when a person brags about their attainments. In truth, self esteem is a self evaluation where an individual values themselves and is not reliant on the positive feedback of others to prop up their self image. Self esteem is not being ego centric where an individual believes they are fabulous merely because they want to believe they are fabulous.

When a person tries to impose their viewpoints on others it reflects low self esteem. If a person cannot adequately advocate for their own needs, it reflects low self esteem. A person with normal or balanced self esteem won't feel driven to convert others to their point of view and they will value themselves enough to take good care of themselves and to equally reach out and take good care of others.

> *Self esteem is a huge factor in maintaining good mental health. Do you have daily practices to improve and heal your self esteem?*

Part of self esteem is inter-relational in that the wellness and caring of others is valued as much as the wellness and caring of self. Reaching this kind of balance in our culture is very difficult because it isn't oriented towards the money metric of success.

In the realm of D/s, humility and self esteem become even more significant. There are many who see only the overt sexual aspects of D/s without seeing the complex psychological struggles that each person makes to create and sustain meaningful and loving relationships in their life.

D/s is an attempt by two people to form a lasting relationship with new kinky features. Both people are unsuccessful when they enter this attempt. If they were successful, they would not be trying to enter this type of relationship now.

Failure is often interpreted by the individual as a blow to the self valuation. This means that most people trying to form D/s relationships have a good chance of having self esteem problems.

A new submissive will often feel obligated to present themselves as extra humble towards a new dominant. The problem here is that this is an artificial presentation designed to acquire the new relationship. The submissive will believe it is a genuine behavior. They will ignore the fact that in their former relationships they used behaviors that were not humble. They didn't feel humble in the past and they interpret their current desire to present themselves as humble as evidence of their submissive qualities.

Practicing humility isn't a bad thing but this perspective is a delusion. Delusions cause suffering. When you create a delusion and invest in it as if it is a fact then eventually, when it is proved to be inaccurate, you will suffer because the delusion sets up unattainable expectations and you build upon this faulty base critical elements of your relationship and of your understanding of self.

The dominant and the submissive are a team. Their union must be a true partnership. Both must desire a non-conflictive interaction style between successful individuals. They attain this through active decisions during the course of every day. In today's society there is strong emphasis on individuality and independence. Money becomes the goal, the indicator of success.

Humility emerges from a recognition of value in all human beings regardless of their good or bad behaviors.

A human being is seen as composed of all of the possibilities that reside in the individual. This offering of understanding, sympathy and empathy towards others equalizes the individual's understanding, sympathy and empathy towards themselves.

Humanity (and the world) benefit when each person performs their tasks well. While our culture preaches independence and status by virtue of money or celebrity, in fact we are all part of a much larger system. Our role within the life system of all things is essential but not unique or individually different from the value of the role of others.

In a relationship, performing the tasks that are yours to perform benefit the overall relationship. Each task should not require outside approval or reward but should be done with genuine joy based on self knowledge of its essential but equal value in benefiting the whole of the relationship.

When any person within a relationship fails to perform their relationship tasks to the fullest of their ability, this negatively effects the health of the relationship. One person cannot pick up the slack for the other.

I like to describe a relationship in this way: Imagine that each person lives in their own world and they are divided from their relationship partner by a stream. To create the relationship each person must build a joint bridge across this stream. In a solid relationship the two people will meet at the top of the bridge. In an unstable or unbalanced relationship one person will build the entire bridge into the world of the other. Because these bridges are in constant decay that person is constantly working to maintain their bridge. This takes lots of energy and at some point they know they are working alone and a relationship isn't about one person working alone on it.

As they spend all of their time working on the bridge and visiting the world of their partner, their own world begins to decay and wither because they don't have the time or energy to tend to themselves. Eventually, they must retreat across the bridge to their world and tend to their dying gardens otherwise they too will die.

Humility is the acts taken by both to constantly build the bridge towards each other.

Sometimes a dominant will ask a submissive to learn humility. Usually this occurs when the dominant believes that the submissive isn't acting deferential enough to meet the ideals of the dominant. While deference is a choice it is also a habit and often a behavior that indicates an evaluation of the person who wants to experience the deference. If a person isn't genuinely offering deference on their own it is likely they don't feel it.

The role of submissive is not a passive existence of someone of diminished status who must automatically genuflect both mentally and physically towards anyone who can self-identify as dominant.

Before a dominant 'blames' the lack of deference on other people, they must examine their own behaviors to see if they are behaving in ways that negate deference. If you are an asshole, and you make poor decisions, and you act out like a three-year-old with tantrums, it's likely that these behaviors are the true source of the lack of deference.

False humility and false deference are merely scripted

behaviors used to temporarily meet personal goals. When a person says things or behaves in a way merely to gain something for themselves, it means they are disingenuous and that the relationship is a lie.

The dominant, for his part, should cherish the strength of the submissive in even attempting to fulfill the many behavior shifts demanded by the role. He should understand the difficulty of not answering back in pride and aggression. He should understand that it is far harder to kneel than to stand, to give than to take.

Some people cannot offer deference. They look at all people skeptically and challenge all behaviors that are slightly questionable. They probably didn't start that way as infants but by the time they reach adulthood they have had hard lessons in trust. This doesn't mean they shouldn't be working on the hardness of their viewpoint. Learning humility and deference is as much choice as experience. It helps if the person, idea or concept you are deferring towards has a constant ethical merit. Over time, value is added by new experiences.

HUMILIATION... *and the female submissive*

Humiliation: *To subject to severe and vexing embarrassment. To shame.*

One of the most delicate practices of the BDSM community is the art form of directed, controlled, willful and consensual humiliation. Shame is a painful emotion cause by consciousness of guilt or impropriety, Within the area of humiliation the dynamics which are at play are in some ways different between the male submissive and the female submissive. Because of this I am speaking mostly to how women experience humiliation first.

You have to start with an understanding that women have lived under the oppression of patriarchy for several thousand years and that part of oppressive practices include using humiliation to diminish and control women.

Propriety is the fear of offending against conventional rules of behavior especially between the sexes. This is the standard of social acceptability. Historically only virginal females had value. Their virginity was literally traded for material goods. A female without virginity had little to no 'real' value. Propriety was the measure used to evaluate female value. Propriety usually relates to how women present and defend themselves in a sexual context towards men.

We are each the product of our gender, upbringing, culture and apparent material status. Positioning within this social structure is often apparent through the teaching and expectations of proper conduct. This is especially true for women. Women tend to be held to a different level of accountability from men where any apparent variation from the acceptable norm is severely punished. Issues relating to female sexuality, exposure, and promiscuity are tied up in cultural language of unacceptability. To be considered decent a woman must cover up, shut up, keep her legs crossed, her eyes down and her indecent opinions to herself. This is of course functional societal control (the patriarchy) at work.

To cross any of the societal boundaries can cause a woman to be cast out of her peer group, be physically, mentally and emotionally exposed to ridicule, cruelty and even physical assaults by virtually anyone and to be without the safeguards and protections given to a decent woman. Violating these boundaries can and does alter a woman's status within her family, friends and community. Stepping outside means she is asking for or deserving of physical, mental and emotional abuse. She becomes a lesser being; discountable and discardable.

Though our society is slowly changing and altering in some of these perspectives, we as human beings adapt to changing perspectives very slowly. Often we carry the same ideas and traditions as our grandparents, only now those ideas are not socially correct in the rhetoric of the day so we hide them and pretend that we are liberal enough to openly accept the variations and differences between us. We are weak. We judge each other. In some form we all jockey for apparent position, rank or status.

When it comes to using humiliation techniques on a female submissive these fundamental dynamics need to be considered and understood. Most men don't understand the experience or conditioning of women. Most men act with unconscious privilege and assault and diminish women without any awareness they are doing so. Adding intentional humiliation to this existing reality is very questionable.

What does the male dominant wish to be the outcome overall? Are you venting against a submissive for how you feel some other woman treated you in the past? By diminishing the female in front of you, do you experience some kind of vindication or vengeance?

The female does not wish to lose status especially with those persons whom she respects and loves such as family, friends and co-workers. That status is generally hard won and of significant value in how that female views herself in her world. However, many females submissives desire, want and need to be taken across these invisible boundaries into the person who lurks inside who enjoys all those naughty pleasures of the flesh that the proper and decent woman on the outside is forbidden to admit to.

The dominant walks a fine line of reinforcing the strong positive mental health and imagery that the submissive female needs to be happy and healthy while overtly violating or consensually forcing this same female to experience taboo language, dress, behavior and responses. Learning the nuances of your submissive female is crucial here. If she has been a victim of past explosively verbally assaultive language coupled to mental, physical or emotional abuse then she will probably have certain language or word triggers which thrust her into potentially severe memories and responses. It is very likely your female submissive has experienced all of the abuses mentioned. Statistics show that most if not all women endure abuse experiences in their lifetime.

This is not what the dominant wants to do. Humiliation, properly done, is part of a freeing process, a way for the sensual, erotic, impulsive woman/child within to escape the bonds of societal behavior and express herself in a completely reprehensible way. The best way to discover what a submissive wants is to ask her. Be specific. Ask or give her a list of words and tell her to talk to you and clearly state which words she wants to hear used on her and which ones bring up hateful or horrifying memories. This may take some time but it is essential to do prior to just jumping in there with words that may do true damage when that is not your intent.

Many apparent aspects of submission are shameful or in opposition to what most females have been taught is appropriate behavior for a modern woman. Coupled to this are the conflicting messages that have been taught over the past 30 years. For many female submissives the simple action of kneeling at the feet of a dominant for the first time is filled with excesses of emotion. She does not want anyone to see her doing this, especially her children and friends. It is the dominant's responsibility to ensure that her status remains inviolate. Never overtly humiliate your female submissive in or near her family, friends or co-workers. It is generally only acceptable to humiliate her in private or within acceptable surroundings such as the atmosphere of other D/s people wherein this is acceptable or non-status reducing conduct.

Most female submissives adapt fairly quickly to kneeling to their master/mistress, addressing them using agreed upon honorific titles and conceptualizing the in-the-presence behavior protocols established between the female submissive and her dominant. With a new submissive female every step is a ledge, a challenge, a mystery and a terror. She must believe that her dominant will not allow injury to befall her at exactly the same moment that she voluntarily agrees to obey instructions which are in direct opposition to everything she has been taught. This is an enormous undertaking. It takes courage, belief and trust. If you are a dominant, don't screw this up. Retain an awareness of the mental challenges at work with what may appear to you to be simple instructions.

If you stumble into anything which summons a lightning fast negative reaction do not rush to discipline or punish but step in and comfort your submissive and insist that she engage in a conversation to reveal the root cause of the reaction. You cannot know her path which she walked up to the moment you met her, you can guess at some, hear some from her but essentially the details of that life will forever remain somewhat mysterious.

The most common forms of humiliation that formerly vanilla women want or ask for are language of their socially unacceptable sisters. Words like slut, whore, and cunt are being reclaimed and desensitized by many women who have a fantasy of expressing the strong sexual sides of their personality and desires. They want the naughty and uncivil part of themselves to fly, to scream, to wear clothing that is too tight, too revealing, too sexy and they want their dominant to find them alluring, sluttish and sexually promiscuous. This is everything they have never been allowed to be. At the very same time they want and need their dominant to revere them. Mutual respect. If their dominant truly disrespects them then the submissive female's ego and self-image can be totally destroyed. Her ability to trust enough to be a slut can disappear and she can and may flee from this activity forever.

Speaking crudely to a submissive as well as handling her firmly can make her enormously aroused. Most female submissives do not wish to experience public humiliation such as being led down a street in their hometown where people may recognize them in a leash and collar. Many do like and want to be challenged into completing a task which places them at risk or in a position of embarrassment. This can be an assignment to go into a pet store *(not in their home town)* to try on various dog leashes in the presence or within view of the shop keeper and other customers. This can be a task such as to board a flight wearing a collar, dressed skimpily *(again a situation where she is relatively anonymous yet exposed)*. These adventures when successfully completed should be rewarded. It takes courage to face down the judging eyes of other people. It also makes the submissive stronger as she learns that she can do these things, the little getting away with something naughtiness.

Humiliating someone in a healthy and positive way is difficult. It is essential to remember that each of us is somewhat different every day. There are days when we are feeling strong and days when we are feeling weak. Crossing into negative diminishment is very easy to do especially at the early stages of a relationship. The objective is to create excitement, enjoyment and pleasure for both yourself and your submissive. It is not to destroy, injure or damage. Women hear words differently. Remember that they never forget negative cuts. These words of power become a litany that they hear forever. Once said you can never call them back. You may apologize and she may forgive but the words will still be there. When using humiliation techniques remember that at some point she may take such commentary out of context. This is especially true if you use language about or commenting to her appearance *(if she is fat etc.)* avoid the common diminishment techniques of society if possible. Humiliation done well reduces a submissive just to the point of sensual erotic free female. Do not use humiliation to punish her *–(language used in anger which* *is similar to 'play' or previously used 'affectionate humiliation language').* Doing this will alter the words or techniques from those of bonding, fun and excitement to verbal abuse - forever.

HUMILIATION... *and the male submissive*

Humiliation: *To subject to severe and vexing embarrassment. To shame.*

Humiliation and the male submissive is often the delivery of shame. As found with the female submissive, shame is a painful emotion cause by consciousness of guilt or impropriety. How this is done with, for and to a male submissive can be quiet different from the techniques that are effective for a female. A male submissive's evaluation of what is shameful, degrading or embarrassing is distinctively different. This is not really a surprise when you consider the diverse attitudes and level of expectation that exist in how a male tends to be raised in our society versus a female.

Where a female may lose status for actions of impropriety such as physical promiscuity, multiple sexual partners, having children outside of marriage, and dressing in a manner that is sexually provocative-a male may actually gain status through these same actions. Prowess is used instead of promiscuity, sometimes a score card of acquisitions is used to compare success in getting a female *(or male)* to put out. It is also important to note that attitudes of diminished status evaluations play into this as well. A man that is successful easily and early with a female will almost always hold that female in diminished respect.

Within kink a male submissive will often reveal a desire to be humiliated by a dominant. Frequently this humiliation includes or is centered on adopting the perceived role of the female. The male will want to be *forced* to dress in female clothing, makeup, hair and particularly high heels. They will also then desire to be sexually objectified in much the same way that they believe they constantly objectify women.

The equating of humiliation to being female cannot be escaped or overlooked as it is perhaps the most common humiliation fetish among male submissives. In addition the male submissive often uses the responsibility shift of a dominant to forcibly allow him to experience male-on-male sex. From this perspective the male submissive isn't responsible for wanting homosexual sex, it is being *forced* upon them.

What is driving these fetishes and desires?

Most men believe that women have enormous sexual power (over men). Most women believe that they only have sexual power if they emulate the perfect female body ideal (a rare temporary body shape). Men want to be wanted in the same way that they have experienced themselves wanting women. They want to be viewed as sexual objects and to feel desirable. They want to be punished for violating ideas of masculinity (homosexual sexual interest and dressing as a female) so that their fetish feels balanced out.

Male submissives do tend to enjoy overt verbal humiliation such as crude language (directed at their female aspect). Since promiscuity is to some extent socially acceptable for a male the language of being sluttish tends to carry an arousing message versus one of humiliation.

You cannot really humiliate a male using female derogatives. No matter how much the male fantasizes about being female, he isn't female. His role is temporary and usually not recognized as female outside of scening. (Exceptions here for transgenders.)

Non-gendered derogatory language is more effective. In addition many male submissives enjoy actions of public humiliation, exposure and parading *(again this is outside of their family, friends, community and co-workers)*. In general a male submissive's tolerance for humiliation is often higher than that of a female submissive. Male submissives do not tend to internalize the verbal language used more frequently in humiliation. The exception here is around past-experience bullying or name-calling.

Their orientation is generally more physical and less emotional, or perhaps more pragmatic and direct versus the often circuitous nature of a female submissive's mindset.

> *How does your lifetime experiences of physical and emotional abuse inform your interests and choices in kink?*

The language tends to be identified as exactly what it is and the male submissive is often quite able to respond to the language strictly as another in-scene toy. This does not mean that all male submissives are impervious to being injured through verbal humiliation. Quite the contrary. A large percentage of kink participants have experienced incidents or events of significant verbal, physical and emotional abuse in their past. To some extent these former events damage the individual in peculiar ways. For many submissives both male and female they have been essentially trained since early childhood to feel and experience things through pain, humiliation, fear, shame and guilt.

You may have an internal message that goes something like: "People who love me call me derogatory names." Doing this in an intentional and consensual way instead of a destructive way is often how many people find their way into kink. The two distinct differences are control and consent. When an action is taken through anger *(striking a child)*, there is a sensation that the abuser is out of control and there is a certainty that the child is not consenting to being hit. However, that same child learns love through these painful touches. As an adult those lessons remain and inform the child's adult relationships and behaviors. In a sense the triggers have been trained (much like Pavlov's dog using 'love' as the reward).

Many D/s people can only feel the sensations of love, desire and security through patterns of similarity. Often people struggle with patterns of selecting abusive people as their relationship 'type' even when they are trying very hard to avoid this type. The same negative behaviors that are so hurtful also summon the strongest feelings and make the individual feel more alive and in the moment. It is impossible to unlearn these early messages completely. If that person is in a relationship with no abuse features they often find it dull and unappealing because they don't feel loved. Kink offers a compromise of intentional 'roughness' coupled with control, consent and caring.

It is essential for the dominant to safeguard the emotional health of their submissive and to carefully identify what their submissive, as a unique individual, needs in order to achieve the experience which is most meaningful to both of you. There are male submissives and female submissives who cannot tolerate any type of humiliation and a dominant should never assume things but instead take the time to learn who that individual submissive is prior to taking generic actions which may trigger or damage them.

Many male submissive's desire for a dominant to take them across societal boundaries by allowing, accepting and enjoying their feminization. They want to believe that the dominant deeply enjoys feminizing them. They will often focus on demanding the dominant's enjoyment as an essential element of the fetish.

For a female dominant this can present conflicts. How does the dominant process the concept that the female is inferior (the object of the male's humiliation) while at the same time she is obviously a female? In addition, most male submissives carry a strong visual fantasy about the appearance of the women who will enjoy feminizing them. In general, this appearance is a highly sexualized doll-like visual with the female wearing slutty dominatrix attire.

As you can see, this type of fetish is all about serving the sexual interests of the male. Yes, some female dominants enjoy dressing their male submissives as females or other things. Women are typically conditioned to dressing dolls. Most women can interpret the male as a large doll. Still, the conflict continues.

How does the female dominant make her clothing

choices? On one hand most women are conditioned to be sexually appealing in any sexual environment. The idea that she would just show up in a t-shirt and jeans (more like how most male dominants show up to a scene) is counter-intuitive and it may present the woman with cognitive dissonance, particularly early in her explorations of kink.

Other factors weigh in here. Many female dominants are prodoms. A prodom is interested in retaining clients by pandering to their fetishes. This means the female is likely to dress up in the way the male expects in order to increase the amount she is paid for her time.

For a lifestyle female dominant the situation rapidly shifts to comfort. While she may want to dress sexy for a scene this desire is likely to subside quickly once she becomes more expert at scening.

Scening for a dominant is very physically hot. This means your body gets hot. You sweat and you are often uncomfortable. The last thing you want to wear is a lot of tight-fitting latex, leather or similar lingerie. You may want to dress up for a particular scene for effect or because you have your own sexual dress fetishes but you won't want to be uncomfortable scening another person.

This means that you will quickly shift to wearing stretchy, comfortable clothing. I happen to prefer leggings and a jogging top. I usually have a larger fan blowing directly on me during the entire scene. This is real life. I don't particularly care if my appearance is sexy at all. I don't wear make-up because it itches and smears when I get sweaty.

What I have learned over the years is that men 'get over' their visual fantasy thing rather fast, particularly if their fem dom isn't having sex with them anyway. The male is interested in his own needs first, regardless of how much he talks about serving the needs of the female dominant. His service is about having his needs met. He is gaining something from serving. The female dominant is interchangeable as a representation.

This shifts when people become life partners and invest deeply in each other's lives. But, early on and for some time every relationship starts out with each person trying to get their own needs met.

Bondage and Caging

Although you will see a lot of bondage images on fetish websites, no one talks about bondage as much as they should.

First, you don't need to be an expert at rope tying or shibari to do bondage. And, you should probably do bondage as it is by far the most popular fetish in kink. Bondage is the fast and easy way to give your partner permission to be naughty. If the person is tied up then they can't be held responsible for enjoying sex. There, that's the critical part of bondage.

Be safe. If you are brand new then you really should get a book on basic BDSM safety. Don't tie joints. Don't tie boobs so that they turn blue. Don't cut off circulation. Don't wrap things around the neck. Use proper cuffs if you put pressure on joints and if you don't know what I'm talking about, get educated before you try things out. Don't use duct tape on hairy places. Don't use shrink wrap too tightly for too long. At any sign of physical distress, remove the bondage. Otherwise, use common sense and have fun.

The desire to cage or be caged can be very strong. For the submissive/slave it can be the culmination of a lifetime of fantasies and dreams. To be captured and dragged off into capture and forced servitude or usage by a dominant is, to many, the ultimate act of desire on the part of the dominant or captor. There is the relinquishment of responsibility and the acknowledgment of acquired possession. Everyone wants to feel valued, desirable and desired. In addition there is the removal of constraint. An element of freedom and release of inhibition are intricately intertwined around the concept of being captured, caged, used, owned, possessed and forced.

The use of a cage denotes several things. It is stating that the captive is worthy of being kept and that this same captive is not quite tame but requires a level of external enslavement to keep them in the active possession of their owner.

Some dominants wish for their submissive/slave to know that they are owned and that their freedom of movement is not assured but granted on the whim of the dominant. There is an element of primal control in keeping a person collared and caged. It allows the dominant to 'feel' that their submissive/slave is there expressly to serve the dominant's pleasure. For many submissives/slaves the true act of being caged allows them to fully experience feelings of being owned in a similar fashion to a treasured pet or animal. Caging often occurs during a period or time of puppy, pet or pony training. The usage of an animal cage is often a significant part of reinforcing aspects of this type of training.

Caging can have other effects both positive and negative. It can create mental silence. Often we are so busy in our lives that our minds are spilling over with information, problems, bills, issues, chores, duties and obligations. We are so full that we haven't a moment to spare to think. We tend to be constantly acting and often reacting to stimuli. Being placed in a position of forced confinement without objects of entertainment can force the submissive to stop cycling and focus. For some, after becoming adapted to being confined, there is a sensation of peace. Within the cage they are free. There are no expectations, no obligations, chores, requirements, duties, issues or problems to deal with. There is only the cage, the silence, the reality of waiting to serve the dominant. Everything else leaves. Many submissives want to go home to their cages, so that the sense of chaos so pervasive in the outer world can be forced away from them. Within the cage they are safe, they are not allowed to deal with the chaos. In the most profound sense, the submissive is freed.

Non-consensual caging, such as forced imprisonment, can cause serious mental health issues. Forcible imprisonment is illegal. This type of non-consensual caging has no place within a consensual D/s relationship.

As with many types of D/s choices it is important for the dominant to remember that consent is not a stable force. If you and your submissive choose to experiment with various forms of restrictive bondage or caging then it is essential to keep in mind that the choices are not made for indefinite time periods. A first trial period should be clearly defined for the experiment. Every submissive will react to caging differently. Some will have loved the fantasy of being caged and detest the reality of it. Caging can be quite uncomfortable. In addition if a submissive/slave is caged then they are not being used. In other words their many and varied attributes, talents and gifts are not being used to actively benefit the relationship.

Often the first type of caging explored is the scene caging. This is where the submissive/slave is caged for an hour or two in a pre-scene state to prepare the for a scene later that day. This type of caging is generally safe if the cage is of sufficient size to allow the submissive/slave ample movement to stretch cramped muscles. It is important to remember that there is no desire to injure and that a cramped submissive/slave will not function well. There are many types of in-scene cages and these cages can be quite restrictive and made from various materials. Use them safely employing the same safety standards of blood flow, tissue damage as necessary in any type of bondage.

The second most common usage of the cage is the sleep caging. This is a cage set up in the home of the dominant exclusively to be used as the sleeping area for the submissive/slave. Buying cages or having them made can be quite expensive. It is important that if you are going to invest in this type of toy that you be very certain that it will enjoy long term usage and not be used once or twice and abandoned. A relatively inexpensive cage can be purchased in most pet stores for less than $100.00. In general the all metal cages are most preferred by dominants as they allow for full viewing of your naked slave and in-cage playing through the cage for short durations of time. These metal cages tend to be flimsy, sometimes with sharp edges, uncomfortable floors and potentially dangerous locking mechanisms. However, they will often do adequately for a short trial period (very short) prior to buying or having a custom cage made.

A typical trail period of first usage of a sleep cage might be for one week. This means that the cage would be used only during the sleep period and that the submissive/slave would be required to maintain a very active exercise regime during this experiment to ensure that muscles and tissues retain their health. In addition the dominant should place a piece of sheet plywood on the floor of the cage to level out the wire. This should be covered with matting or *(as some prefer-a dog bed)* for the nightly comfort of the submissive/slave. In addition the dominant needs to ensure that the submissive/slave is physically capable of such confinement, has all the necessary blankets for warmth and most importantly an escape key.

Most pre-manufactured small animal cages are constructed for external release only. While this may sound erotic and arousing it is extremely dangerous. Long-term caging means that the submissive is within the cage for significant time periods. Problems happen, fires happen. A dominant can provide the key to the cage to the submissive in a manner that will restrict its usage to emergency conditions only. This can be quite simply done. The dominant can place the key in a small envelope which is then sealed and attached to the inside of the cage. This will require the submissive to 'tear open' the envelope revealing any usage of the key if that key is used in a non-emergency situation. A dominant should force the submissive to practice opening the cage door using the key prior to caging them. Make sure that the submissive can do this even in poor to bad lighting conditions. If the locking mechanism is difficult to reach then the cage is poorly designed and may be too dangerous to use with adequate safety.

Assuming that the trial period passes and a reevaluation of the idea occurs, and the dominant and the submissive agree to implement caging on a longer term basis then they should actively seek out and invest in a good, designed-for-human-usage, cage. At that point I would suggest a hard floored *(or one with removable hard floor)* cage, one with adjustable internal stocks for scening, and easily unlockable door from both sides and of a size to comfortably fit the submissive. Expect a custom cage to be expensive so pre-plan on many types of usage to make it as flexible in design as possible.

It is important to listen to your submissive. If for any reason they cease taking pleasure in using the cage then you should not attempt to coerce or force them into imprisonment. Involuntary imprisonment is non-consensual and illegal. Caging should be fun, pleasurable, sexy, erotic, sensual and safe for both people engaged in it. Also, many people are surprised to discover that some submissives long for their cages and can be found inside of them reading books, using a laptop and munching on goodies with the door open. A cage can become a nest, a place of safety surrounded by the physical reality of possession by someone that the submissive loves.

Collars

A collar is exactly what it sounds like, a piece of leather, rubber, metal, rope or other material looped around the neck and connected or tied. In kink, collars are used both functionally and decoratively. It is common to see both dominants and submissives wearing collars or wearing jewelry that indicates a collared relationship. Just because someone is wearing something that appears to be a collar doesn't mean they are kinky, collared or submissive. It means they like collars.

Within kink the word collaring indicates the exchange of a collar from a dominant to a submissive that is used to indicate the status of the relationship. Historically a collar is used to indicate ownership such as placing a collar on a dog to indicate that it is a pet and that someone owns the pet and is responsible for the pet's actions.

American BDSM (culture) is generally identified as emerging from the Old Guard leather groups. The general historical story is that homosexual American soldiers returning from World War II were attracted to the leather garments common to military men who rode motorcycles during the war. After the war these men formed groups or met at gay-friendly bars to associate and the term 'leather-men' grew out of these groups and associations. Because many of the men were post-military they also retained much of their military training and began to incorporate that training in their growing kink interests. These groups became collectively known as the Old Guard. To have been an Old Guard member you would need to have been an adult of 18 in 1944. This means that most members of these groups are likely dead. There is a Leather Museum and Archives in Chicago. You can access more information about early leather at http://www.leatherarchives.org/about/about.htm. The site hosts more in-depth research regarding leather and the Old Guard community and how that community informs modern kink. I am not an expert on the Old Guard and it should be made clear that to the best of my understanding this wasn't a cohesive organization with defined rules, it was many groups and associations across the country with widely varying ideas and practices. My identification of collars and practices is based on my own knowledge received from people I knew when I entered kink.

Collar of Consideration

This collar is given by a dominant, master or top to their relationship partner when they believe the relationship is the equivalent of 'significant friendship'. Historically this collar is blue. Today few collars are blue and most people don't communicate via color in the heterosexual community in the same way that color is used in the homosexual kink community.

If you are considering someone it means they are more than a friend but less than a partner, it is more akin to a friend with benefits with the benefits being kink. It also means that you are thinking about the relationship in more long-term ways. Please note that a kink relationship does not have the same connotations of a vanilla relationship. It is common for people to have multiple partners at the same time who never meet and whose interests vary. This is more like poly-kink that is based on shared kink interests rather than shared love interests.

A collar of consideration does not indicate a lifelong commitment or love. It usually does mean that the relationship is more important than casual play. A person under consideration is likely to be a regular play partner over several months or longer.

In kink public, if a person is wearing a collar or anything remotely like a collar and you are required to interact with that person, ask them how they would like to be addressed. Usually they will offer a name or title to you immediately. Respond with common courtesy.

No person at a kink event is obligated to use honorific titles towards any other person. You are also not to use diminishing labels towards any other person. Just because a person is submissive doesn't mean they are submissive to you.

Training Collar

If a person has been under consideration for some time and the dominant has decided they have more than a friendly interest in that submissive, the dominant may ask the submissive if they want to wear a training collar. Historically a training collar is always made of leather, usually black or red and it is often functional. A functional collar means it will have 1-3 D rings that can be used in scening. It can mean the collar is locked at the back so that the submissive wears it constantly. It is more common today that more permanent or constant collars are made of less obvious materials. You can find seamless metal collars that look like fine jewelry and can be worn in the shower without rusting. These usually have hidden closures.

The objective of a training collar is to remind the submissive in a constant way that they are in the process of moving towards a deeper commitment with their partner and that this commitment includes the behaviors they assign to submission.

It is common for both dominants and submissives to wear identical collars at both the training and formal collaring stages as usually both people are more serious about their relationship and they want to show others their attachments (somewhat like engagement rings).

Similar to any engagement the training phase is usually where two people test out living together and applying their version of D/s on their relationship to see how it works in real life. This can be a long transition with many failures and problems before the couple works through the more difficult issues and is able to think about a more formal and permanent collar.

Formal Collar

At some point many people want the formality of a marriage to their partner. In kink this is called a collaring ceremony. It is increasingly common for both persons to wear identical locking collars to show the depth of their commitments to each other. Again, this reflects the influence of mainstream culture and the expectations of both people towards supporting traditions.

A formal collar is any collar that a person wears that represents the committed state of their kink relationship.

A collar doesn't mean two people are married or even living together 24/7. It doesn't mean two people are in love. It does mean two people are committed to pursuing their kink relationship fully along with its D/s or M/s features.

Many kink collaring ceremonies are big events where people dress up and engage in much the same types of behaviors you might see at a wedding except that there will be nudity, kink and often play happening as part of the environment or event.

If you are invited, bring a gift. Food, wine or other similar conventional gifts are fine. Kink gifts are more fine. Behave yourself as photos are likely to be taken. If the event is held in the couple's home, offer to help with dishes, garbage, vacuuming and similar mundane tasks so that the couple can spend their time enjoying their party rather than working at their party.

Velcro Collar

You don't need to be around any online fetish website for long before you discover the Velcro collar. This euphemism describes the popular online collaring. An online collaring is when two people meet on a fetish site and in a very short time they are collared. Often both people will gush over their big event and they will get quite angry when people question the sincerity of their collaring when people discover they haven't actually met in person. Usually there is a lot of fanfare and they will change their profile status and go in and out of forum message boards offering advice on pretty much everything. And then, a short time later, there will be a big blow up and poof the relationship is ended, the dominant has dropped off the website or simply changed their name, the status is wiped clean and there is a huge drama about 'fake' dominants or 'fake' submissives.

The easier a collar goes on, the easier it comes off too.

If you want to engage in collar and collaring practices that are meaningful you have to invest them with meaning in the first place.

Note: you don't have to collar anyone to be in a serious relationship with them kinky or otherwise. Collaring is something of a fetish, you either think it's essential or you may be a person who ignores it completely or maybe you wear collars because you like the way they look and feel.

Scene Building

People often ask me how to 'do' a scene. It sounds like something mysterious and difficult from the outside. It can be. I have done tightly scripted scenes that took weeks to prepare and I've done spontaneous scenes based on what was in my purse in the car.

A scene is an interaction between two people (usually in role) that has kink elements.

What is kinky? Ahhh, the million dollar question.

See, here's the thing – almost everything can be made kinky.

I tend to drive my car. This means if I am going somewhere with a submissive that they won't be responsible for driving. Sometimes I want to play.

I have been known to pull my car over and use bobby-pins from my purse on the nipples of my submissive during a short drive. This transforms a mundane drive to the grocery store into a scene.

This scene involved two bobby-pins. Yet, we were in public (in my car) and (in the store) and we shared this *secret*. The submissive invariably spaces out even though the stimulation is minor. The *idea* they are being sexually used is very exciting for them.

I offer this scene as a kind of clue. Scening doesn't need to be fancy or detailed every time. Your scening partner is with you hoping to have some adult fun.

Have fun. Be unexpected as long as it is something you can reasonably accomplish without causing problems.

If you really want a big scene (one that lasts several hours) you can script it out. Generally your submissive will have lots of fantasies that they will tell you over time. Keep notes. Anything in the submissive fantasy can make for a fun scene. Get it right. Pay attention to why it is a fantasy for them. Mix it up.

I frequently have men around me who like bondage. What they expect are leather cuffs and being tied spread eagle or hogtied. I've been known to use a simple carabiner from my submissive's collar to my passenger seat headrest (not while driving).

Park in some public park with a view. Your submissive will be self-conscious of people walking by. The carabiner holds them in the seat. You can have their hands under the seat belt and then simply play with their nipples under their shirt. It's fun. Be creative. Giggle while they struggle not to 'look' weird if anyone looks at them.

I write out big scripts and make sure I have everything I need on hand. I play it out in my mind until I know how I want it to go. On the day of the scene I know that my memory will be unstable. I usually keep an index card handy with my notes to refer to in case I forget where I wanted to go. The submissive never knows. Once they start flying their eyes may be closed for most of the time.

Sometimes scenes don't work. It's okay. Stop or change it up. Remember that your submissive may not be in the mood for your big scene. It's okay. There are other days and other times. Sometimes I have a scene planned and the person shows up and needs to talk to me. This is actually common in my life. I attract people who want to talk. Often it isn't kinky talk. It's okay. I can always talk. What is important is the relationship.

Relationships are living things, they need all kinds of tending. Don't rely on scenes as your answer to relating. Scenes are fun. Relationships and life are often serious and sometimes it is necessary to put aside fun and be a good support for other people.

When you are new don't think you can't scene your partner. Your best tools are your body. Touch is, by far, the most critical tool you will ever have. Learn to touch each other in all kinds of ways. You will find that your environment supplies all kinds of fun textures and elements you can turn into fun. Enjoy each other.

STERILE SAFETY

This section is provided to give you an overview of some of the issues related to sterilization and safety. I suggest you use this section to augment, amplify and complement other available texts since this book is not designed to offer comprehensive intense technical data on toys or their usage. I am including this section to make you aware of the potentially serious issues related to sterilization as they relate to play, your health and the health of every person you may scene with. Don't use this text as your sole resource on medical sterilization or safety. I am not offering professional medical advice. It is up to you to seek out professional information regarding the correct sterilization and safety instructions for your specific kink-related toys or practices.

While I've titled this section 'sterility' it is really about the ongoing issues with biohazards in kink. If you are like most people you will build up a kit. In this kit you will have metal, leather, wood, plastic, fibers, cloth, rubber, latex, and other stuff. Each of these items has different cleaning requirements to prevent passing diseases between the people who come into direct contact with your 'stuff'. Most people are not particularly tidy (by nature). Some are very conscientious about cleanliness but, overall, at the end of a scene one or both partners are tired with a primary desire to sleep.

By the following day some toys or objects will have been moved and some will be put away dirty. If you are in a public play space it is likely that most of your stuff will go back into your bag, dirty. You may place all of the soiled items in a to-be-cleaned bag inside your big bag but by the time you reach home you are tired and you leave things for – later.

This is the reality of how life operates. Your kinky stuff is probably 60% dirty this very minute. You know you *should* clean everything and be totally on top of such things but – is it getting done?

In general, if you play with most things and you don't break the skin of your play partner you mostly have skin cells, sweat, slobber and genital excretions on your stuff. All of this is pretty much invisible unless you own a bio-fluids detector (buy one or two). There is a hand-held version called a SteriPEN. This is a UV light that will detect body fluids. If you hold the light over the area for 10 seconds it will kill the bacteria present. This is a good idea for when you are using scene equipment in a public dungeon or play space. Buy a larger version like the Urine-Off Black Light & Spray. This uses similar technology but includes a bio enzymatic spray as well. Scan your gear. Oops, you have splooge...

Use condoms! I know you have heard about using them for STDs (yes) but you should also use them on anything you insert. The condom will provide an additional layer of protection not only for the person but it will help keep your insertables less dirty. Condoms can be expensive. Have your insertees purchase them in bulk and give them to you as a present. I try to have my partners replace all of my consumables including latex gloves, condoms, lubes (many kinds), candles, batteries and more.

Buy your own gear. If you are concerned with your personal biohazards buy your own kit. You can request any dominant, top, sadist to only use items from your personal kit on you. They will generally be happy to comply and they will probably tell you what to add to your collection.

When you buy a new item (hopefully from a quality sex toy shop) ask about the proper cleaning solutions or techniques. If the clerk doesn't know or if you buy stuff online, try to contact the manufacturer for info, if you can't find them (they are in China) then you might want to not buy the item. You have to know how to clean each item in your kit.

In general it is hard to clean leather because it is porous. Use a 50/50 mixture of distilled white vinegar and water to kill bacteria. You can use a toothbrush to get into the small places. Wash with a leather soap and water. Hang to dry completely. Condition with saddle soap. Store your leather in a cool, dry, dark environment out of direct sunlight, moisture or heat. Hang your leathers with the tails down.

Use an autoclave to sterilize metal items (those that are rated for intense cleaning) note that some pot-metal items cannot be cleaned in an autoclave. You can also use the machine to clean glass items, some liquids and other items. Check the specific directions that come with your machine on how to use it and what can be cleaned in the machine.

Purchase all of the cleansers you need for any particular material at the time that you purchase the item.

This will cost you more but you will then have the correct cleaner on hand for each item. Use a sharpie and mark on the bottle of the cleaner what item it is for. You will forget.

Go through your kit regularly looking for broken, damaged and dirty conditions. Make repairs or discard items when they become dangerous to use. Store items separately in zip-lock bags or other small containers after they are clean.

Before scening anyone ask if they are allergic to leather, latex, rope or any other material in your kit. It is usually a good idea to let them look through your stuff and identify what might be a problem.

Soap and water are your friends. Use them on your stuff. When in doubt, soap and water to the rescue. Dry your item well with a clean cloth or by hanging it. Always store your items dry and clean.

Don't wait until ten minutes before your next scene to clean stuff. Wet stuff isn't cool.

When visiting a public play space ask the owner or manager what they prefer to use for cleaning the equipment. Run your UV light over the equipment before you stick your partner on it. If you see bio stuff, use the owner's cleaning liquid to clean the equipment. This means you should always bring a few cleaning towels with you. If the owner doesn't provide cleaning fluid, use the 50/50 vinegar and water bottle sprayer in your kit. Then check the equipment again for bio hazard. Your care will help prevent the spread of disease between strangers and even friends.

Some people have an ikkk factor about using insertables that were formerly used on someone else. Ask well in advance of a scene. Many people have allergies to many of the various materials that common dildos are made from. You don't want to see what an allergic vaginal reaction is and you certainly don't want your female partner to remember the scene based on vaginal hives, lesions, burning and pain.

If your partner goes into the hospital within a few hours of a scene it is likely their body will have marks on it. It is common for some people to hide their kink from their friends and family members. Your partner may ask you to go to the hospital with them. This can be scary for many people. Guess what, people in hospitals are familiar with kink. If your partner needs your support, be supportive. If you have friends in the kink community it is also common for your friends to call you to be supportive of them in the hospital. It's okay. Go and be a good friend.

If the hospital asks you about things they see on your friend's body, explain that your friend is kinky. If you go into the hospital and you have marks, bruises, cuts, abrasions or other issues as a result of scening, tell the nurse or doctor. Explain the nature of the scene if it is important for your treatment. If the scene has nothing to do with why you are in the hospital, merely explain that you are kinky and that you were recently playing with someone.

Don't do breath play. I know it is popular and everyone wants to think that they can be safe while cutting off the air supply to another person. This is a delusion. You cannot scene breath play in the intensive care unit of a hospital and guarantee the safety of the submissive. The fact is that by the time a human being shows problems during breath play, they are *too far gone*. Don't do it. Nothing is worth that level of risk.

Do you know CPR? If not, take a class every year to brush up on your knowledge. This is a minimum if you are going to scene with people who are likely to have physical problems. Every person can have these problems. Take a class with your partners and friends. Learn how to respond when problems happen.

When was your last STD test? If you can't readily answer then it has been too long. Get a complete STD panel including HIV, herpes, genital warts and more. Ask your partners to do the same.

Ask your partners if they have any kind of communicable diseases. There are many. Find out if your partner is allergic to bee stings and if they are, have them show you how to administer the remedy (they usually carry a medical 'pen' with the appropriate remedy), ask about asthma, epilepsy or any other type of medical problem that might surface during a scene.

Find out the medications your partner is using and when they must be taken and under what conditions. Write it down. If your scene or interaction overlaps these time periods you must be aware and able to make sure that the appropriate medications are available and that the conditions are correct for the medication.

Kinky Menopause

Kink has a lot of women who are approaching or in the midst of menopause. Many men don't fully comprehend the magnitude menopause has in the minds, bodies and emotional states of women. On the one hand most women love the idea of never having to bother with a period again. On the other hand, women are told that after menopause they will become dried up old hags whose vagina will resemble a discarded prune.

In the early stages of menopause many women, who are dealing with the last of their eggs, will experience waves of intense sexual interest. It seems reasonable that this is directly related to the waves of hormones that wash over the eggs each month trying to promote reproduction. It is common that this is also the period of time where a lot of women *discover* kink.

Often women in their late 30s, 40s and 50s are less interested in producing children if they already have children. This means they may think about their sexuality in terms of sexual satisfaction rather than in terms of nesting and family building.

The uneven flow of hormones and other physical changes associated with menopause have lots of other symptoms. Here are a few:

- Hot flashes
- Flooding (rapid release of blood)

- Extra long periods
- Changes in vaginal fluids
- Depression
- Feeling less feminine
- Depression
- Weight gain
- Breast tenderness
- Hair growth in odd places
- Fatigue
- Irritability and short temper
- Memory inconsistencies
- Hair loss
- Strong body odors
- Equilibrium changes (dizziness)
- Gas
- Stomach problems
- Confusion
- Achy joints
- Bladder control issues
- Changes in heart beat
- Different nutritional needs
- Skin changes

There are other symptoms. Women should consult with their doctor and talk to other women about their experiences during menopause. There are several 'treatments' for menopause but some of the most familiar treatments are now associated with additional medical problems. You may find something that works well for you but remember that menopause is a normal biological process and at some point you will be mostly done with it. You will be different from how you perceived yourself when you were younger but this doesn't need to be a horror show.

Many women discover their sexuality during menopause and after menopause. They discover their true libido rather than a libido flooded with reproductive hormones. Inevitably this changes their viewpoint on sex, relationships and the future. The question often becomes, what does the individual woman want for *herself* rather than what does she want to *please others*.

Women often have mediocre sexual experiences. Men don't tend to understand how to please a woman and women tend to have trouble advocating for their sexual needs. This means that sex is something many women want but not the same old mediocre sex of their past relationships. Men tend to believe the answer women want is 'oral sex' performed by men. While some women do enjoy receiving oral sex, many women don't find it particularly fun or sexy.

Women tend to have mastery of fake orgasms, mostly to make the boring sex end at some point. It is easy to *sound* orgasmic and men seem to like to think that they are great lovers who can really satisfy women. Women often pander to these fantasies while inside their sex life is not anything to write home about.

A lot of women reach menopause without ever being sure they have ever orgasmed, ever. They hear about women ejaculating and think it is a big damn lie. What happened? Their youth is quickly evaporating and the whole business is disappointing.

Women arrive at kink with a vague idea that scening appears to mean that some future lover (male or female) will spend more than 10 minutes in foreplay. Often women have explored one or more self-help books on improving their sex life, in private, so their current relationship partner doesn't realize the inadequacies of their sex life. Women usually know that foreplay to get them on the sexual field probably takes around 45 minutes. That's just to get them on the field. It takes even more time (frequently) for them to get so turned on that they can actually get near a real, honest-to-Betsy orgasm. They've heard that getting kinky helps.

There are a lot of reasons that women struggle with intimacy and sexual satisfaction. Chief amongst these are how women think and feel. Women tend to carry and hold the messages of each day like a collection of playing cards. If the interactions during the day suck, they bring all of that suckedness into the bedroom and into their sex life. Add to this the punishing self-messages most women dwell on about their body and appearance. Every woman thinks their body isn't particularly attractive, it has something wrong with it, she knows, she can tell, she can feel the wrongness and she desperately feels concerns that she should hide these wrong things.

Over the course of life most women conquer some of these issues and become 'comfortable' with their body unless they are being constantly informed about what is wrong with them. Sometimes they dump the people who can't seem to stop being verbally abusive about body issues. Sometimes these people are their parents, siblings, spouses and children and they can't seem to make people stop.

This is what enters the bedroom, all of the 'stuff' around sex that women deal with on a chronic level. These feelings and thoughts are so ubiquitous that most women never have a single day without having to defend themselves against external and internal arrows battering them.

Menopause adds to all of this. It is a kind of death for most women. They lose their 'attractive cute sexual identity' with the loss of their unborn dead potential babies. They have depended on this sexual identity as part of how they attract and maintain relationships with sexual partners. What happens when that sexy young woman is gone forever?

Most people on kink fetish sites are attracted to the attractive, cute, sexy person, male or female. Yet a large percentage of the actual site members are older. This disparity is noticed by women. How could they escape the constant flood of images 'loved' by everyone on their friend's list and by total strangers?

You won't see many older men and older women and older people with not young, not athletic, not slender bodies in fetish images. You won't see a lot of wrinkled skin, gray or white hair and people in regular clothing. We seem determined, as a culture and as a sub-culture, to pander to the idea that human sexuality is the purview of the young. In fact, during youth, many people have the worst sex of their lives. They may look good having the sex but the actual sex isn't so good. It's all image without substance.

The older woman shouldn't despair. While many potential future lovers are held captive to youth-driven fantasies, there are a few who discover that sex during or after menopause can be quite fun and sometimes a whole lot better than fun.

How to Enhance Dominant or Submissive Traits

If you are in a long-term relationship when you begin exploring kink, it is likely that you will think or ask this question of someone. What happens if you think you are kinky but your relationship partner doesn't seem interested or worse, they even have a negative opinion about kink and they have no desire to explore with you. What do you do? Will your relationship fail if you explore or should you abandon your interest and simply be vanilla even though you aren't feeling very satisfied.

Your worries are valid, but exploring kink doesn't have to doom your relationship. First, I'm going to advocate that you keep your current partner *fully* informed about your growing interest. Don't allow them to shut you down or try to silence or threaten you into stopping. Don't argue. Tell them calmly that your interest isn't a trend or something you are only going to be interested in for ten minutes. Explain that you aren't unhappy in your relationship with them but you are experiencing a desire for other kinds of experiences.

If they become very upset (a reasonable response) set up couple's therapy with a kink friendly therapist. Talk about your motivations and feelings and allow your partner to express their opinion and feelings just as openly.

Most people don't follow my advice and they opt to cheat. They often don't consider online 'dating' or interactions as *real* cheating. Usually they think it is just a fantasy and something they can manage and get over. What actually happens is that they get caught up in the excitement of having a secret, in meeting in a clandestine way online, of receiving strong positive attention from someone new and of having new experiences. All of this is very real energy and time directed away from the primary romantic relationship. Whether the romantic partner knows or not (directly) they will sense the redirection of interest and their trust will erode. Over time this will cause stress on the relationship until someone decides to end the relationship.

Many people fear that their current romantic partner will not understand. It is likely that this fear is valid. But, if your relationship is important to you then you should maintain as much trust with your relationship partner as possible. While being open will invariably be difficult, it also allows you to reassure your partner and even to enroll your partner as an ally in your explorations.

When you begin conversations with your current romantic partner you need to have a few quality books on hand that talk about the aspect of kink that primarily gets your interest.

Your partner is likely to refuse to read or discuss the content initially. Don't give up or walk away from your needs. Keep requesting that they read some of the material so that the two of you can have a mutually educated conversation rather than one person dismissing the other out of hand.

If you are submissive, talk to you partner about your desire to learn about that role in your current relationship. Many newcomers to kink think that their needs can only be served by someone new or someone with lots of experience. This simply isn't true.

The attraction towards kink though, may actually reveal a desire on the part of the individual to escape their current relationship but they don't have good cause so their new attraction is used as a wedge. This is a passive way to exit a relationship and to deny that is what is happening.

The actions and interactions of kink do not markedly benefit from experience. The reality is that all people in kink started out as beginners with no experience. You gain experience by doing. Often the objective people have when they start a kink exploration is to find a loving relationship that incorporates their fetishes or kink fantasies. If you are in a loving relationship then why are you looking for a new loving relationship? Something doesn't jive.

It is possible for two people to have very different sexual needs. If this is the issue then place the issue squarely on the table and work on fixing the issue. There are many, many ways to approach different sexual needs and not all of them have to require destruction of the relationship. It is true that most solutions will require significant growth for the original relationship couple as they learn new ways to relate to each other and their ideas about sexuality and relationships.

In general, if two people love each other they have a desire to please each other. In addition, if they discover that something in a real huge turn on for their partner they are often amenable to considering it. An example of this is simple sensory touch. If pinching your mate's nipples turns them on *(and if you enjoy sex)* then you will pinch their nipples to turn them on more. In addition to doing this in a fun and pleasurable way, you might want to engage in dress up games.

In most cases your spouse will probably know more about this community than they admit to. Purchasing fun erotic clothing and toys can be a way to widen the range of sex play and stimulate new turn-ons that both people may be unaware of. Further conversations should continue.

Many people have trouble advocating for their sexual needs. It requires intention and practice. What do you want? Does your partner know you want this? Can you articulate it clearly without being negative or judgmental? Do they feel secure enough to try things out that they know you like. It can be as simple as saying, "Could you do this?" "I think I might really like that." In this way you impose no judgment on your mate for not doing things before. Also try to ask them, "would you like this?"

If your mate is very vanilla, they will have some struggles with the roles they were taught to follow from their whole background versus what you are asking of them. If they are more open you may desire to move a bit further. Buy some good glossy fetish magazines and a few books like the Loving Dominant, and maybe one of the popular erotic fiction books. Make these books accessible in a private place, but in a place your spouse or romantic partner will find and look at them. Sometimes a private bathroom is a good place People get very bored in the bathroom and are likely to read almost anything. Be prepared for questions. Assuming you can get past that hurdle with at least a 50% "I am sort of interested" response, then move toward what you think is the role you want.

Be aware that your early ideas may not be correct. Your initial desire may change, grow or evolve over time. Try to be as open and natural as possible and see where it can go. Remember that you are still facing all the pre-existing roles that you have become accustomed to over the length of the relationship. Be sure to keep your conversations as open as possible.

If your spouse or partner becomes interested enough, locate your local munch and attend. These are usually held in the banquet room of a restaurant. Everyone dresses normal. Everyone talks rather normal. Go to check it out and see what the energy is like. See if you are uncomfortable.

Spouses can feel very threatened and they are often resistive in many ways. They have a big investment in the relationship and now it appears the understood rules upon which they based their relationship are changing. Care must be taken to keep the relationship stable as both people are learning new things. Do not expect fast or easy results. Do expect hard times and tough decisions and challenging conversations.

Talk, talk, talk. If your spouse feels secure they will be more willing to try new things. If you threaten to leave if they don't do this or that, your relationship will eventually end. If you are a submissive and want your dominant/master/mistress to become more so-you may elect to involve a mutual submissive friend for a simple scene like spanking (non-sexual). During this scene, even if you have been almost a switch in teaching your spouse, you must participate as strongly submissive as possible to reinforce your spouse's sense of being in charge.

This type of cooperative scene can go a long way toward breaking free of inhibitions. Make it fun and funny. Relinquishing your own 'switch' teaching role may be one of the hardest aspects to the whole process. In general, people hate relinquishing personal power. So keep in mind that the hardest battles are probably going to be those inside of yourself.

Also, I need to mention here that during this process I sincerely recommend that cyber relationships be cut way back. The presence of a potential mate in the offing will cause significant problems in making your marriage work. Focus on the one you love.

By experimenting as a couple you have the built-in strength and knowledge of each person aiding in concerns about health and safety. Go slow. There isn't any rush to arrive at some spot. The idea is to remain open and invested in making improvements in your overall life experiences.

Conversions

So, you head into the deli next to your office building at lunch and on your way up to the crowded counter you almost trip over her. *(I will explore the female for this article.)* You take one look at her and want to dominate her. The thought both embarrasses you and intrigues you. *(I will assume here that you have enough chutzpah to engage her in conversation and invite her out.)*

The core of the situation is your desire to introduce a vanilla person into domination and submission. I will explore a few dynamics first. Vanilla is a loose term we use to identify those outside the D/s and BDSM world. Beyond that, it has virtually no other meaning in this context. Human females *(in the United States)* have been raised in a patriarchal society where the father figure was head of the household, women were expected to mind, tend and manage the household and in general adhere to traditional roles.

In the later half of the 1900s there was a huge push to have the American dream which included a big house, a couple of cars, a TV, nice furniture and a couple kids in a nice suburban neighborhood. In order to finance this dream it became necessary for business or industry to redefine the roles and expectations of men and women. These industries piggybacked upon old time female suffragette movements to free the American female and send her into the workforce by the millions. The American female bought into this new freedom and the hint of equality and leaped. Only, a few problems occurred.

Among these were a loss of family integrity, an emasculation of the woman's femininity, conflict between male and female and a blurring of the lines. Women found they were told to dress like men in order to get ahead, and when they did they became bitches. Men were told to be more sensitive and don't look at a woman in an admiring way or you will be brought up on harassment charges. Both genders were forced into new roles and neither had any experience or education in how to manage these roles.

The results are still unfolding. With divorce possible the length of committed nuclear relationships declined. Children, now spending more time away from parents in daycare and school show increasing signs of behavior problems. Prison populations exploded and people struggled to comprehend what their 'goal' might be under all of these new pressures. Women still feel constant pressure to maintain traditional roles of mother and housekeeper along with the new role of provider. Men still feel the constant pressure of provider in a world with decreasing employment opportunities. And men often experience strong challenges in meeting the changing needs and expectations in their romantic relationships.

Both genders find that working together as parents is increasingly difficult. Few thrive as divorced parents and often they struggle to raise their children based on the confusions of their own life. How should they try to prepare their children for the changing world?

Both men and women seek the same thing in relationships — attention. Most seek to gain the attention they crave by performing in the role that their target partner is most likely to desire. This means that each is busy fitting their confusion into any likely role or appearance that appears to give them an advantage in acquiring their goal.

> *You don't need to be in a relationship to receive attention. Try to be clear on what your needs really are instead of what you think they should be.*

When the person has settled on a kink role or persona, they will struggle with how to balance their kink needs with their other vanilla roles. In dating, if they see someone they are attracted to they may immediately try to figure out ways to approach the subject of kink without scaring off the potential partner.

There is no easy answer to this. On the positive side the most popular romance novel recently released was kinky and an enormous amount of women purchased and read the series of books. On the negative side if the woman is interested in exploring kink and she likes the way the guy in the grocery store looks, she is also confronted with questions about how to approach the topic if he is otherwise the right kind of person for a relationship.

First, go on a few dates to see if you really are compatible. Then on a fourth or fifth date bring up the popular book title and ask your potential partner if they have read it. If they haven't (many men have not) then mention how the book is kinky and how do they feel about kink?

It's a conversation. If both people are attracted to each other and if neither person is extremely sexually conservative then it is possible to be open and flexible enough to try out kinky stuff.

Share it together. If you are a veteran kinky person you can be very scary to a new person. Don't lie, say you have some past experience. If your whole home is a faux dungeon you are probably in trouble. Otherwise, take it slow and base your adventures on your new partner's level of interest. By going slowly and letting them adjust to your interest you are more likely to see it through into an exploratory state that works for both of you. Don't impose role.

When fantasy collides with reality

The problem comes when the individual tries to translate a fictional realm into real life. Books, with all of their titillating eroticism, fall far short in conveying reality. In fact, many books get most of their kink – wrong. Authors tend to gloss over the realities of just about everything. Fictional worlds are worlds of unblemished perfection under the tightly held controls of the writer. Real life does not function that way. Someone has to take the children to school, pay the bills and balance the checkbook.

Unrealistic expectations and desires are some of the most difficult challenges faced by those who are experienced in the lifestyle when dealing with those just entering the lifestyle. In many ways we each buy into a particular aspect of some kink fantasy. Be it the control, or the subjugation or the intense eroticism. None of these things are sustainable 24 hours a day. Yet over and over people try to implement the impossible.

The individual puts on the role, be it dominant or submissive. They reach inside just like an actor and pull out that part of themselves that identifies with that aspect and they drape it across themselves like a cloak. And while wearing that cloak, they present themselves in the assumed role fully. In that mode they seek out and engage their opposite, they pull out all those fantasies and dreams and try to fashion them into a workable scenario. And it seems to work. Except that their new relationships tend to fail rather quickly. After a few meetings something happens and they separate to seek another person, ignoring the sensation of personal relief they feel. They willingly attribute that sensation to that person not being *the one*. This may recur for years. Especially if they cling to their fantasies as being the epitome of perfection.

The fantasy of being caged every day is enormously erotic mentally, and extremely challenging in reality. It is boring, uncomfortable and a total waste of the ability and talents of the individual. They do nothing to contribute. There is no computer, no books, no television, no bathroom, no telephone, no attention. The books never talk about how the slave would feel if their mother walked into the room where they were caged naked. The fantasy of having slaves at your beck and call suggests that anyone *(regardless of wealth)*, could live like a king. They could have sex whenever they liked, have other people do chores, make money for them and shower them with compliments. The books never talk about the total responsibility of clothing, housing, feeding, medical, and retirement of each of those individuals. What about the enormous outpouring of attention required to keep a slave happy and healthy? What happens when not-really-poly submissives fight amongst themselves over everything? When they have jealousy issues, personality conflicts, areas of responsibility disagreements and a myriad of other problems?

When the individual reaches their limit, *(the length of time where the role is sustainable)*, then inevitability that role falls away and the rest of their personality shows through. This generally shows up as an argument. The role becomes stressful to sustain and the source or reason for the perceived strain of maintaining that role becomes the focal point for the outburst. This is generally followed by embarrassment and disappointment. The individual realizes they have broken their own word. They have acted in a manner in opposition to what they agreed upon in the relationship, the role they may have thought of as 'natural' is now revealed to be not as natural as they thought. This embarrassment can be so great that they completely sever the relationship, seeing no way to rebuild the previous role illusions.

Roles are often doomed before they begin. Assuming any type of role pressurizes the insides of a person. Maintaining a veneer while hiding other parts of the self creates imbalance. Eventually the psyche tries to reestablish that balance. There are no rules or formula to being either dominant or submissive. There are no requirements. Being a dominant does not mean you have to be a bitch on wheels 24 hours a day. Nor does it mean that should you show vulnerability others will lose respect for you. If you cannot be all sides of yourself then you are reflecting a flawed image outward. If you feel it is un-dominant to smile, laugh, tease, flirt, etc., then that should be a warning to you that you are not being honest with yourself. A sustainable relationship requires the entirety of the person to be involved. Being whole will allow you to project a confidence of self, being sure of who you are with all your warts. No, you will not be dominant or submissive 24 hours a day. You can develop habit roles where your habit maintains the illusion of role without a great deal of stress.

At some point the illusions and expectations must be set aside in lieu of functional choices. There is no Gor with its eternally young women and no children, there is no chateau hidden somewhere with some fabulously wealthy person willing to keep you in luxury and comfort and Mickey Rourke is not waiting to bring you to your knees somewhere. A submissive carrying these illusions may find cleaning a toilet with a toothbrush not to be something they fantasized about doing at all. A dominant whose partner is clinging to them may feel more like a day care nurse of a helpless infant. Most people are completely unprepared for the stress of being totally responsible for someone else's life and happiness. We call that role a parent and even then, we expect our dependent children to grow up and take on responsibility for themselves.

Who is real?

Analyzing who is real, who is play, who is cyber etc., is a waste of time and energy. Essentially when most persons begin to seek out and explore this side of themselves they do so tentatively, with tongue in cheek. They are seeking to fulfill a distant fantasy, an unrealized dream. It isn't truly real. This does not mean they are not real. It merely means they are on a different step in the staircase and should be treated with the respect of one human to another. Exploring oneself is a very difficult process. We don't win by reaching the goal line. There is no goal line.

Life evolves.

While it is true that you may feel disheartened by those that seem to desire only to play on a part time basis, this does not mean you can disparage these people. Maybe you are being approached just for sex. Does it make your possible interaction fake? No. As long as these individuals express their position with clarity and honesty you must and should respect their choices as you would wish them to respect your choices.

If you are in the business of identifying: strong, powerful, intense, true, real or (insert any adjective here) kink persons, then you are doomed to failure. You won't find what you seek because it doesn't exist. What you will find is regular people trying to hook up with other regular people. They just happen to be a little or a lot kinky.

Role Fatigue

Although I've mentioned this a few times in this book it is important enough to take a deeper look at the function of roles.

D/s is dependent on two people adopting roles. The two roles are dominant and submissive. Before either of these two people discovered kink they were raised to fulfill other roles such as mother, father, sibling, worker, employee, service member, boss, spouse and many more. All of these roles require a certain amount of time and energy. Some of these roles we cannot abandon as they are essential to maintaining life within our cultural framework. Before finding kink many people have reached a state where they feel overwhelmed by the obligations they have taken on and the roles that they fill in many people's lives. Inside these obligations it is common to feel that their individual sense of self is being neglected under the pressure of being, doing and performing for everyone else.

This can escalate into the deep need that finally pushes them into kink. Usually they want to escape the sense of pressure and performance. They have role fatigue.

From the outside new and different roles tend to look so much easier than what a person is currently experiencing. In this way a new role offers the appearance of some relief and salvation and it is about the self and not about other people.

Initially, when a person gets into kink role play (such as D/s or M/s or other similar role productions) they are likely to experience relief and a sense of freedom when they can unburden themselves of their regular roles. For a while this works.

But, over time the new role is simply added to the existing roles. In addition, the new role often has new requirements that require a lot more energy, attention and time that are now added to the old burdens. Eventually, you will experience role fatigue.

> *Avoiding role fatigue helps to increase your enjoyment of kink. By relegating D/s to scening rather than to a relationship style you can avoid the stresses of imposed roles.*

This can be compounded by what I described as need frenzies common to everyone in kink. A person in an elevating state of need will push on or require role performance from others. This is experienced as an emotional and psychological burden if your partner is not in exactly the same state of need. If your need levels do not match then role fatigue can quickly become chronic. Most people cannot afford to prioritize kink and kinky roles over their other life obligations. This means they will vanish and shut down the kink role in favor of relief from focusing on their constant obligations. It also means that they will 'be kinky' in waves and that the presentation of role will rise and fall along with their state of need.

While you may be completely committed to pursuing D/s as a relationship style, I encourage you to 'scene' D/s as a fetish, instead of adopting roles and adding stressors to your already complicated life.

Recommended Reading, References and Resources

Screw the Roses, Send Me the Thorns: The Romance and Sexual Sorcery of Sadomasochism by Philip Miller, et al (Paperback-July 1995) **ISBN-10:** 0964596008 **ISBN-13:** 978-0964596009

The Loving Dominant by John Warren (Paperback) **ISBN-10:** 1890159727 **ISBN-13:** 978-1890159726

Different Loving: The World of Sexual Dominance and Submission by Gloria G. Brame, et al (Paperback-January 1996) **ISBN-10:** 0679769560 **ISBN-13:** 978-0679769569

The Topping Book: Or, Getting Good at Being Bad by Dossie Easton, Catherine A. Liszt (Paperback-December 1998) **ASIN:** B001TJV5DW

The New Bottoming Book by Janet Hardy and Dossie Easton **ISBN-10:** 1890159352 **ISBN-13:** 978-1890159351

SM 101: A Realistic Introduction by Jay Wiseman (Paperback-December 1998) **ISBN-10:** 0963976389 **ISBN-13:** 978-0963976383

The Ultimate Guide to Kink: BDSM, Role Play and the Erotic Edge, Tristan Taormino **ISBN-10:** 157344779X

ISBN-13: 978-1573447799

The Masters Manual: A Handbook of Erotic Dominance by Jack Rinella, Joseph W. Bean (Paperback-August 1994) **ISBN-10:** 1881943038 **ISBN-13:** 978-1881943037

The Mistress Manual: The Good Girl's Guide to Female Dominance by Lorelei (Paperback-June 2000) **ISBN-10:** 1890159190 **ISBN-13:** 978-1890159191

Consensual Sadomasochism: How to Talk About It and Do It Safely by William A. Henkin Ph.D., Sybil Holiday (Paperback-September 1996) **ISBN-10:** 1881943127 **ISBN-13:** 978-1881943129

Learning the Ropes: A Basic Guide to Safe and Fun SM Lovemaking by Race Bannon (Paperback-January 1993) **ASIN:** B0093O85Q0

The Ethical Slut, Dossie Easton, **ASIN:** B004JHYRAE

Other Nonfiction Titles
By
F.R.R. Mallory

Extreme Space II: Kink Secrets
ISBN: 9781482053050

The Kinky Feminist
(Available March 2013)

Made in the USA
San Bernardino, CA
11 August 2017